JN444711

Disney Princess

Beauty and the Beast

미녀와 야수

초판 1쇄 2012년 2월 27일
초판 2쇄 2013년 1월 21일

번역 · 해설 | 샤이니
펴낸이 | 조치영
디자인 | 남다희
기획 | 스크린영어사 기획 1팀
인쇄 | 보광문화사
펴낸곳 | 스크린영어사

서울특별시 관악구 대학동 1514번지
TEL (02) 887-8416
FAX (02) 887-8591
http://www.screenplay.co.kr

등록일자 1997년 7월 9일
등록번호 제16-1495

ISBN 978-89-6415-058-0 18740
ISBN 978-89-87915-11-1 18740 (세트)

Copyright © 2012 Disney Enterprises, Inc. All rights reserved.

* 잘못된 책은 구입하신 곳에서 바꾸어 드립니다.
* 이 책은 저작권자의 계약에 따라 발행한 것이므로 본사의 허락 없이는 어떠한 형태와 수단으로도 이 책의 내용을 이용하지 못합니다.

Beauty and the Beast

스크린영어사

〈미녀와 야수〉를 시작하며

다년간 EBS 및 다양한 교육 매체에서 영어 학습 컨텐츠 개발 및 강의를 통해 학생들을 만나면서 가장 많이 들은 말이 있다. "선생님 어떻게 하면 영어를 쉽게 공부할 수 있을까요?" 처음에는 난감했지만 지금은 이 질문이 '어떻게 하면 더 쉽고 더 재미있게 강의할 수 있을까' 하고 나를 항상 연구하게 하는 원동력이 되었다. 생각해 보면 나는 딱히 '영어'라는 과목에 처음부터 거부감이 없었던 것 같다. 어렸을 때부터 목소리가 낭랑하여 성우를 해도 되겠다, 노래를 해 보라는 말을 주위에서 많이 들었던 터라 사람들 앞에서 낭독이나 발표를 많이 해 왔다. 나 또한 모든 어린이들의 로망인 디즈니 만화영화를 보면서 꿈을 키웠고, 나중에는 좋아하던 만화영화의 영어 원음을 들으면서 영어를 '자연스럽게' 받아들이게 되었던 것 같다. 이 덕분에 영어학원이라고는 없던 동네였지만 항상 영어를 곁에 두고 공부할 수 있었다.

대학교에서 전공으로 만난 영어는 나의 시야를 더욱 넓혀지게 해 주었다. 물 만난 고기처럼 신나고 즐겁게 공부했고 자연스럽게 영어교육은 나의 직업으로 이어졌다. 그리고 지금은 하루하루 좋아하는 일을 하며 살아갈 수 있다는 것에 감사하고 있다. '아는 사람은 좋아하는 사람만 못하고, 좋아하는 사람은 즐기는 사람만 못하다'라는 공자님의 말씀을 나는 나의 인생을 통해 체득한 셈이다. 이 덕분에 영어를 죽어라 싫어하는 친구들에게 가장 먼저 해주는 말이자 나의 공부 철학이 된 말이 '즐겨라, 일단 재미있어야 열심히 한다' 이다. 이런 나의 철학과 딱 맞는 공부 방법을 지향하는 스크린영어사와의 인연도 우연은 아닌 것 같다. 몇 년 전부터 스크린 영어사와 인연을 맺어 출판한 〈디즈니 라푼젤〉 교재와 〈Ice Age 2〉, 〈하늘에서 음식이 내린다면〉등의 스크린 강의가 독자들에게 호평을 받아 이번에는 애니메이션의 고전적인 명작이라고 할 수 있는 〈미녀와 야수(Beauty and the Beast)〉로 독자 여러분들을 만나게 되었다.

책을 펼치긴 했는데 어떻게 활용해야 할 지 부담스러운 독자들께서는 우선 '공부'라는 생각을 접고, 부담없이 어떤 내용의 영화인지 일단 즐기며 보기를 바란다. 처음부터 끝까지 스토리 파악 위주로 보았으면 한다. 그 후에 시간을 쪼개어 챕터별로 나누어져 있는 분량을 소화하길 바란다. 이 때도 무조건 많이 학습하겠다는 생각을 버리고 내가 할 수 있는 만큼만, 재미있게, 즐기면서 할 수 있는 분량이면 된다. 그것에 0.5챕터이든 1챕터이든 1.5챕터이든 상관없다. 본인의 집중력이 견딜 수 있는 만큼만 하루에 소화하고 점차 늘려 나가길 바란다. 분량과 시간을 정했으면 책과 영화를 번갈아 보면서 모르는 어휘나 기본 표현을 반드시 학습하길 바란다. 이 때 주의할 점은 절대로 먼저 지문을 보지 말고, 최대한 이야기 속의 등장인물이 '뭐라고 하는지'에 집중하여 들어본 후에 안 들리는 부분만 지문의 도움을 받으라는 것이다. 대부분 들리지 않는 어휘나 기본 표현이 그날의 학습해야 할 분량과 일치할 것이다. 기본 표현을 익힌 후에는 핵심이 될 만한 표현들을 뽑아서 정리해 놓은 Zoom In코너와 다양한 응용 표현이 실린 Key Expression을 보면서 숙달하면 좋겠다.

영어를 학습한 후에 꼭 해야 할 것은 '생활에 응용해 보라'는 것이다. 배운 것을 직접 활용해 보지 않으면 아무런 소용이 없다. 배운 영어표현에서 나온 상황에 나도 처하게 되었다면 혼자서라도 꼭 영어표현을 중얼거려보자. 그런 경험이 쌓이고 쌓인 만큼 영어에 대한 장벽은 낮아지고 나의 자신감은 상승할 것이다. 진정한 사랑의 힘으로 야수에서 왕자로 변하게 되는 이 멋진 이야기를 학습서로 펴내게 되어 기쁘다. 이 책을 통해 많은 독자들이 영어와 좀 더 친해지는 계기를 만들었으면 한다. 나의 마음이 꼭 전해지길 바라며.

2012년 1월 역삼동 자택에서

샤이니 김재영

Contents

MAIN CHARACTERS

BELLE 벨
이야기의 주인공으로 책을 좋아하는 아름다운 소녀이다. 발명가인 아버지를 찾아 나섰다가 야수가 사는 성에 들어가게 된다. 마을 대장인 개스톤의 구애를 거부하고 야수와 사랑에 빠진다.

BEAST 야수
한때 이기적이고 사랑의 의미를 몰랐던 왕자. 요정이 진정한 사랑을 깨달을 때까지 야수로 살도록 마법을 걸어놓았다. 우연히 성으로 들어온 모리스와 벨에게 처음엔 아주 무서운 모습을 보인다.

MAURICE 모리스
벨의 아버지로 발명가이다. 호기심이 많은 그의 행동 때문에 마을 사람들은 그를 미치광이라고 부른다. 어느 날 발명대회에 나가려던 그는 도중에 길을 잃고 야수의 성에 도착하게 된다.

GASTON 개스톤
마을의 두목과도 같은 역할을 하는 개스톤. 우람한 체격과 잘생긴 얼굴 때문에 인기가 많다. 하지만 벨을 좋아하는 그는 그녀와 결혼하기 위해 야비한 일을 계획한다.

LEFOU 르푸
개스톤의 똘마니 역할을 한다. 키가 작고 못생겨 자신과는 다른 개스톤을 왕처럼 따른다. 하지만 가끔씩 개스톤의 비위에 거슬리는 사실을 서슴없이 말해 개스톤에게 호되게 당하기도 한다.

LUMIERE & COGSWORTH 루미에르와 콕스워즈
마법에 걸린 성에 있는 촛대와 시계로 원래는 성의 시종과 집사였다. 벨과 야수의 사랑으로 마법이 풀리자 결국은 다시 사람이 된다.

Beauty and the Beast

Tale as old as time, song as old as rhyme
Beauty and the Beast

Chapter 1

야수가 된 왕자, 책을 좋아하는 벨

A Prince Becomes a Beast and Belle Is Introduced

시간 00:01:01 ~ 00:09:34

EXT. FOREST
A beautiful forest shows up. One little deer is enjoying the peaceful moment drinking water from the stream. Over the trees is seen a magnificent castle. Zoom in to the castle.

NARRATOR : Once upon a time, in a faraway land, a young prince lived in a shining castle. Although he had everything his heart desired, the prince was spoiled, selfish and unkind. But then one winter's night, an old beggar woman came to the castle and offered him a single rose in return for shelter from the bitter cold. Repulsed by her haggard appearance the prince sneered at the gift and turned the old woman away, but she warned him not to be deceived by appearances, for beauty is found within. And when he dismissed her again, the old woman's ugliness melted away to reveal a beautiful enchantress. The prince tried to apologize but it was too late,

외부. 숲 속
아름다운 숲이 보인다. 작은 사슴 한 마리가 개울물을 마시며 평화로운 시간을 즐기고 있다. 나무 너머로 웅장한 성이 보인다. 성의 모습이 점점 커진다.

나레이터 : 오랜 옛날 아주 머나먼 곳에 아름다운 성에 젊은 왕자가 살고 있었다. 그는 자기가 원하는 것은 뭐든지 가졌지만, 성격이 거칠고 이기적이며 차가웠다. 그러던 어느 추운 겨울날, 한 거지 노파가 성을 찾아와서는 추위를 피할 수 있게 해 주면 그 대가로 장미 한 송이를 준다고 하였다. 노파의 초라한 몰골을 본 왕자는 선물을 비웃으며 청을 거절했다. 노파는 진실한 아름다움은 사람의 마음속에 있다고 경고했으나, 왕자는 들은 척도 하지 않았다. 그러자 노파는 초라한 모습을 벗어내고 아름다운 요정으로 바뀌었다. 왕자는 사죄를 하려 했지만 이미 때는 늦었다.

- **selfish**
  이기적인
  If you say that someone is selfish, you mean that he or she cares only about himself or herself, and not about other people
- **shelter**
  주거지, 대피처
  A shelter is a small building or covered place which is made to protect people from bad weather or danger
- **haggard**
  초췌한
  Someone who looks haggard has a tired expression and shadows under their eyes, especially because they are ill or have not had enough sleep
- **enchantress**
  여자 마법사
  In fairy stories and legends, an enchantress is a woman who uses magic to put spells on people and things

for she had seen that there was no love in his heart, and as punishment, she transformed him into a hideous Beast and placed a powerful spell on the castle and all who lived there. Ashamed of his monstrous form, the Beast concealed himself inside his castle with a magic mirror as his only window to the outside world. The rose she had offered was truly an enchanted rose, which would bloom until his twenty-first year. If he could learn to love another and earn her love in return by the time the last petal fell, then the spell would be broken. If not, he would be doomed to remain a Beast for all time. As the years passed, he fell into despair and lost all hope, for who could ever learn to love a Beast?

We have seen a progression of stained glass windows illustrating the narration, as well as the Beast shredding his portrait. The camera slowly zooms out from the castle and we see the title.

TITLE CARD: BEAUTY AND THE BEAST

Fade up on the home of Belle. She exits the front door and begins her walk into town.
Belle comes out of her house holding a basket in her hand. She starts to sing. She walks through the village.

BELLE : (singing) *LITTLE TOWN, IT'S A QUIET VILLAGE*
EVERY DAY LIKE THE ONE BEFORE
LITTLE TOWN, FULL OF LITTLE PEOPLE
WAKING UP TO SAY...

Each and every window of villagers pops open and people chant one by one.

왕자의 마음속에 사랑이 없다는 것을 안 요정은 그 벌로 왕자를 흉측한 야수로 만들었고 성 안의 모든 것들에 마법을 걸었다. 그때부터 야수는 자신의 흉측한 모습을 수치스러워하여 성안에 숨어 살면서 오직 마술 거울로만 바깥세상을 볼 수 있게 되었다. 요정이 남긴 신비한 장미의 마지막 꽃잎이 떨어지는 왕자의 21번째 생일까지, 그가 누군가를 진실하게 사랑하고 또 그녀로부터 사랑을 받게 되면 마법에서 풀려날 것이나, 그렇지 않다면 그는 영원히 야수로 살 수밖에 없었다. 그 이후로 많은 세월이 흘렀고 그는 모든 희망을 잃어버렸다. 과연 누가 그 야수를 사랑할 수 있을 것인가?

지난 이야기를 그린 스테인드글라스에 이어, 자신의 초상화를 찢어버리는 야수의 모습이 보인다. 카메라는 성으로부터 점점 멀어지고, 제목이 등장한다.

타이틀: 미녀와 야수

벨의 집이 점점 뚜렷해진다. 벨은 문 밖으로 나와 마을로 향한다. 벨은 바구니를 손에 든 채 집을 나선다. 그녀는 노래를 부르며, 마을을 걸어 다닌다.

벨 : (노래하며) *작고 조용한 마을, 일상적인 생활 보잘 것 없는 사람들은 깨어나 이렇게 외친다네…*

마을 사람들이 창문을 열고 한 명씩 일제히 외친다.

- **punishment**
  벌, 처벌
  Punishment is the act of punishing someone or of being punished
- **transform**
  변형시키다
  To transform something into something else means to change or convert it into that thing
- **conceal**
  감추다, 숨기다
  If you conceal something, you cover it or hide it carefully
- **spell**
  주문
  A spell is a situation in which events are controlled by a magical power
- **despair**
  절망
  Despair is the feeling that everything is wrong and that nothing will improve

If not, he would be doomed to remain a beast for all time.
If not은 '만약 그렇지 않는다면' 이라는 의미로 이 문장은 가정법이 쓰인 문장이다. be doomed는 '~한 운명을 맞게 되다, 결말을 맞게 되다'라는 의미이다.

Zoom In

If not, he would be doomed to remain a beast for all time.

그렇지 않다면 그는 영원히 야수로 살 수밖에 없었다.

TOWNSFOLK 1 : Bonjour!
TOWNSFOLK 2 : Bonjour!
TOWNSFOLK 3 : Bonjour!
TOWNSFOLK 4 : Bonjour!
TOWNSFOLK 5 : Bonjour!

A Baker is holding a tray of bread, and a merchant is carrying some pumpkins.

BELLE : (singing) *THERE GOES THE BAKER WITH HIS TRAY LIKE ALWAYS*
THE SAME OLD BREAD AND ROLLS TO SELL
EVERY MORNING JUST THE SAME

The Merchant greets Belle and Belle greets him back.

BELLE : (singing) *SINCE THE MORNING THAT WE CAME*
TO THIS POOR PROVINCIAL TOWN...
BAKER: Good morning, Belle!

Belle jumps over to the bakery.

BELLE : Morning monsieur!
BAKER : Where are you off to?

Belle takes out a book from a basket and shows it to the Baker. She sounds very excited about the book.

BELLE : The bookshop! I just finished the most wonderful story, about a beanstalk and an ogre and...
BAKER : That's nice... (ignoring her) Marie, the baguettes! Hurry up!

마을 사람 1 : 안녕!
마을 사람 2 : 안녕!
마을 사람 3 : 안녕!
마을 사람 4 : 안녕!
마을 사람 5 : 안녕!

빵집 아저씨는 빵이 담긴 쟁반을 들고 있고, 상인은 호박들을 나르고 있다.

벨 : (노래하며) *빵장수는 항상 같은 곳에 있고 그의 수레에는 오래된 빵이 있다네 이 평범한 마을에서의 아침은 언제나 같은 풍경이라네*

상인은 벨에게 인사를 건네고, 벨도 상인에게 인사를 한다.

벨 : (노래하며) *우리 마을 아침은 먼 옛날부터 이렇게 시작되었다네*
빵집 아저씨 : 안녕 벨.

벨 빵집으로 달려간다.

벨 : 안녕하세요? 아저씨.
빵집 아저씨 : 어디 가니?

벨은 바구니에서 책을 꺼내 빵집 아저씨에게 보여준다. 그녀는 책을 아주 재미있게 읽은 것 같다.

벨 : 책방이요. 잭과 콩나무라는 재미있는 책을 다 읽었거든요. 그 책은…
빵집 아저씨 : 그래 멋있구나. (무시하며) 마리! 어서 서둘러!

- **tray**
  쟁반
  A tray is a flat piece of wood, plastic, or metal, which usually has raised edges and which is used for carrying things, especially food and drinks

- **merchant**
  상인
  A merchant is a person who buys or sells goods in large quantities, especially one who imports and exports them

- **greet**
  인사하다
  When you greet someone, you say 'Hello' or shake hands with them.

- **provincial**
  마을의, 지방의
  Provincial means connected with the parts of a country away from the capital city

Where are you off to?
간단한 문장이지만 자주 쓸 수 있는 표현이다. Where are you going?을 대신해서 Where are you off to?도 사용해보자.

Zoom In

Where are you off to?
어디 가니?

Belle shrugs her shoulders and starts walking again.

TOWNSFOLK : (singing) *LOOK THERE SHE GOES, THE GIRL IS STRANGE NO QUESTION. DAZED AND DISTRACTED, CAN'T YOU TELL?*

WOMAN 1 : (singing) *NEVER PART OF ANY CROWD*

On the second floor of the building, windows are open. A Barber looks out of the window and sings.

BARBER : (singing) *'CAUSE HER HEAD'S UP ON SOME CLOUD*

TOWNSFOLK : (singing) *NO DENYING SHE'S A FUNNY GIRL, THAT BELLE!*

Belle jumps on the back of a wagon and rides through town.

DRIVER : (singing) *BONJOUR!*

WOMAN 2 : (singing) *GOOD DAY!*

DRIVER : (singing) *HOW IS YOUR FAMILY?*

WOMAN 3 : (singing) *BONJOUR!*

MERCHANT : (singing) *GOOD DAY!*

WOMAN 3 : (singing) *HOW IS YOUR WIFE?*

WOMAN 4 : (singing) *I NEED SIX EGGS!*

MAN 1 : (singing) *THAT'S TOO EXPENSIVE!*

BELLE : (singing) *THERE MUST BE MORE THAN THIS PROVINCIAL LIFE!*

INT. BOOKSHOP
Belle enters the bookshop.

BOOKSELLER : Ah, Belle!

BELLE : Good morning. I've come to return the book I borrowed.

벨은 어깨를 움츠리며 다시 걷기 시작한다.

아줌마들 : (노래하며) *저 소녀를 좀 보아요, 분위기가 이상하고 매력적이지 않나요?*
아줌마 1 : (노래하며) *우리랑은 뭔가 다르죠*

건물 2층 창문이 열린다. 이발사가 창밖을 내다보며 노래한다.

이발사 : (노래하며) *그래서 그녀는 하늘의 구름처럼 보이죠*
사람들 : (노래하며) *벨은 매우 흥미로운 아이예요*

벨 마차에 올라타서 마을을 둘러본다.

마 부 : (노래하며) *안녕하세요?*
아줌마 2 : (노래하며) *날이 좋네요*
마 부 : (노래하며) *식구들은 잘 있나요?*
아줌마 3 : (노래하며) *안녕하세요?*
가게 아저씨 : (노래하며) *좋은 하루*
아줌마 3 : (노래하며) *부인은 어떠세요?*
아줌마 4 : (노래하며) *계란 6개 주세요*
아저씨 1 : (노래하며) *비싸군요*
벨 : (노래하며) *어딘가 더 멋진 곳이 있을 거야*

내부. 책방
벨은 책방에 들어간다.

책방 아저씨 : 안녕. 벨.
벨 : 안녕하세요? 빌린 책 가져 왔어요.

- **shrug**
  으쓱하다
  If you shrug, you raise your shoulders to show that you are not interested in something or that you do not know or care about something
- **strange**
  이상한
  Something that is strange is unusual or unexpected, and makes you feel slightly nervous or afraid
- **wagon**
  마차
  A wagon is a strong vehicle with four wheels, usually pulled by horses or oxen and used for carrying heavy loads
- **return**
  돌려주다
  If you return something that you have borrowed or taken, you give it back or put it back
- **borrow**
  빌리다
  If you borrow something that belongs to someone else, you take it or use it for a period of time, usually with their permission

There must be more than this provincial life!
이 문장에서 must be는 '~임에 틀림없다'로 해석한다. 강한 추측을 나타낼 때 쓰는 표현이다. 얼굴이 창백한 친구를 보고 You must be sick.(너 아프구나)라고도 말할 수 있다.

Zoom In

There must be more than this provincial life!
어딘가 더 멋진 곳이 있을 거야!

She hands over the book to the Bookseller.

BOOKSELLER : (putting the book back on the shelf) Finished already?

BELLE : Oh, I couldn't put it down! Have you got anything new?

She starts to climb up the ladder of the bookshelf.

BOOKSELLER : (laughing) Not since yesterday.

BELLE : (on ladder of bookshelf) That's all right. I'll borrow... this one.

The Bookseller takes a close look at the book and gets surprised.

BOOKSELLER : That one? But you've read it twice!

BELLE : Well, it's my favorite! (Belle swings off side of ladder, rolling down its track) Far-off places, daring swordfights, magic spells, a prince in disguise!

BOOKSELLER : (handing her the book) If you like it all that much, it's yours!

BELLE : But sir!

BOOKSELLER : I insist!

EXT. STREET

BELLE : Well thank you. Thank you very much! (leaves bookshop)

Three guys that were looking in window of the bookshop turn to watch her.

그녀는 책방 아저씨에게 책을 건넨다.

아저씨 : (책을 받아서 놓으면) 벌써 다 읽었니?
벨 : 아, 책을 꺼내기가 힘드네요. 새 책 들어온 것 있나요?

그녀는 책꽂이의 사다리를 올라가기 시작한다.

아저씨 : (웃으면서) 어제 그대로지.
벨 : (사다리 위에서) 상관없어요. 저는… 이걸 빌리겠어요.

책방 아저씨는 책을 가까이 가져가서 보더니 놀란다.

아저씨 : 그건 벌써 두 번이나 읽었잖니?
벨 : 제가 가장 좋아하는 책이거든요. (벨은 사다리 모서리에 매달려서 옆으로 이동한다) 먼 나라에, 멋진 칼싸움에, 마법에 걸린 왕자님!
아저씨 : (벨에게 책을 주며) 그렇게 그 책이 좋다면 가져도 좋아.
벨 : 하지만 아저씨!
아저씨 : 괜찮아!

외부. 거리

벨 : 고마워요. 정말 고마워요. (책가게를 나온다)

창문으로 책방 안을 들여다보던 세 명의 청년들이 벨을 보기 위해 몸을 돌린다.

- **climb up**
  올라가다
  If you climb something such as a tree, mountain, or ladder, or climb up it, you move towards the top of it
- **bookshelf**
  책꽂이
  A bookshelf is a shelf on which you keep books
- **swordfight**
  칼싸움
  A fight or duel using swords
- **disguise**
  변장
  If you are in disguise, you are not wearing your usual clothes or you have altered your appearance in other ways, so that people will not recognize you

Have you got anything new?
thing으로 끝나는 명사인 anything, everything, nothing, something 등은 형용사가 그 단어의 뒤에서 꾸며준다.
ex) I have nothing to give you.

Zoom In

Have you got anything new?
새 책 들어온 것 있나요?

MEN : (singing) *LOOK THERE SHE GOES*
THAT GIRL IS SO PECULIAR!
I WONDER IF SHE'S FEELING WELL!

Belle keeps reading the book while walking. She is deeply engrossed in the book.

WOMEN : (singing) *WITH A DREAMY FAR-OFF LOOK!*
MEN : (singing) *AND HER NOSE STUCK IN A BOOK!*
ALL : (singing) *WHAT A PUZZLE TO THE REST OF US IS BELLE!*

Belle sits on the edge of a fountain singing to the sheep and the washing woman in the background, who leaves.

BELLE : (singing) *OH! ISN'T THIS AMAZING!*
IT'S MY FAVORITE PART BECAUSE YOU'LL SEE!
HERE'S WHERE SHE MEETS PRINCE CHARMING

A sheep tears away the corner of the page.

BELLE : (singing) *BUT SHE WON'T DISCOVER THAT IT'S HIM TILL CHAPTER THREE!*

All the sheep start to run away from a shepherd.
In the shop a lady looks into the mirror and sings about Belle. She is bald.

WOMAN 5 : (singing) *NOW IT'S NO WONDER THAT HER NAME MEANS 'BEAUTY' HER LOOKS HAVE GOT NO PARALLEL!*
MERCHANT : (singing) *BUT BEHIND THAT FAIR FACADE*
I'M AFRAID SHE'S RATHER ODD
VERY DIFFERENT FROM THE REST OF US...

청년들 : (노래하며) *저 소녀 좀 봐. 정말 특별하지. 그녀와 사랑을 할 수 있을까?*

벨은 걸으면서도 계속 책을 읽는다. 그녀는 완전히 책에 몰입해 있다.

아줌마들 : (노래하며) *꿈꾸는 것처럼 보이죠*
남자 1 : (노래하며) *책에서 떨어지질 않아요*
사람들 : (노래하며) *벨은 정말 모를 아이야*

벨은 분수 가에 앉아서 양들에게 노래를 불러준다. 빨래를 하던 한 여자가 자리를 뜬다.

벨 : (노래하며) *아. 놀랍지 않니? 내가 제일 좋아하는 부분이야. 왜냐하면 그녀가 아름다운 왕자님을 만나는 장면이거든*

양이 책장 귀퉁이를 찢는다.

벨 : (노래하며) *하지만 그녀는 3장까지 그가 왕자라는 것을 모르지*

모든 양들이 목동으로부터 도망친다.
가게에서는 한 여자가 거울을 보며 벨에 대해 노래한다. 그녀는 대머리이다.

아줌마 5 : (노래하며) *그녀의 이름이 '미녀'라는 뜻인 건 결코 이상하지 않죠. 그녀만큼 아름다운 사람은 없어요*
모자가게 아저씨 : (노래하며) *그러나 그 뒷면엔 무언가 이상한 것이 있어요. 그녀는 우리랑 달라요*

- **peculiar**
  특이한, 이상한
  If you describe someone or something as peculiar, you think that they are strange or unusual, sometimes in an unpleasant way

- **engrossed**
  몰두한
  If you are engrossed in something, it holds your attention completely

- **fountain**
  분수
  A fountain is an ornamental feature in a pool or lake which consists of a long narrow stream of water that is forced up into the air by a pump

- **bald**
  대머리
  Someone who is bald has little or no hair on the top of their head

Her looks have got no parallel!
parallel은 '평행한, 아주 유사한'이라는 의미를 지닌 단어이다. have no parallel은 '필적할 만한 상대가 없다' 즉, '최고다'라는 의미이다.

Zoom In

Her looks have got no parallel!
그녀만큼 아름다운 사람은 없어요!

ALL : (singing) *SHE'S NOTHING LIKE THE REST OF US*
YES, DIFFERENT FROM THE REST OF US IS BELLE

Geese flying overhead, one is shot and plummets to the ground. Lefou runs over, holds out the bag-and misses, catching the prize. He returns to Gaston.

LEFOU : Wow! You didn't miss a shot, Gaston! You're the greatest hunter in the whole world!

GASTON : I know!

LEFOU : Huh. No beast alive stands a chance against you... And no girl for that matter!

GASTON : It's true, Lefou. And I've got my sights set on that one! (pointing to Belle)

LEFOU : The inventor's daughter?

GASTON : She's the one! The lucky girl I'm going to marry.

LEFOU : But she...

GASTON : The most beautiful girl in town.

LEFOU : I know, but...

GASTON : That makes her the best. And don't I deserve the best?

LEFOU : Well, of course, I mean you do, but I mean...

GASTON: (singing) *RIGHT FROM THE MOMENT WHEN I MET HER, SAW HER*
I SAID SHE'S GORGEOUS AND I FELL
HERE IN TOWN THERE'S ONLY SHE

Belle walks by and away.

GASTON: (singing) *WHO IS BEAUTIFUL AS ME*
SO I'M MAKING PLANS TO WOO AND MARRY BELLE

사람들 : (노래하며) *우리하고는 아주 다르죠*
그래요. 벨은 우리하고는 아주 달라요

거위들이 하늘을 날고 있다. 한 마리가 총에 맞아 땅으로 떨어진다. 르푸는 달려가서 자루를 벌리지만, 잡지 못하고 놓친다. 그는 개스톤에게 돌아간다.

르 푸 : 우와. 정통으로 맞았어. 개스톤. 넌 세상에서 가장 훌륭한 사냥꾼이야.

개스톤 : 그럼.

르 푸 : 어떤 짐승도 네 앞에선 꼼짝 못하지. 어느 여자도.

개스톤 : 그럼. 하지만 나는 한 여자만을 좋아하지. (벨을 가리키며)

르 푸 : 발명쟁이의 딸?

개스톤 : 그녀는 나와 결혼 할 운 좋은 여자야.

르 푸 : 하지만 그녀는…

개스톤 : 마을에서 가장 아름다운 여자이기도 하고.

르 푸 : 나도 알아. 하지만…

개스톤 : 그녀는 최고야. 내가 최고를 가질 자격이 없다고 생각하니?

르 푸 : 아. 물론 그건 아니지. 하지만…

개스톤 : (노래하며) *내가 그녀를 만나볼 때가 왔다네. 그녀는 운이 좋군*
이 마을에서 내게 어울릴 만큼 아름다운 여자는 그녀뿐이지

벨은 점점 멀어져 간다.

개스톤 : (노래하며) *누가 나처럼 훌륭해*
그래서 나는 벨과 결혼할 계획을 세우고 있다네

- **plummet**
  곤두박질치다
  If an amount, rate, or price plummets, it decreases quickly by a large amount

- **deserve**
  ~를 받을 만하다
  If you say that a person or thing deserves something, you mean that they should have it or receive it because of their actions or qualities

- **gorgeous**
  아주 멋진
  If you say that something is gorgeous, you mean that it gives you a lot of pleasure or is very attractive

- **woo**
  구혼하다
  If you woo people, you try to encourage them to help you, support you, or vote for you, for example by promising them things which they would like

I've got my sights set on that one!
have one's sights set on ~은 '~을 눈 여겨 보고 있다'라는 의미이다. 여기서는 본인이 마음에 두고 있는 여인을 말한다.

Zoom In

I've got my sights set on that one!

나는 한 여자만을 좋아하지!

Gaston starts to run to Belle. In the meantime, three Bimbettes sing a worshiping song of Gaston. Gaston stops running, being blocked by a wagon passing by.

BIMBETTES : (singing) *LOOK THERE HE GOES, ISN'T HE DREAMY*
MONSIEUR GASTON, OH HE'S SO CUTE
BE STILL MY HEART, I'M HARDLY BREATHING
HE'S SUCH A TALL, DARK, STRONG AND HANDSOME BRUTE

Belle walks easily through the crowd of people in the town; Gaston struggles to catch up to her.

MAN 1 : Bonjour!
GASTON : Pardon!
MAN 2 : Good day!
MAN 3 : Mais oui!
WOMAN 1 : You call this bacon!
WOMAN 2 : What lovely grapes!
MAN 4 : Some cheese!
WOMAN 3 : Ten yards!
MAN 4 : One pound
GASTON : 'Excuse me!
MAN 4 : I'll get the knife!
GASTON : Please let me through!
WOMAN 4 : This bread!
MAN 5 : Those fish!
WOMAN 4 : It's stale!
MAN 5 : They smell!
MAN 6 : Madame's mistaken!

개스톤은 벨에게 달려가기 시작한다. 그러는 동안 세 여자들이 개스톤을 찬양하는 노래를 부른다. 개스톤은 지나가는 마차에 막혀 달리기를 멈춘다.

여자들 : (노래하며) *저기 봐. 그가 지나간다. 황홀해라. 개스톤! 얼마나 멋진가. 오!*
가슴이 뛰고, 숨이 막히네
어찌나 키도 크고 우람하고 잘 생겼는지

벨은 마을 사람들 사이로 요리조리 잘 걸어간다. 개스톤은 그녀를 따라잡기 위해 애 쓴다.

아저씨 1 : 안녕!
개스톤 : 미안합니다!
아저씨 2 : 좋은 하루!
아저씨 3 : 안녕!
아줌마 1 : 베이컨 주세요!
아줌마 2 : 맛있는 포도요!
아저씨 4 : 치즈 있어요!
아줌마 3 : 10야드요!
아저씨 4 : 1파운드에요.
개스톤 : 실례합니다.
아저씨 4 : 칼 주세요!
개스톤 : 좀 지나갑시다!
아줌마 4 : 빵이요!
아저씨 5 : 생선이요!
아줌마 4 : 빵이 상했네!
아저씨 5 : 냄새나요!
아저씨 6 : 실수했소!

- **worship**
  찬양하다
  If you worship a god, you show your respect to the god, for example by saying prayers
- **block**
  막다
  To block a road, channel, or pipe means to put an object across it or in it so that nothing can pass through it or along it
- **struggle**
  애쓰다
  If you struggle to do something, you try hard to do it, even though other people or things may be making it difficult for you to succeed
- **stale**
  싱싱하지 못한
  Stale food is no longer fresh or good to eat

I'm hardly breathing.
hardly는 '거의~가 아니다'라는 의미로 준부정어로 해석한다. breathe는 '숨쉬다, 호흡하다'라는 동사. 거기에 ing를 붙여 '숨쉬기, 호흡하기'로 이해하면 된다.

Zoom In

I'm hardly breathing.
숨이 막히네.

BELLE : (singing) *THERE MUST BE MORE THAN THIS PROVINCIAL LIFE!*

GASTON : (singing) *JUST WATCH, I'M GOING TO MAKE BELLE MY WIFE!*

Town people gather around Gaston, and eventually surround him.

ALL : (singing) *LOOK THERE SHE GOES A GIRL WHO'S STRANGE BUT SPECIAL*
A MOST PECULIAR MADEMOISELLE
IT'S A PITY AND A SIN
SHE DOESN'T QUITE FIT IN!

GROUP 1 : (singing) *BUT SHE REALLY IS A FUNNY GIRL*

GROUP 2 : (singing) *A BEAUTY BUT A FUNNY GIRL*

ALL : (singing) *SHE REALLY IS A FUNNY GIRL! THAT BELLE!*

TOWNSFOLK 1 : Bonjour!

TOWNSFOLK 2 : Bonjour!

TOWNSFOLK 3 : Bonjour!

TOWNSFOLK 4 : Bonjour!

TOWNSFOLK 5 : Bonjour!

TOWNSFOLK 6 : Bonjour!

Gaston goes up to the roof of a house to see where Belle is going, and jumps to the ground right in front of Belle.

GASTON : Hello, Belle.

BELLE : Bonjour Gaston.

Gaston grabs the book from Belle.

벨 : (노래하며) *어딘가 더 멋진 곳이 있을 거야!*

개스톤 : (노래하며) *두고 봐요. 벨과 결혼할 테니!*

마을 사람들은 개스톤의 주변으로 모여들더니, 결국 그를 둘러싼다.

사람들 : (노래하며) *봐요. 그녀가 가고 있어요*
얼마나 이상하고 특별한 아이인가. 불쌍해
그녀는 이 마을과 어울리지 않아

그룹 1 : (노래하며) *그러나 그녀는 흥미로운 아이죠*

그룹 2 : (노래하며) *아름답지만 재미있죠*

사람들 : (노래하며) *벨은 정말 재미있는 아이에요. 벨!*

마을 사람 1 : 안녕!

마을 사람 2 : 안녕!

마을 사람 3 : 안녕!

마을 사람 4 : 안녕!

마을 사람 5 : 안녕!

마을 사람 6 : 안녕!

개스톤은 벨이 어디로 가는지를 보기 위해 지붕 위로 올라가서는 바로 벨 앞에 뛰어 내린다.

개스톤 : 안녕, 벨.

벨 : 안녕하세요.

개스톤 벨로부터 책을 빼앗는다.

- **gather**
  모이다
  If people gather somewhere or if someone gathers people somewhere, they come together in a group

- **surround**
  둘러싸다
  If a person or thing is surrounded by something, that thing is situated all around them

- **fit**
  어울리다
  If something fits, it is the right size and shape to go onto a person's body or onto a particular object

- **grab**
  잡아채다
  If you grab something, you take it or pick it up suddenly and roughly

It's a pity and a sin.
pity는 '연민, 동정, 유감, 측은히 여김'이라는 의미로, 무언가 안타까운 일에 대해 말할 때 자주 쓰인다. What a pity!(참 안됐구나)라는 문장도 기억해 두었다 사용해 보자.

Zoom In

It's a pity and a sin.
불쌍해.

BELLE : Gaston, may I have my book, please?

GASTON : How can you read this? There's no pictures!

Belle speaks in a proud voice with her arms folded.

BELLE : Well, some people use their imaginations.

GASTON : Belle, it's about time you got your head out of those books (tossing book into the mud) and paid attention to more important things... like me!

The Bimbettes, who are looking on, sigh.

GASTON : The whole town's talking about it.

Belle has picked up the book and is cleaning off the mud.

GASTON : It's not right for a woman to read. Soon she starts getting ideas... and thinking.

BELLE : Gaston, you are positively primeval.

GASTON : (putting his hand around her shoulders) Why thank you, Belle. Hey, what do you say you and me take a walk over to the tavern and take a look at my trophies.

Gaston tries to take her out.

BELLE : Maybe some other time.

The Bimbettes, who are in love with Gaston, can't understand Belle's attitude toward him.

BIMBETTE 1 : What's wrong with her?

벨 : 개스톤, 제 책 좀 돌려주시겠어요?
개스톤 : 어떻게 이런 책을 읽지? 그림이 하나도 없잖아!

벨은 팔짱을 낀 채 자신 있는 목소리로 말한다.

벨 : 상상을 하면서 읽으면 다 보여요.
개스톤 : 벨. 이런 책 따위는 집어치워. (책을 진흙탕에 빠뜨리며) 이제는 더 중요한 곳에 신경을 써 봐. 바로 나 같은.

바라보던 여자들은 황홀해한다.

개스톤 : 마을 모두가 그걸 얘기하고 있어.

벨은 책을 들어올려서 진흙을 털어낸다.

개스톤 : 여자가 책을 보면 생각이 많아져서 안 돼. 생각해봐.
벨 : 개스톤, 당신은 구제불능이군요.
개스톤 : (그녀의 어깨를 두드리며) 고맙군, 벨. 자 이제 우리 주막에 가서 내가 받은 트로피나 구경해볼까?

개스톤은 그녀를 데려가려고 한다.

벨 : 다음에요.

개스톤에게 반한 여자들은 벨의 태도를 이해할 수가 없다.

여자 1 : 말도 안 돼.

■ **proud**
자랑스러운
If you feel proud, you feel pleased about something good that you possess or have done, or about something good that a person close to you has done

■ **imagination**
상상력
Your imagination is the ability that you have to form pictures or ideas in your mind of things that are new and exciting, or things that you have not experienced

■ **sigh**
한숨쉬다, 탄식하다
When you sigh, you let out a deep breath, as a way of expressing feelings such as disappointment, tiredness, or pleasure

■ **primeval**
원시적인
You use primeval to describe things that belong to a very early period in the history of the world

■ **tavern**
주막
A tavern is a bar or pub

Maybe some other time.
어떤 일을 지금이 아닌 다음 기회로 미룰 때 쓸 수 있는 표현이다. Maybe next time. 또는 Maybe some other time. 이라고 말할 수 있다.

Zoom In

Maybe some other time.
다음에요.

BIMBETTE 2 : She's crazy!

BIMBETTE 3 : He's gorgeous!

Belle shakes his hands off and steps back.

BELLE : Please, Gaston. I can't. I have to get home to help my father. Good-bye.

LEFOU : Ha ha ha. That crazy old loon! He needs all the help he can get!

Gaston and Lefou laugh heartily.

BELLE : Don't you talk about my father that way!

GASTON : Yeah, don't talk about her father that way!

Gaston conks Lefou on the head.

BELLE : My father is not crazy! He's a genius!

Right at that moment, there is an explosion in the background. Gaston and Lefou continue laughing.

GASTON, LEFOU : Ha ha ha!

Belle rushes home and descends into the basement.

여자 2 : 미쳤어.
여자 3 : 개스톤은 정말 멋져.

벨은 그의 손을 뿌리치고 뒷걸음질 친다.

벨 : 제발, 개스톤. 집에 가봐야 해요. 집에 가서 아버지를 도와드려야 해요. 안녕.
르 푸 : 하하하. 그 미친 늙은 발명쟁이가 도움이 필요한가 보군.

개스톤과 르푸는 박장대소한다.

벨 : 우리 아버지를 그런 식으로 말하지 말아요!
개스톤 : 맞아, 그녀의 아버지를 그런 식으로 말하지 마!

개스톤은 르푸의 머리를 한 대 친다.

벨 : 아버지는 미치지 않았어요. 그는 다만 천재일 뿐이라구요!

바로 그 순간 폭발음이 들린다. 개스톤과 르푸는 계속해서 웃는다.

개스톤, 르푸 : 하하하!

벨은 집에 달려가서 지하실로 내려간다.

- **loon**
  미치광이
  A simple-minded or stupid person
- **genius**
  천재
  Genius is very great ability or skill in a particular subject or activity
- **explosion**
  폭발
  An explosion is a sudden, violent burst of energy, for example one caused by a bomb
- **descend**
  내려가다
  If you descend or if you descend a staircase, you move downwards from a higher to a lower level
- **basement**
  지하실
  The basement of a building is a floor built partly or completely below ground level

Key Expressions

18 If you like it all that much, it's yours!

그렇게 그 책이 좋다면 가져가도 좋아!

'If 주어+동사'는 '만약 ~한다면'이라는 뜻의 조건의 부사절을 이끈다. it's yours라는 표현은 이제 네 것이라는 의미이므로, 가져도 좋다는 허가의 뜻도 나타낼 수 있다.

· If you need this pen, it's yours. 이 펜이 필요하다면 가져가도 좋아.

20 It's no wonder that her name means 'BEAUTY'.

그녀의 이름이 미녀라는 뜻인 건 결코 이상하지 않죠.

wonder는 궁금증이라는 뜻이므로 It's no wonder that~이라고 하게 되면, '~해도 궁금하지 않다' 즉, '~해도 이상하지 않다'는 의미를 갖게 된다.

· It's no wonder that he became angry. 그가 화나는 것도 이상하지 않지.

22 You're the greatest hunter in the whole world!

넌 세상에서 가장 훌륭한 사냥꾼이야.

형용사 뒤에 est를 붙이면(3음절 이상의 경우 most를 붙이면) '가장 ~한'이라는 뜻의 최상급을 표현할 수 있다. 또한 최상급의 의미를 강조해주기 위해서 'in the whole world(전 세계에서)'와 같은 표현을 더해줄 수도 있다.

· She is the kindest girl in the whole world.
그녀는 세상에서 가장 친절한 여자야.

26 I'm going to make BELLE my wife!

벨을 내 아내로 만들고 말겠어.

I'm going to~는 앞으로 ~하겠다는 미래의 계획과 예정을 나타내는 표현이다. 'make'라는 동사 뒤에는 목적어와 목적보어가 올 수 있으므로, 목적어를 목적보어로 만들다는 의미로 써줄 수 있다.

· My parents are going to make my sister a doctor.
부모님은 여동생을 의사를 만들 계획이다.

28 with her arms folded 팔짱을 낀 채

with one's arms folded라는 표현은 '팔짱을 낀 채'라는 관용적 표현으로 외워두면 좋다. one's의 자리에 소유격을 써주면 된다.

· With his arms folded, he asked me why I was late for school.
그는 팔짱을 낀 채, 나에게 왜 지각을 했느냐고 물었다.

28 It's about time you paid attention to more important things like me! 이제는 바로 나 같은 더 중요한 곳에 신경을 쓸 때야!

It's about time that뒤에는 주어와 동사의 과거형이 와서 '~할 때이다'라는 가정법 과거 문형으로 쓰인다. 동사의 과거형이 온다는 데 주의해야 한다. about대신에 high를 써도 같은 의미이다.

· It's about time I broke up with him. 이제 그와 헤어질 때이다.

Movie Talk

영어의 특징

미국의 브로드웨이 뮤지컬가수이자 배우인 Paige O'Hara(페이지 오하라)가 ≪미녀와 야수≫에서 벨의 역할을 맡았다. 그녀는 미녀와 야수 1 · 2 및 번외 시리즈를 통해 전세계인의 사랑을 받았다. 한편, 야수의 목소리를 맡은 Robby Benson(로비 벤슨)은 일부 비평가들로부터 벤슨의 목소리이라고 믿기 어려울 정도로 뛰어난 목소리 연기였다고 호평을 받기도 했다.

그 외에도 개스톤(리처드 화이트, Richard White), 모리스(렉스 에버하트, Rex Everhart), 칩(브래들리 피어스, Bradley Pierce), 포트 부인(안젤라 랜스베리, Angela Lansbury) 등 다양한 연령층의 남성과 여성들이 골고루 출연하기 때문에, 학습자들은 다채로운 영어를 접해볼 수 있다. 따라서 특정 연령층이나 성별만 집중적으로 등장하는 영화보다 ≪미녀와 야수≫는 실제 영어권 환경에 적응하기에 훨씬 더 적합한 영화라고 할 수 있겠다.

영화에는 고풍스러운 단어들이 등장하여 고급스러운 표현들도 익힐 수 있는 한편, 실생활에서 바로 활용할 수 있는 간단하고 유용한 표현들이 많이 등장한다. 특히 콕스워즈와 루미에르의 빠르고 재미있는 대화로부터 많은 구어체 표현들도 익힐 수 있을 것이다.

이렇듯 ≪미녀와 야수≫에는 다양한 연령층의 남녀가 사용하는 유용한 실생활 표현들과 재미있는 구어체 표현들을 익힐 수 있는 장치가 곳곳에 마련되어 있다. 또한 노래가 자주 등장하여 더욱 생동감 있게 상황을 이해하고, 노래를 여러 번 듣는 것만으로도 살아있는 영어가 귀에 맴도는 암기 효과도 누릴 수 있을 것이다.

영어 난이도 The Degree of Difficulty ★★☆☆☆

속도(Speed) ★★☆☆☆ **표현**(Expression)★★☆☆☆ **어휘**(Vocabulary)★☆☆☆☆

L'ARGENT

Chapter 2

모리스, 야수의 성에 가다

Maurice Enters the Beast's Castle

시간 00:09:35 ~ 00:17:33

INT. BASEMENT

BELLE : Papa?

MAURICE : How on earth did that happen? Dog gonnit!

He pulls a barrel off his waist, along with his pants.

BELLE : Are you all right, Papa?

MAURICE : I'm... about ready to give up on this hunk of junk! (kicking machine)

BELLE : You always say that.

MAURICE : I mean it this time. I'll never get this boneheaded contraption to work.

He angrily points to the machine.

BELLE : Yes, you will. And you'll win first prize at the fair tomorrow.

내부. 지하실

벨 : 아빠?
모리스 : 세상에 어떻게 이럴 수가! 제기랄!

그는 허리에서 통을 빼내려는데 바지가 함께 벗겨진다.

벨 : 괜찮아요, 아빠?
모리스 : 이놈의 기계덩어리, 포기하기 일보 직전이야! (기계를 발로 차며)
벨 : 늘 그러셨잖아요.
모리스 : 이번엔 정말이야. 이 고물덩어리는 틀려먹었어.

그는 기계를 가리키며 화가 나서 말한다.

벨 : 아빠는 꼭 해낼 수 있어요. 내일 발명가 대회에서도 1등 하실 거예요.

- **barrel**
  통
  A barrel is a large, round container for liquids or food

- **give up**
  포기하다
  to stop trying to do something, usually because it is too difficult

- **junk**
  고물, 쓰레기
  Junk is old and used goods that have little value and that you do not want any more

- **contraption**
  기계, 장치
  You can refer to a device or machine as a contraption, especially when it looks strange or you do not know what it is used for

- **fair**
  대회, 박람회
  A county, state, or country fair is an event where there are, for example, displays of goods and animals, and amusements, games, and competitions

MAURICE : Hmmmph!

BELLE : ...and become a world famous inventor!

MAURICE : You really believe that?

BELLE : I always have.

MAURICE : Well, what are we waiting for? I'll have this thing fixed in no time.

He slides under the machine.

MAURICE : Hand me that ...The dog-legged clincher there... So, did you have a good time in town today?

BELLE : I got a new book. Papa, do you think I'm odd?

MAURICE : My daughter? Odd? (appears from under machine with bizarre goggle contraption on his head distorting his eyes) Where would you get an idea like that?

BELLE : Oh, I don't know. It's just that I'm not sure I fit in here. There's no one I can really talk to.

MAURICE : What about that Gaston? He's a handsome fellow!

BELLE : He's handsome all right, and rude and conceited and... Oh Papa, he's not for me!

Belle sits down helplessly.

MAURICE : Well, ha ha... don't you worry, 'cause this invention's gonna to be the start of a new life for us. (comes out from under machine) I think that's done it. Now, let's give it a try.

Maurice pulls down the lever of the machine and it whirs and chops wood, just as it should. The machine works well.

모리스 : 흠…

벨 : …이 세상 제일가는 발명가가 될 걸요!

모리스 : 정말 그렇게 생각하니?

벨 : 전 언제나 그렇게 생각하고 있었는걸요.

모리스 : 자. 그렇다면 이러고 있을 때가 아니지. 사설이나 늘어놓고 있을 순 없지.

그는 기계 밑으로 들어가 눕는다.

모리스 : 저기 굽은 연장 좀 다오. 그래, 오늘 마을에서는 즐거웠니?

벨 : 새 책을 얻어 왔어요. 아빠. 제가 좀 이상하다고 생각하세요?

모리스 : 우리 딸이? 이상해? (눈을 일그러지게 하는 이상한 고글 장치를 머리에 쓰고 기계 밑에서 나오면서) 왜 그런 터무니없는 생각을 하니?

벨 : 모르겠어요. 저는 이곳에 어울리지 않는 사람 같아요. 말이 통하는 사람도 없구요.

모리스 : 개스톤은 어떻더냐? 미남이던데.

벨 : 잘 생겼지만, 무례하고 잘난 척하고… 아빠, 제 타입은 아니에요.

벨은 힘없이 걸터앉는다.

모리스 : 하하… 걱정마라. 발명이 잘 되면 새 출발을 할 수 있을 테니. (기계 밑에서 나온다) 이제 됐다. 이제 시험해보자.

모리스는 기계의 레버를 당기자, 도끼가 요란한 소음과 함께 나무를 베기 시작한다. 기계는 잘 작동한다.

- **odd**
  이상한
  If you describe someone or something as odd, you think that they are strange or unusual

- **fellow**
  친구
  You use fellow to describe people who are in the same situation as you, or people you feel you have something in common with

- **conceited**
  자만하는
  If you say that someone is conceited, you are showing your disapproval of the fact that they are far too proud of their abilities or achievements

- **whir**
  윙 소리를 내다
  When something such as a machine or an insect's wing whirrs, it makes a series of low sounds so quickly that they seem like one continuous sound

Where would you get an idea like that?
get an idea는 '영감을 얻다, 생각을 하게 되다'는 뜻이므로 위 문장은 직역하면 어디서 그런 생각을 얻게 되었냐는 의미이다. 상대방이 어떻게 해서 그런 생각을 하게 되었는지를 물을 수 있다.

Zoom In

Where would you get an idea like that?

왜 그런 터무니없는 생각을 하니?

BELLE : It works!

MAURICE : It does? It does!

BELLE : You did it! You really did it!

MAURICE : Hitch up Phillipe, girl. I'm off to the fair!

Log strikes him in the head, knocking him out. Fade to later in the day.

EXT. IN FRONT OF BELLE'S COTTAGE
The next morning, Maurice heads to the fair riding Phillipe with a wagon.

BELLE : Goodbye, Papa! Good luck!

MAURICE : Goodbye, Belle. And take care while I'm gone!

Maurice and Phillipe continue on their journey until they become lost. It's getting darker and darker.

MAURICE : We should be there by now. Maybe we missed a turn. I guess I should have taken a... wait a minute.

Maurice lifts lantern to illuminate sign giving various directions.

MAURICE : No! Let's go this way!

Phillipe looks right at a dark overgrown path, then left towards a more inviting route, then begins to go left.

MAURICE : Come on, Phillipe! It's a shortcut. We'll be there in no time!

Maurice forces Phillipe to go through the dark path and they continue through the dark.

벨 : 아빠, 움직여요.

모리스 : 그래? 정말 움직이네!

벨 : 해냈어요. 정말로 해냈어요.

모리스 : 말을 끌고 와, 얘야. 대회장에 가야지.

모리스는 나무토막에 머리를 맞고 정신이 혼미해진다. 날이 저문다.

외부. 벨의 집 앞
다음 날 아침, 모리스는 필립에 짐수레를 싣고 대회장으로 향한다.

벨 : 잘 다녀오세요. 아빠. 행운을 빌어요.

모리스 : 잘 있거라. 벨. 내가 없는 동안 몸 건강하고.

모리스와 필립은 길을 잃을 때까지 여행을 계속한다. 날이 점점 어두워진다.

모리스 : 지금쯤 도착할 때가 되었는데. 길을 잘못 들었나? 이 길로 갔어야 했… 잠깐.

모리스는 손전등으로 에어하임과 발렌시아를 가리키는 표지판을 비춘다.

모리스 : 이쪽으로 가자!

필립은 어둡고 잡초가 무성한 오른쪽 길과, 가기 편한 왼쪽 길을 휘휘 돌아본다. 그러고 나서는 왼쪽으로 가기 시작한다.

모리스 : 왜 그래, 필립! 이쪽이 지름길이야. 이제 곧 도착할거야!

모리스는 필립에게 어두운 길로 가게 한다. 그들은 어둠 속을 계속 헤쳐 간다.

- **knock out**
  의식을 잃게 하다
  to make somebody fall asleep or become unconscious

- **journey**
  여행, 여정
  When you make a journey, you travel from one place to another

- **illuminate**
  비추다
  To illuminate something means to shine light on it and to make it brighter and more visible

- **shortcut**
  지름길
  A short cut is a quicker way of getting somewhere than the usual route

Take care while I'm gone!
Take care!하면 헤어질 때 쓸 수 있는 인사말로, '건강해! 몸 조심해!'라는 뜻이다. 친한 사이에서는 Bye.뒤에 Take care!을 더하여 사용해보자.

Zoom In

Take care while I'm gone!
내가 없는 동안 몸 건강하고!

MAURICE : This can't be right. Where have you taken us, Phillipe? We'd better turn around... and...

Out of fear Phillipe starts to step back suddenly. Maurice tries to keep the balance not to fall off.

MAURICE : Whoa... whoa, boy, whoa, now whoa Phillipe. Oh, oh! Look out! No!

A swarm of bats fly out of a tree. Phillipe. runs through the forest avoiding everything until he almost runs over the edge of a cliff.

MAURICE : Whoa... whoa boy. Back up! Back up! Back up! Good boy, good boy. That's good, that's... back up! Steady. Steady! Hey now. Steady.

But Phillipe is still freaked out about some scary forces in the forest and finally bucks off Maurice.

MAURICE : Phillipe! Oh!

Phillipe runs away leaving Maurice on the edge of the cliff.

MAURICE : Phillipe! Oh no!

He looks up and sees Wolves growling at him. Maurice runs away being chased by the Wolves. He stumbles down a hill and lands at the gate of a castle. He grabs the locked gate and tries to shake it open.

MAURICE : Help! Is someone there? Help!

The gate opens and Maurice runs in. He slams the gate in the faces of the Wolves. Leaving his hat on the ground as the rain begins to fall, Maurice runs to the castle and bangs on the door. It creaks open and he enters cautiously.

모리스 : 이게 아닌데. 도대체 여기가 어디지, 필립? 돌아가는 게 낫겠…

겁에 질린 필립이 갑자기 뒷걸음을 치기 시작한다. 모리스는 떨어지지 않기 위해 균형을 잡아보려 애 쓴다.

모리스 : 진정해. 천천히 필립. 어, 어! 조심해!

나무에서 박쥐 떼가 날아간다. 필립은 다른 동물들을 피해 숲 속을 달리다가 거의 벼랑 끝에 이른다.

모리스 : 워워… 뒤로! 뒤로! 그래, 좋아. 뒤로! 천천히, 천천히! 진정해.

그러니 필립은 숲속의 무언가 무시무시한 분위기에 흥분해서, 결국 모리스를 떨어뜨린다.

모리스 : 필립! 오!

필립은 모리스를 벼랑 끝에 놔둔 채 도망간다.

모리스 : 필립! 오, 안 돼!

위를 올려다보니 늑대가 그를 향해 으르렁대고 있다. 모리스는 늑대들에게 쫓겨 도망간다. 그는 언덕에서 굴러 성 문 앞에 떨어진다. 그는 잠긴 철문을 열어 보려고 성문을 붙잡고 흔든다.

모리스 : 도와줘요. 누구 없어요? 도와줘!

성 문이 열리고 모리스는 그 안으로 들어간다. 그는 늑대들을 앞에 두고 성문을 쾅 닫는다. 비가 쏟아지기 시작하는데, 모자를 땅에 떨어뜨린 채 모리스는 성 안으로 달려가서 문을 두드린다. 문이 삐걱거리면서 열리자 그는 조심스럽게 들어간다.

- **swarm**
  떼, 무리
  A swarm of bees or other insects is a large group of them flying together
- **avoid**
  피하다
  If you avoid something unpleasant that might happen, you take action in order to prevent it from happening
- **steady**
  조심해!
  You say 'steady on' to someone to tell them to calm down or to be careful about what they are saying
- **chase**
  쫓다
  If you chase someone, or chase after them, you run after them or follow them quickly in order to catch or reach them
- **bang**
  쾅쾅 치다
  If something bangs, it makes a sudden loud noise, once or several times

Where have you taken us, Phillipe?
여기서 take는 '데리고 가다'라는 의미로, 우리를 어디로 데리고 갔냐는 뜻이므로, '도대체 여기가 어디지?'라는 의미로 쓸 수 있다. 간단하게 Where are we?라고 말할 수도 있다.

Zoom In

Where have you taken us, Phillipe?

도대체 여기가 어디지, 필립?

INT. INSIDE THE CASTLE

MAURICE : Hello? Hello?

Maurice's voice echoes in the darkness.
Watching from a table near the entrance are Lumiere and Cogsworth.

LUMIERE : (barely whispering) Poor fellow must have lost his way in the woods.

COGSWORTH : (also whispering) Keep quiet! Maybe he'll go away.

MAURICE : Is someone there?

COGSWORTH : Not a word, Lumiere. Not one word!

MAURICE : I don't mean to intrude but I've lost my horse and I need a place to stay for the night.

Lumiere looks at Cogsworth like a child having just found a lost puppy.

LUMIERE : Oh! Cogsworth, have a heart.

COGSWORTH : Shush shhhhh!

Cogsworth puts hand over Lumiere's mouth, who promptly proceeds to touch his lit candle hand to Cogsworth's hand.

COGSWORTH : Ow ow Ow OW OW OUCH!!!!!

LUMIERE : Of course, monsieur, you are welcome here.

Maurice looks around in confusion.

MAURICE : Who said that?

He picks up the candlestick for light, not realizing that the speaker is in his hand.

내부. 성 안

모리스 : 계세요? 아무도 없어요?

모리스의 목소리가 어둠 속에서 울려 퍼진다. 입구 근처의 테이블에서 루미에르와 콕스워즈가 그를 바라보고 있다.

루미에르 : (작게 속삭이며) 노인이 숲속에서 길을 잃었나봐.

콕스워즈 : (역시 속삭이며) 조용히 해! 아마 곧 돌아가겠지.

모리스 : 아무도 없어요?

콕스워즈 : 조용히 있어. 가만히 있으라구.

모리스 : 실례합니다만, 말도 잃어버리고, 하룻밤 묵을 곳이 필요해요.

루미에르는 잃어버린 강아지를 막 찾은 아이와 같은 표정으로 콕스워즈를 바라본다.

루미에르 : 콕스워즈. 도와주자.

콕스워즈 : 쉿!

콕스워즈가 손으로 루미에르의 입을 막자, 루미에르는 바로 촛불을 켜서 콕스워즈의 손에 닿게 한다.

콕스워즈 : 아, 아, 아 뜨거!

루미에르 : 물론 괜찮아요. 어서 오세요.

모리스는 혼란스러워서 주변을 둘러본다.

모리스 : 누구세요?

그는 말하는 사람이 손에 있는 것을 알아차리지 못한 채 불을 밝히려고 촛대를 들어 올린다.

- **echo**
  메아리치다
  If a sound echoes, it is reflected off a surface and can be heard again after the original sound has stopped

- **entrance**
  출입구
  The entrance to a place is the way into it, for example a door or gate

- **intrude**
  침범하다
  If you say that someone is intruding into a particular place or situation, you mean that they are not wanted or welcome there

- **candlestick**
  촛대
  A candlestick is a narrow object with a hole at the top which holds a candle

I've lost my horse and I need a place to stay for the night.
have lost는 잃어버려서 지금 없다는 현재완료 시제가 사용된 문장이다. stay for the night은 "하룻밤 묵다"는 뜻으로, stand overnight, spend a night, put up for the night역시 같은 뜻의 숙어이다.

Zoom In

I've lost my horse and I need a place to stay for the night.

말도 잃어버리고 하룻밤 묵을 곳이 필요해요.

LUMIERE : (tapping him on the shoulder) Over here!

MAURICE : (spins around, pulling Lumiere to the other side) Where?

LUMIERE : (taps Maurice on the side of the head. Maurice looks at Lumiere) Hello!

MAURICE : Oh!!!!

Startled, Maurice drops Lumiere onto the floor.

MAURICE : Incredible!

COGSWORTH : (hopping over) Well, now you've done it, Lumiere. Splendid just peachy... aaarrrgghh!

Maurice picks up Cogsworth.

MAURICE : How is this accomplished? (he fiddles with Cogsworth)

COGSWORTH : Put me down! At once! Stop that! Stop that, I say!

Maurice tickles the bottoms of Cogsworth's feet. He laughs. He begins to wind the spring on the back of Cogsworth's head, twisting his face around with the clock hands. Maurice opens the front of Cogsworth and begins to play with his pendulum. Cogsworth slams the door shut on his finger.

COGSWORTH : Sir, close that at once, do you mind!

MAURICE : I beg your pardon, it's... it's just that I've never seen a clock that... aah... I mean... aah aah aah-chooo!!!!

Maurice sneezes in the face of Cogsworth, who proceeds to wipe his face off using his clock hands in a very anachronistic windshield wiper manner. Maurice sniffles indicating the cold he has caught from being in the rain.

LUMIERE : Oh, you are soaked to the bone, Monsieur. Come, warm yourself by the fire.

루미에르 : (그의 어깨를 툭툭 치며) 여기에요.

모리스 : (빙글 돌면서 루미에르를 다른 쪽으로 비추어본다) 어디요?

루미에르 : (모리스의 머리를 톡톡 친다. 모리스가 루미에르를 본다) 안녕하세요?

모리스 : 오!

놀란 모리스는 루미에르를 바닥에 떨어뜨린다.

모리스 : 믿을 수 없어!

콕스워즈 : (뛰어 오면서) 결국 일을 저질렀군, 루미에르. 잘했어, 아주 장하다. 아!

모리스가 콕스워즈를 들어 올린다.

모리스 : 어떻게 만들었지? (콕스워즈를 만지작거린다)

콕스워즈 : 내려줘요! 빨리! 멈춰요! 멈추라고 말하잖아요!

모리스는 콕스워즈의 발을 간지럽히고, 콕스워즈는 낄낄댄다. 그가 콕스워즈의 머리 뒤에 있는 태엽을 돌리자, 그의 얼굴이 시계바늘 때문에 일그러진다. 모리스는 콕스워즈 뚜껑을 열고 시계추를 건드리기 시작한다. 콕스워즈는 모리스의 손가락을 끼운 채 뚜껑을 닫아버린다.

콕스워즈 : 당장 문 닫아요. 허락도 없이.

모리스 : 미안합니다. 나는 그저 본 적이 없던 거라··· 에··· 에··· 에··· 에취!

모리스는 콕스워즈의 얼굴에 재채기를 하자, 시계바늘이 구식 와이퍼처럼 시계판을 닦는다. 모리스는 훌쩍이는데, 비 때문에 감기에 걸린 것처럼 보인다.

루미에르 : 저런. 흠뻑 젖으셨군요, 아저씨. 이리 오셔서 몸을 좀 녹이세요.

- **incredible**
  놀라운
  If you describe something or someone as incredible, you like them very much or are impressed by them, because they are extremely or unusually good

- **splendid**
  장한, 훌륭한
  If you say that something is splendid, you mean that it is very good

- **accomplish**
  성취하다
  If you accomplish something, you succeed in doing it

- **tickle**
  간지럼을 태우다
  When you tickle someone, you move your fingers lightly over a sensitive part of their body, often in order to make them laugh

- **soak**
  젖다
  If you soak something or leave it to soak, you put it into a liquid and leave it there

Well, now you've done it.
have done은 현재완료 시제가 쓰인 것으로, 이미 일을 저지른 것이 완료되었다는 의미를 함축한다. 따라서 You've done it.은 결국 일을 저질러서 지금 손 쓸 방도가 없음을 탓하는 표현으로 쓰일 수 있다.

Zoom In

Well, now you've done it.

결국 일을 저질렀군.

MAURICE : Thank you.

Lumiere and Maurice head towards the den, with Cogsworth running after them.

COGSWORTH : No, no, no, you know what the master would do if he finds him here.

Beast is watching the action from an overhead walkway and rushes off as the trio enters the den.

COGSWORTH : I demand that you stop... right... there!

Cogsworth tumbles down the steps. Maurice takes a seat in a large chair in front of a roaring fire.

COGSWORTH : Oh no no, not the master's chair!

Footstool rushes past Cogsworth, barking up a storm.

COGSWORTH : I'm not seeing this, I'm not seeing this!

MAURICE : (as Footstool rushes up to him) Well, hello there, boy.

Footstool props himself up under the feet of Maurice. Coatrack enters and removes his cloak.

MAURICE : What service!

COGSWORTH : All right, this has gone far enough. I'm in charge here, and...

While saying this, Cogsworth is run over by the anachronistic Indycar sounding teacart of Mrs. Potts.

모리스 : 고맙습니다.

루미에르와 모리스는 방 쪽으로 향하고, 콕스워즈가 그들 뒤를 쫓아간다.

콕스워즈 : 안 돼. 안 돼. 주인님이 보면 어떻게 될지 알잖아.

야수는 이들의 행동을 저 위에서 바라보고 있다가 그들이 방으로 들어가자 빠르게 자리를 뜬다.

콕스워즈 : 안 돼. 이제 그만 해!

콕스워즈는 계단에서 굴러 떨어진다. 모리스는 벽난로 앞에 있는 큰 의자에 앉는다.

콕스워즈 : 이런, 주인님 의자는 안 돼!

발 깔개(풋스툴)가 짖으면서 콕스워즈 옆으로 빠르게 지나간다.

콕스워즈 : 난 못 본거야. 난 몰라!
모리스 : (풋스툴이 그에게 달려오자) 안녕 꼬마야.

풋스툴은 모리스의 발밑으로 들어와 받침대가 된다. 옷걸이대가 들어와서 망토를 둘러준다.

모리스 : 친절하군요!
콕스워즈 : 자, 이제 이쯤에서 그만하자. 내가 여기 책임자이고…

말하는 도중에 콕스워즈는 포트 부인이 끄는 티 왜건 밑에 깔린다.

- **tumble**
  굴러 떨어지다
  If someone or something tumbles somewhere, they fall there with a rolling or bouncing movement
- **roaring**
  타오르는
  A roaring fire has large flames and is sending out a lot of heat
- **prop**
  받침대
  If you prop an object on or against something, you support it by putting something underneath it or by resting it somewhere
- **remove**
  제거하다
  If you remove something from a place, you take it away
- **cloak**
  망토
  A cloak is a long, loose, sleeveless piece of clothing which people used to wear over their other clothes when they went out

All right, this has gone far enough.
All right은 '자, 그래, 알았어'와 같이 상황을 정리하고 새로운 말을 시작하려고 할 때 쓰이는 표현이다. has gone far enough는 너무 멀리 가버렸다는 뜻이므로, 이제 그만하자는 의미를 나타낼 수 있다.

Zoom In

All right, this has gone far enough.
자, 이제 이쯤에서 그만하자.

MRS. POTTS : (arriving by the side of Maurice) How would you like a nice spot of tea, sir? It'll warm you up in no time.

She pours tea into cup (Chip), which hops over into Maurice's open hand.

COGSWORTH : (from face down position on carpet) No! No tea, no tea!!!

CHIP : (as Maurice sips the tea) Ha ha! His moustache tickles, momma!

MAURICE : (startled by the cup) Oh! Hello!

The door to the den slams open and a strong gust of wind blows into the room, extinguishing Lumiere's flames and the fire in the fireplace. Cogsworth dives for cover. Mrs. Potts begins to shake. Chip jumps back onto the tea cart and takes refuge from behind his mother.

CHIP : Uh oh!

Beast enters. We see him in full for the first time. He is on all fours. He looks around in the darkness.

BEAST : (growling his words) There's a stranger here.

LUMIERE : (who has relit his flames) Master, allow me to explain. The gentleman was lost in the woods and he was cold and wet so...

Lumiere's last sentence is drowned out by the very loud growl of Beast which puts out his flames once again. Lumiere looks down dejected.

COGSWORTH : (coming out from under a rug) Master, I'd like to take this moment to say... I was against this from the start. It was all his fault. I tried to stop them but would they listen to me? No, no...!

포트 부인 : (모리스 옆으로 와서) 차를 드시겠어요? 금방 몸이 따뜻해질 거예요.

그녀는 찻잔에 차를 따르고, 찻잔은 모리스의 손바닥까지 뛰어오른다.

콕스워즈 : (카펫에 얼굴을 묻고 있다가) 안 돼. 차는 안 돼!

칩 : (모리스가 차를 홀짝이자) 하하. 턱수염이 간지러워요. 엄마.

모리스 : (찻잔을 보고 놀라서) 오. 안녕?

방문이 쾅 열리더니 방 안으로 거센 돌풍이 불어온다. 루미에르의 불꽃과 벽난로의 불이 꺼진다. 콕스워즈는 몸을 숨기기 위해 뛰어든다. 포트 부인은 고개를 흔든다. 칩은 티 카트로 다시 뛰어올라가 엄마 뒤에 숨는다.

칩 : 이런!

야수가 등장한다. 처음으로 그의 전신이 보인다. 그는 네 발로 서 있다. 그는 어둠 속에서 주위를 둘러본다.

야 수 : (으르렁거리며) 이 자는 누구냐?

루미에르 : (불을 다시 밝히며) 주인님, 제가 설명할게요. 이 분이 숲에서 길을 잃으셨는데 추워 보이고 비에 젖어서…

야수가 크게 으르렁거리자 루미에르의 마지막 말은 묻히고, 다시 그의 불이 꺼진다. 루미에르는 실의에 빠져 바닥을 내려다본다.

콕스워즈 : (깔개에서 나오며) 주인님, 제 말을 들어 주세요… 저는 처음부터 절대 안 된다고 했습니다. 막아보려 했지만 제 말을 들어야 말이죠. 전 아니에요!

- **mustache**
  콧수염
  A man's moustache is the hair that grows on his upper lip. If it is very long, it is sometimes referred to as his moustaches

- **extinguish**
  끄다
  If you extinguish a fire or a light, you stop it burning or shining

- **refuge**
  피신
  If you take refuge somewhere, you try to protect yourself from physical harm by going there

- **growl**
  으르렁거리다
  When a dog or other animal growls, it makes a low noise in its throat, usually because it is angry

I was against this from the start.
be against는 '반대하다'라는 뜻으로 자주 사용되는 표현이다. 이외에도 object, disagree, oppose도 같은 뜻의 동사이다. 반면에 찬성을 나타낼 때는 support, agree, approve, support와 같은 동사들을 쓴다.

Zoom In

I was against this from the start.
저는 처음부터 절대 안 된다고 했습니다.

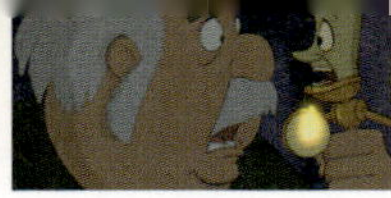

Again Beast's growl drowns out Cogsworth.
Maurice looks to one side of the chair then to the other and sees Beast.

BEAST : Who are you! What are you doing here?

Being very scared Maurice backs away from the advancing Beast.

MAURICE : I… I… I was lost in the woods and... (stares at Beast)

BEAST : (advancing on him) You are not welcome here!

MAURICE : I... I'm... I'm sorry

BEAST : What are you staring at?

MAURICE : (cowering under Beast) Nothing... (turns to leave)

BEAST : (racing around and blocking the entrance with surprising speed) So, you've come to stare at the Beast, have you?

MAURICE : Please, I meant no harm! I just needed a place to stay .

BEAST : I'll give you a place to stay!

MAURICE : No, no, please! No! No!

Beast picks up Maurice, carries him out of the room and slams the door, plunging the den... along with Cogsworth, Lumiere, Mrs. Potts-and Chip... into darkness. Fade out.

또 다시 야수가 으르렁거려 콕스워즈의 말을 삼켜 버린다. 모리스는 의자 한 쪽을 쳐다보고, 다른 한 쪽을 보려는데 야수가 눈에 띈다.

야 수 : 넌 누구냐! 여기서 뭘 하고 있지?

겁에 질린 모리스는 다가오는 야수로부터 뒷걸음질 친다.

모리스 : 저… 저… 저는 숲에서 길을 잃어서… (야수를 본다)

야 수 : (모리스를 향해 전진하며) 여긴 네가 올 곳이 아니야!

모리스 : 죄송합니다.

야 수 : 뭘 쳐다봐!

모리스 : (야수에게 몸을 숙이며) 아… 아… 아무것도 아니에요! (도망치려 한다)

야 수 : (뛰어다니며 놀라운 속도로 입구를 막으면서) 야수를 구경하러 왔지?

모리스 : 제발. 아니에요. 다만 머물 곳이 필요했을 뿐입니다.

야 수 : 네가 묵을 곳을 마련해 주지.

모리스 : 제발, 제발! 안돼! 안돼요!

야수는 모리스를 집어 들어 그를 방 밖으로 데리고 나간 뒤 문을 쾅 닫는다. 어둠 속에 콕스워즈, 루미에르, 포트 부인, 칩이 나란히 서있다. 화면이 점점 희미해진다.

- **drown**
  삼키다
  When someone drowns or is drowned, they die because they have gone or been pushed under water and cannot breathe

- **advance**
  다가가다
  To advance means to move forward, often in order to attack someone

- **stare**
  빤히 쳐다보다
  If you stare at someone or something, you look at them for a long time

- **harm**
  해치다
  To harm a person or animal means to cause them physical injury, usually on purpose

Key Expressions

40 How on earth did that happen?

도대체 어떻게 이런 일이 일어날 수 있지?

의문문에 on earth를 삽입하면 '도대체'라는 의미를 더해주어 물어보는 문장을 강조해 준다. 따라서 How on earth did that happen?이라고 물어보면 도대체 어떻게 이런 일이 일어날 수 있는지 기가 막혀 하면서 묻는 표현이 된다.

· What on earth are you doing? 너 도대체 뭐 하는 거니?

42 So, did you have a good time in town today?

그래, 오늘 마을에서 좋은 시간 보냈니?

여기서 So는 '그래'라는 뜻으로 well과 같이 대화를 시작할 때 문장 첫머리에 자주 붙는 표현이다. have a good time은 '좋은 시간을 보내다'라는 숙어이다.

· We had a good time in Hawaii. 우리는 하와이에서 즐거운 시간을 보냈어.

44 It's getting darker and darker. 점점 더 어두워지고 있다.

'get 비교급 and 비교급'은 '점점 더 ~해지다'라는 중요한 비교급 관용어구이다. 현재진행형으로 써주면 현재 그 상태가 더욱 발전되고 있음을 강조할 수 있다.

· Finding a job is getting harder and harder.
일자리를 찾는 것이 점점 더 어려워지고 있다.

46 **We'd better turn around.** 돌아가는 게 좋겠어.

'had better 동사원형'은 '~하는 편이 더 낫겠다'는 충고를 나타내는 표현이다. 주어와 had를 줄여서 주어'd와 같은 축약형으로도 자주 쓰인다.

· You'd better go home now. 너는 지금 집에 가는 편이 낫겠다.

48 **Poor fellow must have lost his way in the woods.**
나이든 친구가 숲속에서 길을 잃은 게 틀림없어.

must have p.p.는 '~했었음에 틀림없다'는 과거에 대한 강한 추측을 나타내는 조동사를 활용한 중요한 표현이다.

· She was absent from school. She must have been sick.
그녀는 결석을 했다. 그녀는 아팠던 것이 틀림없다.

54 **How would you like a nice spot of tea, sir?**
맛있는 차 좀 드시겠습니까?

would like가 들어가면 정중하게 권유하는 표현이 된다. 뒤에 명사가 와도 좋고, 동사를 쓰고 싶을 경우에는 to부정사를 쓰면 된다.

· Would you like something hot to drink?
따뜻한 것 좀 드실래요?

Chapter 3

개스톤의 끔찍한 프러포즈

Gaston's Terrible Proposal

시간 00:17:34 ~ 00:21:05

EXT. NEAR BELLS'S HOUSE

Fade in to Belle's cottage seen from POV of Gaston and Lefou. Gaston and Lefou have a talk, peeping at Belle's house through the branches.

LEFOU : Heh! Oh boy! Belle's gonna get the surprise of her life, huh Gaston?

GASTON : Yep. This is her lucky day!

Gaston lets go of a branch, which swings back and hits Lefou in the mouth. Gaston turns to the band, wedding guests and others apparently just out of sight of Belle's cottage.

GASTON : I'd like to thank you all for coming to my wedding. But first, I'd better go in there and... propose to the girl!

Minister, Baker, and Others laugh heartily. Camera pans quickly to show Bimbettes crying their eyes out. Gaston presses Lefou's nose and talks to him in a threatening manner. Pointing at Belle's house he gives directions to Lefou.

외부. 벨의 집 근처
개스톤과 르푸의 시야에 벨의 오두막집이 점점 뚜렷하게 보인다. 개스톤과 르푸는 나뭇가지 사이로 벨의 집을 엿보면서 대화를 나눈다.

르 푸 : 하하, 친구. 벨이 깜짝 놀라겠지? 개스톤.

개스톤 : 그럼. 그녀에겐 행운의 날이지.

개스톤이 구부리고 있던 나뭇가지를 놓자, 가지가 다시 휘어지면서 르푸의 입을 친다.
개스톤은 벨의 오두막집 바로 밖에서 밴드와 결혼식 손님에게 다가간다.

개스톤 : 결혼식에 와주셔서 감사합니다. 하지만 먼저, 벨의 집에 들어가서… 청혼을 해야지!

목사, 빵집 주인, 다른 사람들 모두가 배꼽을 잡고 웃는다. 카메라는 눈물을 흘리는 여자들을 빠르게 비춘다. 개스톤은 르푸의 코를 누르며 그에게 위협적으로 말한다. 벨의 집을 가리키며 르푸에게 지시를 내린다.

- **POV**
  (영화 장면에서) 시점
  Point of view
- **cottage**
  오두막집
  A cottage is a small house, usually in the country
- **peep**
  훔쳐보다
  If you peep, or peep at something, you have a quick look at it, often secretly and quietly
- **threatening**
  위협적인
  You can describe someone's behaviour as threatening when you think that they are trying to harm you
- **direction**
  지시
  A direction is the general line that someone or something is moving or pointing in

GASTON : And, you Lefou, now, when Belle and I come out that door...

LEFOU : Oh I know, I know! I strike up the band.

He turns and begins directing the band in "Here Comes the Bride." Gaston slams a baritone over his head.

GASTON : Not yet!

LEFOU : (from inside the instrument, with his lips sticking out the mouthpiece) Sorry!

INT. BELLE'S COTTAGE

Cut to interior of cottage. Belle is sitting in a chair reading her new book. There is a knock at the door. She puts the book down and walks to the door. She reaches up and pulls down a viewing device. She peeks through and sees an anachronistically accurate fish-eye view of Gaston. She moans and pushes the door open.

BELLE : Gaston, what a pleasant... surprise.

Gaston takes a step forward to Belle and Belle takes a step backwards.

GASTON : Isn't it though? I'm just full of surprises. You know, Belle. There's not a girl in town who wouldn't love to be in your shoes. This is the day...

Gaston pauses by a mirror and licks his teeth clean.

GASTON : This is the day your dreams come true.

Belle keeps stepping back. She seems to be scared.

BELLE : What do you know about my dreams, Gaston?

개스톤 : 잘 들어, 르푸. 벨과 내가 함께 저 문으로 나오면…
르 푸 : 그래, 알았어. 연주를 시작해.

그는 돌아서서 밴드에게 '결혼행진곡'을 연주할 것을 지시하기 시작한다. 개스톤은 바리톤으로 그의 머리를 내리친다.

개스톤 : 아직 아니야!
르 푸 : (악기 부는 부분으로 입술만 빠져 나와서) 미안!

내부. 벨의 집
오두막집 내부 장면. 벨은 새 책을 읽으면서 의자에 앉아있다. 문을 두드리는 소리가 난다. 그녀는 책을 내려놓고 문 쪽으로 걸어간다. 그녀는 다가가서 바깥을 볼 수 있는 장치를 당겨본다. 힐끔 보니 구식인 어안렌즈로 개스톤의 얼굴이 선명하게 보인다. 그녀는 투덜거리면서 문을 연다.

벨 : 개스톤, 갑자기 무슨 일이에요.

개스톤은 벨에게 한 걸음 다가오고, 벨은 한 발 뒷걸음질 친다.

개스톤 : 그래? 난 놀라운 사람이지. 알다시피, 벨. 이 마을 모든 여자들이 당신을 부러워하고 있어. 오늘이 바로…

개스톤은 거울 옆에 잠시 멈춰 서서 혀로 이를 깨끗이 훑는다.

개스톤 : 오늘은 바로 당신의 꿈이 실현되는 날이야.

벨은 계속 뒷걸음질 친다. 그녀는 두려워하는 것 같아 보인다.

벨 : 당신이 나의 꿈을 어떻게 알아요, 개스톤?

- **slam**
  쾅 닫다, 세게 밀다
  If you slam a door or window or if it slams, it shuts noisily and with great force
- **device**
  장치
  A device is an object that has been invented for a particular purpose, for example for recording or measuring something
- **peek**
  재빨리 훔쳐보다
  If you peek at something or someone, you have a quick look at them, often secretly
- **pause**
  잠시 멈추다
  If you pause while you are doing something, you stop for a short period and then continue
- **lick**
  핥다
  When people or animals lick something, they move their tongue across its surface

This is the day your dreams come true.
dreams come true는 '꿈이 실현되다'라는 표현으로 다양하게 많이 쓰인다. 특히 make one's dreams come true(~의 꿈이 실현되게 하다)의 형태로도 자주 사용되니 알아둔다.
ex) I will do my best to make my dreams come true.

Zoom In

This is the day your dreams come true.
오늘은 바로 당신의 꿈이 실현되는 날이야.

GASTON : Plenty. Here, picture this.

Gaston plops down in the chair and props his mud-covered feet up on Belle's book. He begins to kick off his boots and wiggle his toes through his holey socks.

GASTON : A rustic hunting lodge. My latest kill roasting on the fire and my little wife, massaging my feet, while the little ones play on the floor with the dogs.

Belle looks positively disgusted. Gaston's feet smell so bad that she holds her nose.
Gaston gets up next to her face.

GASTON : We'll have six or seven.

BELLE : Dogs?

GASTON : No, Belle! Strapping boys, like me!

BELLE : Imagine that.

She picks up her book, places a mark in it and puts it on the shelf.

GASTON : And do you know who that wife will be?

BELLE : Let me think.

GASTON : You, Belle!

BELLE : (ducking under Gaston's arms) Gaston, I'm… I'm speechless. I really don't know what to say.

He pushes chairs and things out of the way until he reaches Belle and traps her against the door.

GASTON : Say you'll marry me.

개스톤 : 다 알지. 들어봐.

개스톤은 의자에 앉아 그의 진흙투성이 발을 벨의 책 위에 올려놓는다. 그는 부츠를 발로 차서 벗어버리고는 구멍 난 양말 사이로 빠져나온 발가락을 꼼지락거린다.

개스톤 : 사냥꾼의 오두막에서 내가 갓 잡아온 짐승을 불에 구우며, 아이들이 개와 노는 동안에 내 발을 주무르는 귀여운 부인.

벨은 역겨워한다. 개스톤의 발 냄새가 심해서 그녀는 코를 움켜쥐고 있다.
개스톤은 일어나서 그녀의 얼굴 옆으로 들이댄다.

개스톤 : 여섯 일곱은 있어야지.
벨 : 개 말이에요?
개스톤 : 아니. 벨. 나를 닮은 우리 건강한 아이들 말이야.
벨 : 꿈도 크군요.

그녀는 책을 들어 표시를 해둔 뒤 책꽂이에 집어넣는다.

개스톤 : 그 여자가 누군지 알아?
벨 : 글쎄요.
개스톤 : 당신이야, 벨!
벨 : (개스톤의 팔 밑으로 빠져나오며) 개스톤, 할 말이 없네요. 무슨 말을 해야 할 지 정말 모르겠어요.

그는 의자와 물건들을 밀치고 벨에게 다가가서, 그녀를 문 쪽으로 밀고 가 움직이지 못하게 한다.

개스톤 : 나랑 결혼할거라고 말 해.

- **plop**
  툭 떨어뜨리다
  If something plops somewhere, it drops there with a soft, gentle sound

- **wiggle**
  꼼지락거리다
  If you wiggle something or if it wiggles, it moves up and down or from side to side in small quick movements

- **lodge**
  오두막
  A lodge is a house or hut in the country or in the mountains where people stay on holiday, especially when they want to shoot or fish

- **strapping**
  건장한
  If you describe someone as strapping, you mean that they are tall and strong, and look healthy

I really don't know what to say.
'what to부정사'는 '무엇을 ~할지'라는 뜻이다. 이렇게 의문사(who, when, where, what, which, how) 뒤에 to부정사가 나오면, '누가, 언제, 어디서, 무엇을, 어떤 것을, 어떻게 ~할지'라는 뜻으로 각각 해석한다.

Zoom In

I really don't know what to say.
무슨 말을 해야할 지 정말 모르겠어요.

Belle reaches for the doorknob.

BELLE : I'm very sorry, Gaston. But but... I just don't deserve you.

She twists the knob and the door opens (this time outward). Belle ducks under Gaston as he tumbles out the door and into the mud.

EXT. OUTSIDE OF BELLE'S COTTAGE

The wedding band begins to play "Here Comes the Bride." Gaston falls into the mud and gets dirty. Gaston's boots are thrown out of the door (now opened inward) and the door is slammed shut. Lefou, who is directing the band, looks down and sees Gaston's legs sticking out of the mud and Pierre's head sticking up. Lefou cuts off the band and Gaston's head pops up with the pig on top of him. He tilts his head and the pig slides down his back.
Lefou picks up Gaston's hair with his baton and asks him.

LEFOU : So, how'd it go?

Gaston picks up Lefou by the neck.

GASTON : I'll have Belle for my wife. make no mistake about that!

Gaston drops Lefou into the mud.

LEFOU : (to Pierre) Touchy!

PIERRE : Grunt. Grunt.

Gaston walks off dejected and the focus returns to the cottage. A waterwheel in front of Belle's house turns, round. Belle pokes her head out the door.
Belle starts a conversation with a rooster which is drinking water.

BELLE : (to the chickens) Is he gone?

Roosters fly and crow. Belle lifts a bucket and gives food to roosters.

벨은 문고리로 손을 뻗는다.

벨 : 미안해요. 개스톤. 하지만… 나는 당신에게 어울리지 않아요.

그녀는 문고리를 돌려 문을 연다(바깥쪽으로). 벨은 개스톤으로부터 빠져나오고, 그는 문 쪽으로 굴러 떨어져 진흙탕에 빠진다.

외부. 벨의 집 밖
웨딩 밴드는 '결혼행진곡'을 연주하기 시작한다. 개스톤은 진흙탕에 빠져 더러워진다. 개스톤의 부츠가 문 밖으로 던져지고(이번에는 문이 안쪽으로 열린다), 문이 쾅 닫힌다. 밴드를 지휘하던 르푸가 아래를 내려다보니, 진흙탕에 개스톤의 다리가 빠져있고 돼지가 고개를 들고 나온다. 르푸는 밴드 연주를 중단시킨다. 개스톤의 머리가 튀어 나오는데, 위에 돼지가 앉아있다. 그가 머리를 뒤로 젖히자 돼지는 개스톤의 등 쪽으로 미끄러진다.
르푸는 지휘봉으로 개스톤의 머리를 들어 올리고 그에게 묻는다.

르 푸 : 그래, 어떻게 됐어?

개스톤은 르푸의 목을 움켜쥐고 그를 들어 올린다.

개스톤 : 벨을 꼭 내 아내로 만들고 말겠어. 절대 포기하지 않아!

개스톤은 르푸를 진흙탕에 떨어뜨린다.

르 푸 : (돼지에게) 저 다혈질.

돼 지 : 꿀꿀.

개스톤은 낙담해서 걸어가고, 다시 오두막집 풍경이 보인다. 벨의 집 앞에 있는 물레방아가 돌아가고 있다. 벨은 문 밖으로 머리를 내민다.
벨은 물은 마시고 있는 닭과 대화를 시작한다.

벨 : (닭들에게) 돌아갔지?

닭들은 꼬꼬댁 거리면서 날아다닌다. 벨은 양동이를 들고 닭들에게 모이를 준다.

- **knob**
  손잡이
  A knob is a round handle on a door or drawer which you use in order to open or close it
- **baton**
  지휘봉
  A baton is a light, thin stick used by a conductor to conduct an orchestra or a choir
- **grunt**
  꿀꿀거리다
  When an animal grunts, it makes a low rough noise
- **deject**
  낙담시키다
  to have a depressing effect on; dispirit; dishearten
- **rooster**
  수탉
  A rooster is an adult male chicken

I just don't deserve you.
deserve는 '~할 가치가 있다, ~을 받을만 하다'라는 뜻이므로, 당신의 사랑을 받을만한 사람이 아니라는 의미가 된다. 그밖에 "어울리다"는 뜻의 동사로는 fit, suit, go well등이 있다.

Zoom In

I just don't deserve you.
나는 당신에게 어울리지 않아요.

BELLE : Can you imagine, he asked me to marry him. Me, the wife of that boorish, brainless...

Belle puts down the bucket on the lid of a barrel and picks up her scarf. She wraps a scarf round her head and kicks off the lid. Two buckets fly away. She ties a scarf which was on her head.

BELLE : (singing) *MADAME GASTON, CAN'T YOU JUST SEE IT?*
MADAME GASTON, HIS LITTLE WIFE
NO SIR, NOT ME I GUARANTEE IT
I WANT MUCH MORE THAN THIS PROVINCIAL LIFE...

Belle walks into the pen and feeds the animals, then runs off singing into an open field overlooking a beautiful valley.

BELLE : (singing) *I WANT ADVENTURE IN THE GREAT WIDE SOMEWHERE*
I WANT IT MORE THAN I CAN TELL
AND FOR ONCE IT MIGHT BE GRAND

The dandelions are swaying in the soft breeze. Belle picks a dandelion. The seeds are dispersed by the wind.

BELLE : (singing) *TO HAVE SOMEONE UNDERSTAND*
I WANT SO MUCH MORE THAN THEY'VE GOT PLANNED

Belle hears a horse neighing. Phillipe runs into the open field. Belle looks at him, disturbed that Maurice is not with him.

BELLE : Phillipe! What are you doing here? Where's where's... Papa? Where is he, Phillipe? What happened? Oh, we have to find him. You have to take me to him!

벨 : 말도 안 돼, 나에게 결혼을 해달라니. 나보고 그런 한심하고 모자란 사람의 아내가 되라는 거야?

벨은 양동이를 물통 뚜껑 위에 두고 스카프를 집어 든다. 그는 머리에 스카프를 두르고 뚜껑을 걷어찬다. 양동이 두 개가 날아간다. 그녀는 머리에 있던 스카프를 날려 버린다.

벨 : (노래하며) *개스톤 부인이라니 생각 해봐*
개스톤 부인, 그의 부인이라니 정말 싫어
나는 자신 있게 말할 수 있어
더 멋진 삶을 살 거야…

벨은 우리에 들어가서 동물들에게 먹이를 주고는 아름다운 계곡을 바라보면서 넓은 들판으로 노래하며 달려간다.

벨 : (노래하며) *나는 어딘가 넓은 곳으로 모험을 떠나고 싶어*
내가 말한 것보다 더 굉장한 걸 원해
정말 대단할거야

민들레꽃들이 부드러운 바람에 흩날린다. 벨은 민들레 한 송이를 꺾는다. 씨앗들이 바람에 널리 퍼진다.

벨 : (노래하며) *먼 훗날에는 이해할거야*
내가 더 큰 희망을 가진 것을

벨은 말이 우는 소리를 듣는다. 필립은 넓은 들판을 달려온다. 벨은 모리스가 말과 함께 없어서 불안해한다.

벨 : 필립! 여기서 뭐해? 아빠는 어디에 계시니? 어디에 계셔, 필립? 무슨 일이야? 오, 아빠를 찾으러 가야겠어. 나를 아빠에게 데려다 줘.

- **boorish**
  천박한
  Boorish behaviour is rough, uneducated, and rude
- **guarantee**
  보장하다
  If one thing guarantees another, the first is certain to cause the second thing to happen
- **dandelion**
  민들레
  A dandelion is a wild plant which has yellow flowers with lots of thin petals. When the petals of each flower drop off, a fluffy white ball of seeds grows
- **sway**
  흔들리다
  When people or things sway, they lean or swing slowly from one side to the other
- **breeze**
  산들바람
  A breeze is a gentle wind

Key Expressions

64 I'd like to thank you all for coming to my wedding.

여러분들 모두 제 결혼식에 와주셔서 감사드립니다.

'I'd like to 동사원형'은 '~하고 싶다'는 정중한 표현이다. thank for은 '~해주어 고맙다'는 뜻으로 뒤에 명사나 동명사를 써주면 된다.

· I'd like to thank my teacher for encouraging me.
선생님께 나를 격려해주셔서 감사드리고 싶다.

64 Minister, Baker, and Others laugh heartily.

목사, 빵집 주인, 다른 사람들 모두가 배꼽을 잡고 웃는다.

heartily는 '실컷, 마음껏'이라는 부사이다. laugh heartily라고 하게 되면 '배꼽을 잡고 웃다, 박장대소하다'라는 표현이 된다.

· He laughed heartily, exposing his white teeth.
그는 하얀 치아를 드러내며 배꼽을 잡고 웃었다.

66 There's not a girl in town who wouldn't love to be in your shoes. 이 마을 모든 여자들이 당신을 부러워하고 있어.

in one's shoes는 '~의 입장, 상황'이라는 뜻도 가지고 있다. 따라서 위 문장은 당신의 입장이 되기 싫어하는 여자가 없다는 의미이므로, 모든 여자들이 당신을 부러워하고 있다고 해석된다.

· I wish I were in your shoes. 네 처지가 제일 부럽다.

66 **Belle keeps stepping back.** 벨은 계속해서 뒷걸음질 친다.

keep ~ing는 '계속해서 ~하다'라는 중요한 숙어이다. keep on ~ing, continue to/ing와도 비슷한 의미이다.

· I kept thinking about the problem. 나는 그 문제에 대해 계속 생각했다.

66 **She seems to be scared.** 그녀는 겁에 질린 것처럼 보인다.

'seem to 동사원형'은 '~한 것처럼 보이다'라는 표현이다. seem의 보어로는 to부정사 외에도 형용사가 올 수 있다. 'It seems that 주어+동사'로도 바꾸어 쓸 수 있다.

· He bought a brand-new car. He seems to be rich.
그는 최신형 차를 샀다. 그는 부자인 것처럼 보인다.

72 **Belle hears a horse neighing.** 벨은 말이 히힝 우는 소리를 듣는다.

hear(듣다)과 같은 지각동사 뒤에 목적어가 나오면, 목적격 보어 자리에는 동사원형 또는 현재분사가 쓰인다. 현재 주어가 감각을 느끼고 있다는 진행의 의미를 강조하고 싶은 경우에 현재분사를 쓰면 된다.

· I heard you whispering to him. 네가 그에게 속삭이는 것 다 들었어.

Movie Talk

영화 소개

미녀와 야수는 애니매이션이지만, 이후 할리우드 멜로 영화의 골격을 세웠다고 해도 과언이 아닐 정도로 영향력이 큰 작품이다. 아이들뿐만 아니라 어른들이 더 큰 감동을 받고, 세계적으로 대단한 인기를 누린 애니메이션 최초로 아카데미 작품상 후보에 까지 오른 웰메이드(well-made) 영화이다.

마법에 걸려 야수로 변한 왕자는 21세 생일까지 진실한 사랑을 찾지 못하면 마법을 풀 수 없다. 벨은 미치광이 취급을 받는 아버지를 정성껏 모시고 살아가는 책을 좋아하는 아름다운 소녀이다. 마을에서 가장 잘생기고 힘센 개스톤은 그녀와 결혼하고 싶어 하지만, 벨은 자신을 이해하지 못하는 개스톤이 마음에 들지 않는다. 벨의 아버지는 발명품을 전시회에 출품하려고 마을을 떠나지만 길을 잃고 늑대들에게 쫓겨 마법의 성에 이른다.

아버지를 찾아 야수의 성에 온 벨은 아버지를 풀어주면 자신이 대신 갇혀 있겠다고 약속한다. 야수가 가지 말라던 서쪽 탑에 갔다가 야수와 크게 싸운 벨은 성을 떠나지만, 추운 겨울 늑대들을 만나 위험해 지고 이 때 야수가 나타나 벨을 구하게 된다. 그 이후 벨과 야수는 점차 가까워지고 야수는 벨에 대한 사랑이 싹튼다. 야수는 벨이 아버지를 만나고 싶어 하자 마법의 거울을 가져와 아버지를 보여준다. 그리고 눈보라 속에서 딸을 찾아다니며 고생하는 아버지를 보고 슬픔에 잠긴 벨을 놓아준다. 개스톤은 정신병원 원장을 데려와 아버지를 끌고 가려 한다. 개스톤은 마을 사람들을 선동해 흉측한 야수를 없애자며 성으로 쳐들어간다. 개스톤과의 싸움으로 상처를 입은 야수는 죽음의 순간에 이른다. 벨이 눈물을 흘리며 사랑한다고 고백한 순간, 마법의 장미 꽃잎이 떨어지고 하늘에서 내리던 비가 유성으로 바뀐다. 쓰러져 있던 야수의 몸은 손, 발, 차례로 인간의 모습으로 변한다. 벨이 키스를 하자 하늘 높이 폭죽이 터지며 성의 마법이 풀리고, 해피엔딩으로 영화는 막이 내린다.

이렇게 내면의 아름다움을 통한 진정한 사랑을 가르쳐주는 미녀와 야수야 말로 현대 사회에 일침을 가하고 교훈을 일깨워줄 수 있는 작품일 것이다. 초라한 노파를 무시하던 이기적인 태도의 왕자가 벨을 통해 진정한 사랑을 깨닫는 아름답고 감동적인 사랑 이야기 속에 잊어서는 안 되는 삶의 가치들이 녹아내려 있다. 이런 좋은 작품과 아름다운 노래를 통해 영어공부를 할 수 있게 된 것은 여러모로 행운이 아닐까 싶다.

Chapter 4

벨, 아버지를 찾아 집을 떠나다

Belle Leaves Home to Find Her Father

시간 00:21:06 ~ 00:26:41

EXT. IN FRONT OF THE CASTLE
Belle unhitches the wagon from Phillipe. Cut to exterior of the castle gate. (How Phillipe brought Belle there is a mystery seeing as Phillipe never made it to the castle with Maurice.)
Belle rides on Phillipe and arrives at the castle. She has a puzzled look on her face.

BELLE : What is this place?

Phillipe snorts, then begins to buck as if something is scaring him.
Belle dismounts and comforts him.

BELLE : Phillipe, please, steady... steady...

She enters the gate and sees Maurice's hat on the ground. She picks up her father's hat.

BELLE : Papa!

외부. 성 앞
벨은 필립에게서 짐수레를 떼어 낸다. 성문 바깥 장면.
(어떻게 필립이 벨을 그곳으로 데려다 주었는지는 미스터리하다. 알다시피 필립은 모리스와 함께 성에 와본 적이 없다.)
벨은 필립을 타고 성에 도착한다. 그녀는 어리둥절한 표정이다.

벨 : 여기는 뭐하는 곳일까?

필립은 마치 무엇인가로 부터 겁을 먹은 듯이 힝힝 울면서 날뛴다.
벨은 그에게서 내려 그를 진정시킨다.

벨 : 필립. 진정해. 진정해…

그녀는 성문으로 들어가 모리스의 모자가 땅에 떨어져 있는 것을 본다. 그녀는 아빠의 모자를 집어 든다.

벨 : 아빠!

- **unhitch**
  떼어내다
  unfasten or release from or as if from a hitch

- **puzzled**
  어리둥절한
  Someone who is puzzled is confused because they do not understand something

- **snort**
  (말 등이) 힝힝거리다
  When people or animals snort, they breathe air noisily out through their noses

- **dismount**
  내리다
  If you dismount from a horse or a bicycle, you get down from it

- **comfort**
  진정시키다
  If you comfort someone, you make them feel less worried, unhappy, or upset, for example by saying kind things to them

INT. IN THE CASTLE

Cut to interior of castle with Cogsworth and Lumiere discussing events.

COGSWORTH : Couldn't keep quiet could we? Just had to invite him to stay, didn't we? Serve him tea, sit in the master's chair pet the pooch.

LUMIERE : I was trying to be hospitable.

Cut back to door opening and Belle entering castle.

BELLE : Hello? Is anyone here? Hello? Papa? Papa, are you here?

We follow as Belle ascends the grand staircase and searches for her father. Cut to kitchen where Mrs. Potts is standing next to a tub of hot water. Chip hops in.

CHIP : Momma. There's a girl in the castle!

MRS. POTTS : Now, Chip, I'll not have you making up such wild stories.

CHIP : But really, momma, I saw her.

MRS. POTTS : (disgusted) Not another word. Into the tub.

She lifts Chip into the tub. Featherduster enters.

FEATHERDUSTER : A girl! I saw a girl in the castle!

Chip pokes his head out from the water.

CHIP : See, I told you ya!

Cut back to Cogsworth and Lumiere bickering.

내부. 성 안
콕스워즈와 루미에르가 대화를 나누는 성 내부 장면.

콕스워즈 : 가만히 있을 수 없다 이거지. 들어오게 할 수밖에 없었잖아, 그렇지? 차도 주고, 주인님 의자에 앉게 하고, 개를 쓰다듬게 하고…

루미에르 : 난 호의를 베풀었을 뿐이야.

문이 열리고 벨이 성으로 들어오는 장면.

벨 : 계세요? 누구 없어요? 아빠, 여기 계세요?

벨이 큰 계단을 올라 아빠를 찾는 장면이다. 포트 부인이 뜨거운 물이 담긴 대야 옆에 서있는 부엌 장면. 칩이 욕조에 뛰어 들어간다.

칩 : 엄마. 성에 여자가 들어 왔어요.

포트 부인 : 떽. 이야기를 지어내면 못써요.

칩 : 하지만 엄마. 진짜 봤어요.

포트 부인 : (찌푸리며) 그만 해라. 욕조에 들어가.

그녀는 칩을 들어서 욕조에 넣어준다. 페더더스터(빗자루)가 들어온다.

페더더스터 : 성에 여자가 들어 왔어요.

칩이 물 밖으로 고개를 내민다.

칩 : 거 봐요. 내 말이 맞죠.

루미에르와 콕스워즈가 말다툼하는 장면.

- **pooch**
  개
  A pooch is a dog
- **ascend**
  올라가다
  If you ascend a hill or staircase, you go up it
- **staircase**
  계단
  A staircase is a set of stairs inside a building
- **bicker**
  말다툼하다
  When people bicker, they argue or quarrel about unimportant things

I was trying to be hospitable.
'try to 동사원형'은 '~하기 위해 노력하다'라는 뜻이다. hospitable은 '호의적인, 환대하는'이라는 뜻의 형용사로 hostile(적대적인)과 철자가 비슷하니 반드시 둘을 구별해서 알아두도록 한다.

Zoom In

I was trying to be hospitable.
난 호의를 베풀었을 뿐이야.

COGSWORTH : Irresponsible, devil-may-care, waxy eared, slack-jawed...

BELLE : Papa?

Cogsworth and Lumiere turn to look at the new arrival.

LUMIERE : Did you see that?

He runs to the door, poking his head around the corner with Cogsworth.

LUMIERE : It's a girl!

COGSWORTH : I know it's a girl.

LUMIERE : Don't you see? She's the one. The girl we have been waiting for. She has come to break the spell!

He chases after her.

COGSWORTH : Wait a minute, wait a minute!

Belle advances down a narrow hallway. Cogsworth and Lumiere sneak up behind her and open the door that leads to the tower where Maurice is being kept. The door creaks open and Belle hears the sound.

BELLE : Papa? Papa?

Cogsworth hides behind the door and Lumiere rushes off.

BELLE : Hello? Is someone here? Wait! I'm looking for my father! I...

She begins up the stairs but doesn't realize that Lumiere is watching her.

콕스워즈 : 무책임하고, 대책 없고, 귀 얇고, 입이 떡 벌어지는…

벨 : 아빠?

콕스워즈와 루미에르는 새로운 손님을 보고 몸을 돌린다.

루미에르 : 봤어?

그는 문 쪽으로 뛰어 들어가 콕스워즈와 구석에서 머리를 내민다.

루미에르 : 여자야!

콕스워즈 : 여잔 건 나도 알아.

루미에르 : 생각해봐. 이 성에 나타난 최초의 여자란 말이야. 우리가 기다리던 아가씨라구. 그녀가 우리의 마법을 풀어줄 거야!

그는 벨을 뒤쫓아 간다.

콕스워즈 : 이봐, 기다려!

벨은 좁은 복도를 걸어 내려온다. 콕스워즈와 루미에르는 살금살금 그녀의 뒤를 쫓고, 모리스가 갇혀 있는 탑으로 가는 문을 열어준다. 끽 소리를 내며 문이 열리고 벨은 그 소리를 듣는다.

벨 : 아빠? 아빠?

콕스워즈는 문 뒤에 숨고, 루미에르는 도망간다.

벨 : 여보세요, 여기 누구 있어요? 기다려요! 아빠를 찾고 있어요!

그녀는 계단을 올라가기 시작하지만, 루미에르가 그녀를 보고 있는 것은 알아차리지 못한다.

- **irresponsible**
  무책임한
  If you describe someone as irresponsible, you are criticizing them because they do things without properly considering their possible consequences
- **poke**
  쿡 찌르다
  If you poke someone or something, you quickly push them with your finger or with a sharp object
- **sneak**
  살금살금 가다
  If you sneak somewhere, you go there very quietly on foot, trying to avoid being seen or heard
- **creak**
  삐걱거리다
  If something creaks, it makes a short, high-pitched sound when it moves

The girl we have been waiting for.
we have been waiting for이 앞에 있는 the girl을 꾸며주는 구조이다. wait for은 '기다리다'라는 동사구로, 현재완료진행형(have been ~ing)으로 쓰여 과거에서부터 지금까지 기다려왔음을 나타낸다.

Zoom In

The girl we have been waiting for.
우리가 기다리던 아가씨라구.

BELLE : That's funny, I'm sure there was someone... I... I... Is anyone here?

Maurice's voice echoes from his cell.

MAURICE : Belle?

Belle rushes up to the cell to find him.

BELLE : Oh, Papa!

MAURICE : How did you find me?

Belle holds her father's hand through the iron grating. She guides his hand to her face.

BELLE : Oh, your hands are like ice. I have to get you out of there.

Maurice coughs. He seems to become weak.

MAURICE : Belle, I want you to leave this place.

BELLE : Who's done this to you?

MAURICE : No time to explain. You must go... now!

BELLE : I won't leave you!

Suddenly, Beast grabs Belle's shoulder and whips her around. She drops the torch she was carrying into a puddle and the room is dark except for one beam of light from a skylight.

BEAST : What are you doing here?

MAURICE : Run, Belle!

BELLE : Who's there? Who are you?

벨 : 이상하네, 분명히 누군가 있는 것 같은데… 아무도 없어요?

모리스의 목소리가 감옥에서 퍼져 나온다.

아 빠 : 벨?

벨은 아빠를 찾기 위해 감옥까지 뛰어 올라간다.

벨 : 아빠!
아 빠 : 어떻게 찾아 왔니?

벨은 철창 틈으로 아빠의 손을 잡는다. 그녀는 아빠의 손을 자신의 얼굴에 가져다 댄다.

벨 : 아빠 손이 얼음장 같아요. 여기서 나가야만 해요.

모리스는 기침을 한다. 그는 몸이 쇠약해진 것 같다.

아 빠 : 벨, 나는 네가 여길 떠나면 좋겠구나.
벨 : 누가 이런 짓을.
아 빠 : 설명할 시간이 없다. 어서 도망가. 당장!
벨 : 아빠를 두고 떠날 수 없어요!

갑자기 야수가 벨의 어깨를 잡아채고 그녀를 확 돌린다. 그녀는 들고 있던 횃불을 웅덩이에 떨어뜨려, 방 안은 천장에서 들어오는 한 줄기 빛을 제외하고는 어두컴컴하다.

야 수 : 여기서 뭐하는 거야?
아 빠 : 뛰어, 벨!
벨 : 누구죠? 누구세요?

- **grating**
  창살
  A grating is a flat metal frame with rows of bars across it, which is fastened over a window or over a hole in a wall or the ground
- **cough**
  기침하다
  When you cough, you force air out of your throat with a sudden, harsh noise
- **torch**
  횃불
  A torch is a long stick with burning material at one end, used to provide light or to set things on fire
- **puddle**
  웅덩이
  A puddle is a small, shallow pool of liquid that has spread on the ground

No time to explain.
'time to 동사원형'은 '~할 시간'이라는 뜻으로 매우 자주 사용되는 표현이다. 앞에 부정어 No가 붙어서 '~할 시간이 없음'을 나타낸다.
ex) It's time to go to bed.

Zoom In

No time to explain.
설명할 시간 없다.

BEAST : The Master of this castle.

Being dropped to the floor, Belle appeals for mercy. However, Beast yells at her, getting close to her.

BELLE : I've come for my father. Please let him out! Can't you see he's sick?

BEAST : Then he shouldn't have trespassed here.

BELLE : But he could die. Please, I'll do anything!

BEAST : There's nothing you can do. He's my prisoner.

BELLE : Oh, there must be some way I can... wait! Take me, instead!

BEAST : You! You would take his place?

MAURICE : Belle! No! You don't know what you're doing!

BELLE : If I did would you let him go?

BEAST : Yes, but you must promise to stay here forever.

Belle ponders the situation and realizes she can't see the captor.

BELLE : Come into the light.

Beast drags his legs then his whole body into the beam of light. Belle looks, her eyes growing wider until she can stand no more and falls back to Maurice. Belle puts her hand over her mouth with fright. She turns her head toward her father and closes her eyes.

MAURICE : No, Belle. I won't let you do this!

Belle regains her composure then steps into the beam of light, giving her a very virgin-ish look.

야 수 : 이 성의 주인이다.

바닥에 떨어진 벨은 애원하지만, 야수는 그녀에게 가까이 다가가 소리친다.

벨 : 아빠를 찾으러 왔어요. 제발 그를 보내 주세요! 병이 드셨잖아요.
야 수 : 그럼 애초에 여길 들어오지 말았어야지.
벨 : 곧 돌아가실지도 몰라요. 제발, 뭐든 할게요!
야 수 : 네가 할 수 있는 일은 아무 것도 없어. 그는 나의 포로야.
벨 : 제가 할 수 있는 게 있을 거예요… 잠깐! 나를 대신 가둬줘요.
야 수 : 네가! 네가 대신 있겠다고?
모리스 : 벨! 안 돼! 그런 소리 마라!
벨 : 그럼 아빠를 풀어줄 건가요?
야 수 : 좋아, 하지만 넌 영원히 이곳에 갇혀 있어야 해.

벨은 상황을 곰곰이 생각하다가 그녀가 야수를 제대로 볼 수 없다는 것을 깨닫는다.

벨 : 어두워서 안 보여요.

야수는 다리를 끌고 들어와서는 그의 몸 전체에 빛이 비추도록 해 보인다. 야수를 본 벨의 눈이 점점 커진다. 더 이상 서 있을 수가 없는 벨은 모리스 쪽으로 넘어진다.
벨은 겁에 질려 손으로 입을 가린다. 그녀는 고개를 아빠 쪽으로 돌리고 눈을 감는다.

모리스 : 안 된다. 벨. 널 이렇게 두고 갈순 없어.

벨은 평정을 되찾고는, 불빛이 비추는 곳으로 걸어간다.

- **appeal**
  애원하다
  If you appeal to someone to do something, you make a serious and urgent request to them

- **yell**
  소리치다
  If you yell, you shout loudly, usually because you are excited, angry, or in pain

- **prisoner**
  포로
  A prisoner is a person who has been captured by an enemy, for example in war

- **captor**
  포획자
  You can refer to the person who has captured a person or animal as their captor

- **composure**
  평정
  Composure is the appearance or feeling of calm and the ability to control your feelings

You don't know what you're doing!
직역하면 '네가 무슨 짓을 하고 있는지 모르지!'라는 뜻으로 상대방이 하는 일을 막고자 할 때 쓸 수 있는 표현이다.

Zoom In

You don't know what you're doing!

그런 소리 마라!

BELLE : You have my word.

BEAST : (quickly) Done!

Beast moves over to unlock the cell and Belle collapses to the floor with her head in her hands. We hear the door being unlocked, then Maurice rushing over to Belle.
Maurice grabs Belle and tries to persuade her.

MAURICE : No, Belle. Listen to me. I'm old, I've lived my life...

Beast grabs him and drags him downstairs.
Belle stretches her hand to Maurice and cries out.

BELLE : Wait!

MAURICE : Belle!

BELLE : Wait!

Cut to ext. of castle. Beast drags Maurice towards Pallenquin.

MAURICE : No, please spare my daughter! Please!

BEAST : She's no longer your concern.

Beast throws Maurice into the Pallenquin.

BEAST : Take him to the village.

The Pallenquin breaks the ivy holding it to the ground, then slinks off like a spider with Maurice inside.

MAURICE : Let me out please, let me out, please! please!

Cut to Belle looking out cell window at the Pallenquin crossing the bridge over the moat. She begins to cry. Cut to Beast walking up the stairs. Lumiereis still at his post.

벨 : 약속할게요.
야 수 : (재빨리) 좋아!

야수는 감옥 문을 열기 위해 가고, 벨은 손으로 머리를 감싼 채 바닥에 주저앉는다. 문이 열리고 모리스가 벨에게 달려온다. 모리스는 벨을 붙잡고 그녀를 설득하려고 한다.

모리스 : 안 돼, 벨. 내 말 들어. 나는 살 만큼 살았어…

야수는 그를 낚아채서 아래층으로 끌고 간다. 벨은 그녀의 손을 모리스 쪽으로 뻗으며 외친다.

벨 : 기다려요!
모리스 : 벨!
벨 : 잠깐만!

성 바깥 장면. 야수는 모리스를 가마로 끌고 간다.

모리스 : 안 돼요. 제발 딸을 보내줘요!
야 수 : 더 이상 딸한테 신경 쓰지 마.

야수는 모리스를 가마 안으로 던져 넣는다.

야 수 : 마을까지 데리고 가라.

가마는 땅에 엉켜있던 덩굴을 자르고 나서, 모리스를 태운 채 거미처럼 슬금슬금 움직인다.

모리스 : 제발, 내보내줘요, 제발!

벨이 감옥 창문을 통해 가마가 해자를 지나 다리를 건너는 것을 보는 장면. 그녀는 울기 시작한다. 야수가 계단을 올라오는 장면. 루미에르는 여전히 그 위치에 있다.

- **cell**
  감옥
  A cell is a small room in which a prisoner is locked
- **collapse**
  무너지다
  If a building or other structure collapses, it falls down very suddenly
- **stretch**
  뻗다
  Something that stretches over an area or distance covers or exists in the whole of that area or distance
- **spare**
  피하게 해주다
  If a person or a place is spared, they are not harmed, even though other people or places have been
- **slink**
  살금살금 움직이다
  If you slink somewhere, you move there quietly because you do not want to be seen

You have my word.
You have my word.는 '약속할게요.' 라는 표현으로 반드시 기억해둔다. have a word를 사용해서 I give you my word.라고 해도 상대방에게 약속한다는 의미가 된다. 물론 I promise.라고 간단히 말해도 좋다.

Zoom In

You have my word.
약속할게요.

LUMIERE : Master?

BEAST : (angrily) What!

LUMIERE : Since the girl is going to be with us for quite some time, I was thinking that you might want to offer her a more comfortable room.

Beast growls angrily at him.

LUMIERE : Then again, maybe not.

Beast enters the cell where Belle is still crying.

BELLE : You didn't even let me say goodbye. I'll never see him again. I didn't get to say goodbye.

Feeling bad, Beast scratches his head. He seems to be guilty and feel sorry for Belle.

BEAST : I'll show you to your room.

BELLE : (surprised) My room? (indicating the cell) But I thought...

BEAST : You wanna... you wanna stay in the tower?

BELLE : No.

BEAST : Then follow me.

Beast leads Belle to her room. As they proceed, Belle begins to lag behind. She looks at the hideous sculptures on the walls and the light casting shadows on them. Frightened, she gasps and runs to catch up with Beast, who is carrying Lumiere as a light source. Beast looks back at Belle and sees a tear form at the corner of her eye.

LUMIERE : Say something to her.

BEAST : Hmm? Oh.

루미에르 : 주인님.

야 수 : (화가 나서) 뭐야 ?

루미에르 : 아가씨가 여기서 오랜 시간을 보낼 텐데, 좀 더 편한 곳에 있게 하는 것이 어떨지…

야수가 화가 나서 으르렁댄다.

루미에르 : 안 되면 할 수 없구요.

야수가 벨이 여전히 울고 있는 감옥 안으로 들어간다.

벨 : 당신은 아빠에게 작별 인사도 못하게 했어요. 다신 볼 수 없을 텐데. 작별 인사도 못 했다구요.

마음이 안 좋은 야수는 머리를 긁적인다. 그는 벨에게 죄책감과 미안한 감정을 느끼는 듯하다.

야 수 : 당신에게 방을 보여 주겠소.

벨 : (놀라서) 제 방이요? (감옥을 가리키며) 하지만 저는…

야 수 : 그럼 당신은 이 탑에 있기를 원하오?

벨 : 아니요.

야 수 : 그렇다면 나를 따라 오시오.

야수는 벨을 그녀의 방까지 안내한다. 벨은 뒤에서 천천히 따라간다. 그녀는 벽에 있는 흉측한 조각들과 그것들에 그림자가 드리워지는 것을 본다. 겁이 난 벨은 숨을 헐떡이며 야수를 따라잡기 위해 달리고, 야수는 루미에르로 빛을 비추고 있다. 야수가 뒤돌아서 벨을 보니 그녀의 눈가에 눈물이 맺혀있다.

루미에르 : 뭐라고 말 좀 해줘요.

야 수 : 음? 아…

- **comfortable**
  편안한
  If a piece of furniture or an item of clothing is comfortable, it makes you feel physically relaxed when you use it, for example because it is soft

- **scratch**
  긁다
  If you scratch yourself, you rub your fingernails against your skin because it is itching

- **guilty**
  죄책감
  If you feel guilty, you feel unhappy because you think that you have done something wrong or have failed to do something which you should have done

- **lag**
  천천히 걷다
  If one thing or person lags behind another thing or person, their progress is slower than that of the other

- **sculpture**
  조각상
  A sculpture is a work of art that is produced by carving or shaping stone, wood, clay, or other materials

You didn't even let me say goodbye.
let이라는 사역동사는 'let+목적어+목적격 보어(동사원형)'의 형태로 쓰여서, '~가 ~하는 것을 허락하다, 하게 하다'라는 뜻을 나타낸다. say goodbye는 '작별인사를 하다'라는 숙어이다.

Zoom In

You didn't even let me say goodbye.

당신은 아빠에게 작별인사도 못하게 했어요.

Beast talks to her in much a more gentle voice.

BEAST : (to Belle) I... um... hope you like it here.

He looks at Lumiere for approval. Lumiere motions Beast to continue.

BEAST : The castle is your home now, so you can go anywhere you like except the West Wing.

BELLE : (looking intrigued) What's in the West Wing?

BEAST : (growing angry) It's forbidden!

Beast continues and Belle reluctantly follows. Cut to int. of Belle's dark room. The door opens and light spills in.

BEAST : (tenderly) Now, if you need anything. my servants will attend you.

LUMIERE : (whispering in his ear) Dinner... invite her to dinner.

BEAST : (growing angry) You... will join me for dinner. That's not a request!

Beast leaves slamming the door behind him. Belle, terrified, runs over to the bed and flings herself onto it finally breaking down and crying. Fade to tavern in the town.
Outside the castle it snows and the cold wind sweeps through.

야수는 훨씬 더 부드러운 목소리로 말한다.

야 수 : (벨에게) **난… 이곳이 당신의 마음에 들었으면 좋겠소.**

그는 루미에르를 보며 동의를 구한다. 그는 야수에게 계속하라고 손짓한다.

야 수 : **이 성은 당신의 집이니, 어느 곳이나 가도 좋소. 서쪽 탑만 빼고.**

벨 : (궁금해 하며) **서쪽 탑은 왜 안 되죠?**

야 수 : (화를 내며) **금지구역이오.**

야수는 계속 걷고, 벨은 하는 수 없이 뒤따른다. 어두운 벨의 방 장면. 문이 열리고 빛이 들어온다.

야 수 : (부드럽게) **이제, 필요한 것이 있으면 하인들이 도와줄 거요.**

루미에르 : (야수의 귀에 속삭이며) **저녁. 저녁식사에 초대하세요.**

야 수 : (화를 내며) **당신은 나와 저녁을 함께 하게 될 거요. 이건 명령이오!**

야수는 떠나고 그의 뒤로 문이 쾅 닫힌다. 두려운 벨은 침대로 달려가 풀썩 쓰러진다. 결국 울음을 터뜨린다. 마을의 주막에 조명이 비춘다.
성 바깥쪽은 눈이 오고 거센 바람이 분다.

- **approval**
  동의, 승인
  If you win someone's approval for something that you ask for or suggest, they agree to it

- **except**
  제외하고
  You use except to introduce the only thing or person that a statement does not apply to, or a fact that prevents a statement from being completely true

- **forbidden**
  금지된
  If something is forbidden, you are not allowed to do it or have it

- **request**
  요청
  If you request something, you ask for it politely or formally

Key Expressions

82 Phillipe never made it to the castle with Maurice.

필립은 모리스와 성에 도착해본 적이 없다.

make it to는 '~에 이르다, 도착하다'라는 중요한 숙어이다. get to, arrive at, reach와 비슷하게 사용된다.

· Did you make it to your destination? 목적지까지 잘 도착했어?

84 Just had to invite him to stay, didn't we?

들어오게 할 수밖에 없었잖아, 그렇지?

위 문장에서의 didn't we와 같은 부가의문문은 평서문 뒤에 붙어서 확인이나 동의를 구하는 의미를 더해준다.

· Wow! He is cool, isn't he? 우와! 멋있다, 그렇지 않니?

90 Then he shouldn't have trespassed here.

그러면 그는 이곳을 지나가지 말았어야지.

should have p.p.는 '~했었어야 했다'는 과거에 대한 후회를 나타내는 의미로, 이 문장에서처럼 부정문이 되면 '~하지 말았어야 했다'는 뜻이 된다.

· I should have bought it online. 온라인으로 샀어야 했는데.

92 She's no longer your concern. 더 이상 그녀에 대해 신경 쓰지 마.

no longer은 '더 이상 ~않다'는 의미이다. 이 문장에서는 '그녀는 더 이상 네 관심사가 아니다'는 의미이므로 곧 더 이상 그녀에게 신경 쓰지 말라는 경고의 표현이다.

· **It's no longer fun to be with you.** 이제 너와 있어도 더 이상 즐겁지 않아.

96 Beast talks to her in much a more gentle voice.

야수는 그녀에게 훨씬 더 부드러운 목소리로 말을 건넸다.

형용사에 -er 또는 more이 붙으면 비교급이 되어 '더 ~하다'라는 뜻이 되는데, much는 이러한 비교급을 꾸며주는 '훨씬'이라는 의미의 비교급 강조부사이다. much 외에도 even still, far, a lot을 쓸 수 있다.

· **The new drugs are much more effective.** 신약이 훨씬 더 효과적이에요.

96 I hope you like here. 당신이 이곳을 마음에 들어 하면 좋겠소.

'I hope that 주어+동사'는 '주어가 동사하면 좋겠다'는 희망을 나타내는 표현이다. 이 경우 that은 생략 가능하다.

· **I hope that this reply is helpful.** 이 대답이 도움이 되면 좋겠네요.

Chapter 5

모리스, 개스톤에게 도움을 요청하다

Maurice Asks Gaston for Help

시간 00:26:42 ~ 00:31:51

INT. A BAR IN THE VILLAGE
Gaston sits in front of the fireplace. Unable to control his anger, he fumes. Lefou carries two glasses of beer to Gaston.

GASTON : Who does she think she is? That girl has tangled with the wrong man. No one says 'no' to Gaston!

LEFOU : Darn right!

GASTON : Dismissed. Rejected. Publicly humiliated.

Gaston takes glasses and throws them into the fireplace.

GASTON : Why, it's more than I can bear. (turns chair away)

LEFOU : (runs in front of him) More beer?

GASTON : (turns chair away again) What for? Nothing helps. I'm disgraced.

LEFOU : Who, you? Never. Gaston, you've got to pull yourself together. (singing) *GOSH IT DISTURBS ME TO SEE YOU, GASTON*

내부. 마을의 술집

개스톤은 벽난로 앞에 앉아있다. 분노를 주체할 수 없는 그는 씩씩거린다. 르푸는 개스톤에게 맥주 두 잔을 가지고 온다.

개스톤 : 도대체 자기가 얼마나 잘났다고 생각하는 거야? 그런 여자는 못된 놈과 좀 엮여봐야 돼. 그 누구도 개스톤을 거절할 수 없어!

르 푸 : 그럼.

개스톤 : 바람맞고! 거절당하고! 공개적으로 망신만 당하고!

개스톤은 맥주잔을 받아서 그것들을 벽난로에 던져버린다.

개스톤 : 왜지, 도저히 참을 수가 없어. (의자를 돌린다)

르 푸 : (그의 앞으로 달려간다) 더 마실래?

개스톤 : (의자를 다시 돌린다) 뭐하러? 다 필요 없어. 창피해.

르 푸 : 누가? 네가? 절대 아니야. 절망하지 마. (노래하며) *왜 그렇게 우울해 하지, 개스톤*

- **fume**
  씩씩대다
  If you fume over something, you express annoyance and anger about it
- **tangle**
  얽히게 하다
  If something is tangled or tangles, it becomes twisted together in an untidy way
- **humiliated**
  창피를 당한
  subdued or brought low in condition or status
- **disgraced**
  망신을 당한
  suffering shame

With his fingers, Lefou opens Gaston's mouth, and tries to make him laugh with his gums showing. Gaston throws a punch to Lefou. Lefou flies away and falls on the table.

LEFOU : (singing) *LOOKING SO DOWN IN THE DUMPS*
EVERY GUY HERE'D LOVE TO BE YOU, GASTON (cheering from the gallery) *EVEN WHEN TAKING YOUR LUMPS*
THERE'S NO MAN IN TOWN AS ADMIRED AS YOU
YOU'RE EVERYONE'S FAVORITE GUY
EVERYONE'S AWED AND INSPIRED BY YOU (Lefou turns chair back to face forward)
AND IT'S NOT VERY HARD TO SEE WHY!

Three girls cling to Gaston's sleeves.

LEFOU : (singing) *NO ONE'S SLICK AS GASTON, NO ONE'S QUICK AS GASTON*
NO ONE'S NECK'S AS INCREDIBLY THICK AS GASTON
FOR THERE'S NO MAN IN TOWN HALF AS MANLY
PERFECT, A PURE PARAGON!
YOU CAN ASK ANY TOM, DICK, OR STANLEY
AND THEY'LL TELL YOU WHOSE TEAM THEY'D PREFER TO BE ON!

Lefou has pulled a man's belt off, whose pants fall to the ground. Lefou jumps up and wraps the belt around Gaston's neck, who flexes and breaks it off. Lefou continues to dance around. Lefou steps on Old Cronies heads one by one and keeps singing. Old Cronies pick him up and swing him around.

OLD CRONIES : (singing) *NO ONE'S BEEN LIKE GASTON, A KINGPIN LIKE GASTON*

르푸는 손가락으로 개스톤의 잇몸이 보이도록 입 꼬리를 끌어 웃음 짓게 한다. 개스톤은 르푸에게 주먹을 날린다. 르푸는 붕 떴다가 테이블 위에 쿵 떨어진다.

르 푸 : (노래하며) *어서 기운을 내*
모두 널 부러워하지, 개스톤 (한쪽에서 응원을 하며)
그러니 용기를 내
이 마을에 너만큼 존경받는 사람은 없어
모든 사람들이 너를 좋아해
모두가 널 부러워하지 (르푸는 의자를 앞으로 돌린다)
왜 그런지는 척 보면 알 수 있어!

세명의 여자들은 개스톤의 소매에 매달린다.

르 푸 : (노래하며) *누구도 이렇게 잘생기지 않고,*
누구도 이렇게 재빠르지 않아
누구도 너만큼 우람하지 않지
너의 남자다움의 반도 못 따라가
완벽한 표본의 결정체야!
모두에게 물어봐
모두들 너를 좋아한다고 말할 걸

르푸가 어떤 남자의 벨트를 당기자, 바지가 땅에 떨어진다. 르푸는 점프해서 벨트로 개스톤의 목을 감싸고, 개스톤은 그것을 툭 끊어버린다. 르푸는 계속해서 춤을 추며 돌아다닌다. 르푸는 추종자들의 머리를 한 명씩 밟고 지나가며 계속 노래를 부른다. 추종자들은 그를 들어 올려 앞뒤로 흔든다.

추종자들 : (노래하며) *그 누구도 개스톤만큼 중요 인물이 될 순 없지*

- **admired**
  존경받는
  regarded with admiration
- **awed**
  외경심에 휩싸인
  inspired by a feeling of fearful wonderment or reverence
- **cling**
  매달리다
  If you cling to someone or something, you hold onto them tightly
- **paragon**
  귀감
  If you refer to someone as a paragon, you mean that they are perfect or have a lot of a good qualities

There's no man in town as admired as you.
'부정어 as 원급 as'구문으로, '~만큼 ~한 사람(것)은 없다'라는 의미가 된다. 결국 '~가 가장 ~하다'는 최상급의 의미를 함축한다.

Zoom In

There's no man in town as admired as you.
이 마을에 너만큼 존경받는 사람은 없어.

LEFOU : (singing) *NO ONE'S GOT A SWELL CLEFT IN HIS CHIN LIKE GASTON*

GASTON : (singing) *AS A SPECIMEN, YES, I'M INTIMIDATING!*

OLD CRONIES : (singing) *MY, WHAT A GUY THAT GASTON!*

Old Cronies swing Lefou back and forth into the camera. Lefou tickles Gaston's chin, who stands with pride.
Gaston shows off the biceps of his.

OLD CRONIES : (singing) *GIVE FIVE HURRAHS, GIVE TWELVE HIP-HIPS*

LEFOU : (singing) *GASTON IS THE BEST AND THE REST IS ALL DRIPS!*

Lefou swings up his arm in dance and throws a mug of beer in Gaston's face who socks Lefou in the face.

ALL : (singing) *NO ONE FIGHTS LIKE GASTON, DOUSES LIGHTS LIKE GASTON*

WRESTLER : (singing) *IN A WRESTLING MATCH, NOBODY BITES LIKE GASTON*

BIMBETTES : (singing) *FOR THERE'S NO ONE AS BURLY AND BRAWNY*

GASTON : (singing) *AS YOU SEE I'VE GOT BICEPS TO SPARE*

LEFOU : (singing) *NOT A BIT OF HIM SCRAGGLY OR SCRAWNY*

GASTON : (singing) *THAT'S RIGHT! AND EVERY LAST INCH OF ME'S COVERED WITH HAIR!*

Gaston fights with the men then lifts a bench with the Blimbettes on it. He drops the bench on Lefou then turns to the camera and reveals his hairy chest.

OLD CRONIES : (singing) *NO ONE HITS LIKE GASTON, MATCHES WITS LIKE GASTON*

LEFOU : (singing) *IN A SPITTING MATCH NOBODY SPITS LIKE GASTON!*

르 푸 : (노래하며) *아무도 그의 턱에 있는 흉터를 흉내 낼 순 없지*
개스톤 : (노래하며) *그래, 이 몸은 남자로 완벽해!*
추종자들 : (노래하며) *멋진 사나이, 개스톤*

추종자들은 르푸를 카메라 앞뒤로 흔든다. 르푸는 개스톤의 턱을 간질이고, 개스톤은 자랑스럽게 일어난다.
개스톤은 팔 근육을 과시한다.

추종자들 : (노래하며) *환호를 지르고 만세를 부르세*
르 푸 : (노래하며) *개스톤만 최고이고 나머지는 모두 얼간이*

르푸는 그의 팔을 흔들며 춤을 추다가 개스톤의 얼굴에 맥주를 뿌리고, 개스톤은 르푸의 얼굴에 주먹을 날린다.

사람들 : (노래하며) *아무도 개스톤만큼 싸움을 못하지. 깨물지 못하지*
레슬러 : (노래하며) *레슬링 경기에서 누구도 개스톤처럼 깨물지 못하지*
여자들 : (노래하며) *아무도 개스톤만큼 우람하고 튼튼하지 않지*
개스톤 : (노래하며) *보다시피 엄청난 근육을 가졌지*
르 푸 : (노래하며) *허약한 모습은 그에겐 없어*
개스톤 : (노래하며) *맞아. 그리고 난 털도 많다네*

개스톤은 사람들과 싸우고 나서 여자들이 앉아 있는 벤치를 들어 올린다. 그는 벤치를 르푸 위에서 떨어뜨리고, 카메라로 몸을 돌려 그의 털이 많은 가슴을 드러낸다.

추종자들 : (노래하며) *아무도 개스톤 만큼 잘 때리지도 영리하지도 않지*
르 푸 : (노래하며) *씨 멀리 뱉기 게임에서도 일등이야*

■ cleft
턱의 움푹 들어간 부분
If someone has a cleft chin, they have a prominent indentation below their lips

■ intimidating
위협적인
If you describe someone or something as intimidating, you mean that they are frightening and make people lose confidence

■ biceps
이두박근
Your biceps are the large muscles at the front of the upper part of your arms

■ spit
뱉다
If someone spits, they force an amount of liquid out of their mouth, often to show hatred or contempt

In a spitting match, nobody spits like Gaston!
앞에서 본 '부정어 as 원급 as'와 같은 표현이다. '부정어 like~'라고 쓰면 역시 '~처럼 ~하는 사람(것)도 없다'는 의미가 되어 최상급의 의미를 나타낸다. 최상급을 쓰지 않아도 부정어를 사용해서 최상의 의미를 표현 가능하니 연습해보자.

Zoom In

In a spitting match, nobody spits like Gaston!
씨 멀리 뱉기 게임에서도 일등이야.

GASTON : (singing) *I'M ESPECIALLY GOOD AT EXPECTORATING!*
PTOOEY!

ALL : (singing) *TEN POINTS FOR GASTON!*

Gaston plays a chess game with a man, then hits the board, sending it and pieces all over. He takes a bite of leather from the belt once wrapped around his neck, chews it and spits it into a spittoon, which falls and gets stuck on the head of Lefou.

GASTON : (singing) *WHEN I WAS A LAD I ATE FOUR DOZEN EGGS*
EVERY MORNING TO HELP ME GET LARGE!
AND NOW THAT I'M GROWN, I EAT FIVE DOZEN EGGS
SO I'M ROUGHLY THE SIZE OF A BARGE!

Gaston juggles a number of eggs then swallows them whole. Lefou attempts the trick and is hit in the face by three eggs.
Gaston shows his biceps again. He puts his finger into the trigger and spins the gun with only one finger.

ALL : (singing) *NO ONE SHOOTS LIKE GASTON, MAKES THOSE BEAUTS LIKE GASTON*

LEFOU : (singing) *THEN GOES TROMPING AROUND WEARING BOOTS LIKE GASTON*

GASTON : (singing) *I USE ANTLERS IN ALL OF MY DECORATING!*

Gaston takes three shots at a beer barrel, which begins leaking into the mugs of onlookers. He returns stomping to his chair, where we see the fireplace surrounded by the heads of the animals he has killed. The mystery cut of music is here! Cut to ending of "Gaston Reprise".

ALL : (singing) *MY WHAT A GUY! GASTON!!!!!!!*

The Old Cronies have picked up the chair and carry Gaston around in it.

개스톤 : (노래하며) *난 침 뱉는데도 선수라구. 퉤!*
사람들 : (노래하며) *10점 만점. 개스톤*

개스톤은 어떤 사람과 체스 게임을 하다가 체스판을 쳐서 모든 말들을 날려버린다. 그는 한때 그의 목에 둘렀던 벨트의 가죽을 깨물어 타구에 뱉는다. 그것은 르푸의 머리 위로 떨어진다.

개스톤 : (노래하며) *내가 어렸을 때 난 매일 아침 48개의 계란을 먹어 몸을 키웠지*
그리고 지금 난 60개의 계란을 먹는다네
그래서 근육이 이렇게 나오는 거야

개스톤은 계란들을 가지고 저글링을 하다가 모두 삼켜버린다. 르푸도 시도하지만, 세 개의 계란에 얼굴을 맞는다.
개스톤은 그의 근육을 다시 보여준다. 손가락을 방아쇠에 넣고 한 손가락만으로 총을 빙글빙글 돌린다.

사람들 : (노래하며) *아무도 개스톤만큼 총을 잘 쏘아 이런 걸 만들지 못하지*
르 푸 : (노래하며) *아무도 개스톤만큼 부츠를 신고 힘차게 걷지 못하지*
개스톤 : (노래하며) *내가 잡은 사슴뿔들은 모두 장식해 두었어!*

개스톤이 맥주 통에 총 세 발을 쏘자, 구경꾼들의 잔으로 맥주가 흘러 들어간다. 그는 쿵쿵 거리며 의자로 간다. 벽난로 주변에는 그가 사냥한 동물들의 머리들이 걸려있다. 음악은 여기서 멈춘다! "개스톤 반복부분"의 엔딩 장면.

사람들 : (노래하며) *대단한 사나이! 개스톤!!!*

추종자들은 개스톤이 앉은 의자를 들어 올려 나른다.

- **expectorate**
  가래를 뱉다
  to cough up and spit out (sputum from the respiratory passages)
- **spittoon**
  타구
  a receptacle for spit, usually in a public place
- **barge**
  너벅선
  A barge is a long, narrow boat with a flat bottom. Barges are used for carrying heavy loads, especially on canals
- **tromp**
  짓밟다
  If you tromp somewhere, you walk there slowly and with regular, heavy steps, for a long time
- **antler**
  사슴뿔
  A male deer's antlers are the branched horns on its head

I'm roughly the size of a barge!
barge는 '바지선(강 등에서 사람이나 화물을 싣고 다니는 배)'이라는 뜻이다. 위 장면에서는 개스톤이 자신의 근육을 자랑하며 거의 배에 필적하는 크기라고 과장하는 비유적인 표현으로 쓰였다.

Zoom In

I'm roughly the size of a barge!
그래서 근육이 이렇게 나오는 거야!

Lefou tries to flee but they toss the chair into its normal place and Lefou is pinned underneath. Maurice bursts in frantically.

MAURICE : Help! Someone help me!

OLD CRONIES : Maurice?

In a hurry Maurice grabs Old Cronies by the collars and asks for their help. However everyone laughs at him.

MAURICE : Please! Please, I need your help! He's got her... He's got her locked in the dungeon.

LEFOU : Who?

MAURICE : Belle. We must go. Not... not a minute to lose!

GASTON : Whoa! Slow down, Maurice. Who's got Belle locked in a dungeon?

MAURICE : A Beast! A horrible, monstrous Beast!

Maurice has gone from person to person pleading his case until he is thrown at the feet of Gaston. A moment of silence then the Old Cronies begin to laugh and mock him.

CRONY 1 : Is it a big Beast?

MAURICE : Huge!

CRONY 2 : With a long, ugly snout?

MAURICE : Hideously ugly!

CRONY 3 : And sharp, cruel fangs?

MAURICE : Yes, yes. Will you help me?

GASTON : All right, old man. We'll help you out.

MAURICE : You will? Oh thank you, thank you! Thank you! Oh!

The Old Cronies pick up Maurice and help him out by throwing him through the door.

르푸가 도망가려고 해보지만, 그들은 의자를 제자리에 던지고, 르푸가 의자 밑에 깔린다. 제정신이 아닌듯한 모리스가 갑자기 나타난다.

모리스 : 제발. 누가 좀 도와줘.

추종자들 : 모리스?

모리스는 급하게 나이든 추종자들의 멱살을 잡고 도움을 요청한다. 그러나 모든 사람들이 그를 비웃는다.

모리스 : 제발. 제발, 도움이 필요하다네. 그녀가 잡혀갔다구. 그 놈이 성 안에 가뒀어.

추종자들 : 누구를?

모리스 : 벨 말이야. 우리가 어서 가야해. 시간이 얼마 없다네.

개스톤 : 오. 진정하세요. 모리스. 누가 벨을 성에 가뒀다는 말입니까?

모리스 : 야수가! 끔찍하게 징그러운 야수가.

모리스는 한 사람씩 다니면서 그의 사정을 설명하다가, 개스톤의 발밑으로 던져진다. 잠시 침묵이 흐른 뒤, 추종자들이 웃으면서 그를 놀리기 시작한다.

사람 1 : 야수는 덩치가 커다랗던가?

모리스 : 아주 커!

사람 2 : 길고 못생긴 코를 가졌고?

모리스 : 그래. 무시무시하게 못 생겼다구.

사람 3 : 날카롭고 잔인한 이빨을 가졌고?

모리스 : 그래, 맞아. 나를 도와주겠나?

개스톤 : 그럼요. 노인 양반. 우리가 나가는 걸 도와주지요.

모리스 : 정말 그래주겠나? 고맙네, 고마워!

추종자들은 모리스를 들어 올려 그를 문 밖으로 던져 그를 내쫓는다.

- **flee**
  도망가다
  If you flee from something or someone, or flee a person or thing, you escape from them
- **frantically**
  미친 듯이
  in an uncontrolled manner
- **dungeon**
  지하 감옥
  A dungeon is a dark underground prison in a castle
- **snout**
  코
  The snout of an animal such as a pig is its long nose
- **fang**
  송곳니
  Fangs are the two long, sharp, upper teeth that some animals have

Not a minute to lose!
'time to부정사'가 '~할 시간'이라는 것은 이미 살펴보았다. time자리에 a minute를 써주면 짧은 시간을 표현할 수 있다. 위 표현은 1분도 지체할 시간이 없다는 의미로 상황이 급박하니 서두르라는 의미이다.

Zoom In

Not a minute to lose!
시간이 얼마 없다네.

Maurice is dumped on snow.

CRONY 1 : Crazy old Maurice. He's always good for a laugh!

GASTON : (very pensive) Crazy old Maurice, hmm? Crazy old Maurice. Hmmm. (singing) *LEFOU, I'M AFRAID I'VE BEEN THINKING*

Lefou is still under the chair. Lefou puts his head out of the chair and talks to Gaston under the chair.

LEFOU : (singing) *A DANGEROUS PASTIME...*

GASTON : (finishing line) (singing) *I KNOW,*
BUT THAT WACKY OLD COOT IS BELLE'S FATHER
AND HIS SANITY'S ONLY SO-SO
NOW THE WHEELS IN MY HEAD HAVE BEEN TURNING
SINCE I LOOKED AT THAT LOONY OLD MAN
SEE, I PROMISED MYSELF I'D BE MARRIED TO BELLE
AND RIGHT NOW, I'M EVOLVING A PLAN!

Gaston picks Lefou out from under the chair and holds his head close and whispers. Gaston sings a song while lifting up Lefou and throws him away.
He starts to talk to Lefou in whispers.

GASTON : If I... (whisper)

LEFOU : Yes?

GASTON : Then we... (whisper)

LEFOU : No, would she?

GASTON : (whispering) ...Guess!

LEFOU : Now I get it!

BOTH : Let's go!

모리스는 눈에 파묻힌다.

사람 1 : 미친 모리스 영감 같으니라구. 언제 봐도 웃기단 말이야.

개스톤 : (깊게 생각하더니) 미친 모리스? 미친 모리스 영감. 흠. (노래하며) *르푸, 내가 생각을 한다는 건 두려운 일이야*

르푸는 여전히 의자 밑에 깔려있다. 르푸는 의자 밑으로 머리를 내밀고 개스톤에게 말을 건다.

르 푸 : (노래하며) *항상 사고를 쳤잖아*

개스톤 : (말을 자르며) (노래하며) *나도 알아*
하지만 저 이상한 늙은이는 벨의 아버지란 말이야
더군다나 정신도 오락가락해
저 미친 영감을 본 이후로 내 머리는 비상하게 돌아가고 있어
두고 봐. 난 벨과 결혼하고 말거야
그러려면 계획을 세워야 해

개스톤은 르푸를 의자 밑에서 꺼내 그의 얼굴을 가까이 가져다 대고 속삭인다. 개스톤은 르푸를 들어 올린 채 노래를 부르다가 그를 던져 버린다.
그는 르푸에게 귓속말을 하기 시작한다.

개스톤 : 만약 내가… (귓속말)

르 푸 : 응?

개스톤 : 그 다음 내가… (귓속말)

르 푸 : 그녀가 할까?

개스톤 : (속삭이며) 생각해봐!

르 푸 : 이제 알았어!

개스톤, 르푸 : 좋았어, 가자!

- **pastime**
  취미
  A pastime is something that you do in your spare time because you enjoy it or are interested in it

- **wacky**
  괴짜의
  If you describe something or someone as wacky, you mean that they are eccentric, unusual, and often funny

- **loony**
  미친
  If you describe someone's behaviour or ideas as loony, you mean that they seem mad, strange, or eccentric. Some people consider this use offensive

- **evolve**
  발전시키다
  If something evolves or you evolve it, it gradually develops over a period of time into something different and usually more advanced

He's always good for a laugh!
good for a laugh는 '웃음을 나게 하는, 웃고 싶어지는'이라는 구어체 표현이다. 위 문장은 항상 우스갯거리를 가지고 있는 모리스에게 개스톤이 비웃으며 한 말이다.
ex) My brother's joke is good for a laugh.

Zoom In

He's always good for a laugh!

언제 봐도 웃기단말이야.

They begin a waltz around the floor as they sing.

BOTH : (singing) *NO ONE PLOTS LIKE GASTON*
TAKES CHEAP SHOTS LIKE GASTON

LEFOU : (singing) *PLANS TO PERSECUTE HARMLESS CRACKPOTS*
LIKE GASTON

ALL : (singing) *SO HIS MARRIAGE WE SOON WILL BE CELEBRATING!*
MY WHAT A GUY, GASTON!!!

Camera zooms out through window to snow-covered square, empty except for Maurice.
Maurice asks for help, lonely in the blinding snow. The wind blows hard.

MAURICE : (to no one in particular) Will no one help me?

그들은 노래를 하면서 바닥을 돌며 왈츠를 추기 시작한다.

개스톤, 르푸 : (노래하며) *아무도 개스톤만큼 음모를 잘 꾸미지 못하지*

르 푸 : (노래하며) *미친놈을 괴롭히는 기발한 계획도 못 세우지*

사람들 : (노래하며) *그의 곧 있을 결혼을 축하하며. 우리의 멋진 사나이, 개스톤!!!*

카메라 눈 덮인 광장에서 점점 멀어진다. 모리스만 그곳에 덩그러니 있다.
모리스는 눈 속에서 홀로 도움을 요청한다. 바람이 세차게 분다.

모리스 : (정해진 듣는 이 없이) 누구 날 좀 도와줄 사람 없소?

- **plot**
  음모를 꾸미다
  If people plot to do something or plot something that is illegal or wrong, they plan secretly to do it
- **persecute**
  귀찮게 굴다
  If someone is persecuted, they are treated cruelly and unfairly, often because of their race or beliefs
- **crackpot**
  괴짜
  If you describe someone or their ideas as crackpot, you disapprove of them because you think that their ideas are strange and crazy
- **celebrate**
  축하하다
  If you celebrate, you do something enjoyable because of a special occasion or to mark someone's success

Key Expressions

108 Gaston shows off the biceps of his.

개스톤은 그의 팔 근육을 과시한다.

show off는 '과시하다, 자랑하다, 으스대다'라는 의미의 숙어이다. boast나 brag와도 같은 의미이다.

· He visited us to show off his gorgeous girlfriend.
그는 예쁜 여자 친구를 자랑하려고 들른 것 같아.

110 I'm especially good at expectorating!

난 침 뱉는 데도 선수라구!

be good at은 '~을 잘하다'라는 표현으로 at뒤에 명사 또는 동명사를 써줄 수 있다. 반대로 잘 하지 못하는 일은 be bad at이라고 표현하면 된다.

· She's really good at singing and dancing.
그녀는 정말 노래도 잘하고 춤도 잘 춰.

112 He's got her locked in the dungeon.

그가 그녀를 성 안의 지하 감옥에 가뒀어.

'get+목적어+목적격보어'의 문형에서, 위에서 그녀가 감옥에 갇힌 상황과 같이 목적어와 목적격보어가 수동의 관계이면 목적격보어 자리에 과거분사가 사용된다. 만약 능동의 관계라면 to부정사가 쓰인다.

· My car has broken. I should get my car fixed.
차가 고장났어. 차를 수리해야겠어.

114 I'm afraid I've been thinking. 내가 생각을 한다는 건 두려운 일이야.

I'm afraid~는 '나는 ~하는 것이 두렵다, ~하게 되어 유감이다'라는 의미로, 뒤에 절이 오거나 of+명사가 온다.

· I'm afraid I can't help you. 당신을 도와주지 못해서 유감입니다.

114 The wheels in my head have been turning since I looked at that loony old man.

저 미친 영감을 본 이후로 내 머리는 비상하게 돌아가고 있어.

The wheels in my head have been turning이라고 하면 머리 속에 있는 바퀴가 돈다는 의미이므로, 두뇌 회전이 비상하게 되고 있음을 비유적으로 나타내는 표현이다. 특히 위 문장에서는 since와 함께 현재완료진행형(have been ~ing)의 시제가 쓰여, 과거의 한 시점부터 현재까지 계속되는 일을 나타낸다.

· It has been raining cats and dogs since yesterday.
어제부터 비가 억수같이 계속 내리고 있다.

116 No one plots like Gaston, takes cheap shots like Gaston. 아무도 개스톤만큼 음모를 잘 꾸미지 못하지.

cheap shot는 '치사한 행동, 음모'를 일컫는 관용적인 표현이다. 또한 위 문장은 누구도 개스톤만큼 음모를 잘 꾸미지 못한다는 의미이므로, 결국 개스톤이 가장 치사한 음모를 잘 계획한다는 최상급의 의미를 나타낸다.

· No one is picky like her. She's not easily satisfied.
그녀만큼 눈 높은 사람도 없어. 쉽게 만족하는 법이 없다니깐.

Movie Talk

영화 정보

게리 트러스데일, 커크 와이즈 감독의 《미녀와 야수(Beauty and the Beast)》는 프랑스 작가 잔마리 르 프랭스 드 보몽 (Jeanne-Marie Le Prince de Beaumont) 부인이 쓴 동명 소설을 원안으로 하였다. 1991년 개봉된 월트디즈니사의 30번째 작품이다. 디즈니 르네상스 시절의 업적을 격상시켜준 작품으로 평가 받고 있으며, 이 영화에서 본격적으로 시작한 전통 2D 애니메이션과 컴퓨터 그래픽의 융합은 이후의 애니메이션 영화에도 큰 영향을 주었다.

아름다운 화면과 음악으로 전세계 사람들을 사로잡은 《미녀와 야수》는 골든글로브 뮤지컬코미디 부분 작품상을 비롯하여 음악상과 주제가상을 수상하였다. 무엇보다 애니메이션 최초로 아카데미상에서 작품상을 비롯하여 6개 부분에 후보로 올랐으며, 음악상과 작곡상을 수상한 기록을 보유하고 있다.

박스 오피스에서 엄청난 성공을 거둔 《미녀와 야수》는 미국 내에서만 1억 4천 500만 달러 이상, 전 세계에서는 4억 300만 달러 이상의 수익을 달성하였다. 《미녀와 야수》는 사상 처음으로 미국 박스 오피스에서 1억 달러 이상의 수익을 달성한 애니메이션 영화로, 당시 디즈니 영화중에서 가장 성공한 작품이었다. 우리나라에서도 1992년 개봉하여 큰 흥행을 거두어 서울 지역 영화관을 기준으로 60만 명 가까이 되는 관객을 동원한바 있다.

이후 영화를 각색하여 제작한 동명의 브로드웨이 뮤지컬은 1994년부터 2007년까지 공연하였으며, TV 어린이 시리즈, 스페셜 에디션도 제작되었다. 뒤를 이어 중편인 《미녀와 야수 : 마법에 걸린 크리스마스》가 비디오로 발매되어 호평을 받았고, 또 다른 중편인 《벨과 마법의 성》이 발매되었다. 최근 미국에서는 《미녀와 야수 3D》로 21년 만에 3D로 컨버팅되어 개봉하는 등 계속해서 그 인기가 지속되고 있다.

Chapter 6

야수의 성 안에서의 생활

Life in the Beast's Castle

시간 00:31:52 ~ 00:37:21

INT. BELLE'S ROOM IN THE CASTLE
Fade back to the bedroom of the castle where Belle is still crying. She faces down and sobs into the pillow. There is a 'clink clink clink' at the door. She gets up and walks over to open the door.
Mrs. Potts enters with Chip and their entourage.

BELLE : Who is it?

MRS. POTTS : (from outside the door) Mrs. Potts, dear. (Door opens) I thought you might like a spot of tea.

Belle is amazed at the fact that she is listening to a walking tea set.

BELLE : But you... ah... but... you're a...

Being so surprised, Belle bumps into the Wardrobe.

WARDROBE : Oof. Careful!

Belle is surprised at the talking closet.

내부. 성 안에 있는 벨의 방

성 안의 침실에서 벨이 여전히 울고 있다. 그녀는 베개에 얼굴을 파묻고 훌쩍인다. 문에서 짤랑짤랑 소리가 난다. 그녀는 일어나서 문을 열러 간다.
포트 부인이 칩과 다른 식기들과 함께 들어온다.

벨 : 누구세요?

포트 부인 : (문 밖에서) 포트 부인이에요. (문이 열린다) 차 드시고 싶을 것 같아서요.

벨은 걸어들어오는 다기 세트가 말하는 것을 듣고 있다는 사실에 놀란다.

벨 : 하지만 당신은…

너무 놀란 벨은 옷장과 부딪친다.

워로브 : 오. 조심하세요.

벨은 말하는 옷장을 보고 놀란다.

- **sob**
  훌쩍이다
  When someone sobs, they cry in a noisy way, breathing in short breaths

- **pillow**
  베개
  A pillow is a rectangular cushion which you rest your head on when you are in bed

- **clink**
  쨍그랑[짤랑] 소리를 내다
  If objects made of glass, pottery, or metal clink or if you clink them, they touch each other and make a short, light sound

- **entourage**
  수행단
  A famous or important person's entourage is the group of assistants, servants, or other people who travel with them

BELLE : (sits on bed) This is impossible.

Wardrobe leans 'shoulder' on bed, popping other end and Belle into the air.

WARDROBE : I know it is, but here we are!

Sugar and cream are being poured into Chip.

CHIP : Told ya she was pretty, mama, didn't I?

MRS. POTTS : All right, now, Chip. That'll do.

Chip hops over to Belle, who is sitting on the floor.

MRS. POTTS : Slowly, now. Don't spill!

BELLE : Thank you.

She picks up Chip and is about to take a sip of tea.

CHIP : (to Belle) Wanna see me do a trick?

Chip takes a big breath then puffs out his cheeks and blows bubbles out the top of the cup.

MRS. POTTS : (admonishingly) Chip!

CHIP : (looking guilty) Oops. Sorry.

MRS. POTTS : (to Belle) That was a very brave thing you did, my dear.

WARDROBE : We all think so.

BELLE : But I've lost my father, my dreams, everything.

All servants in the room feel sorry to see Belle being sad and console her.

벨 : (침대에 앉아서) 말도 안 돼.

워로브가 침대에 어깨를 기대자, 다른 쪽 끝이 튀어 올라 벨은 공중에 뜬다.

워로브 : 우리도 알아요. 하지만 이렇게 있잖아요.

설탕과 크림이 칩 안으로 들어간다.

칩 : 예쁘다고 그랬죠, 엄마?
포트 부인 : 그렇구나, 칩. 정말이네.

칩은 벨에게 통통 뛰어가고, 벨은 바닥에 앉아있다.

포트 부인 : 천천히. 흘리지 않게!
벨 : 고마워요.

그녀는 칩을 들어 올리고, 차를 한 모금 마시려고 한다.

칩 : (벨에게) 내 묘기 좀 볼래요?

칩은 크게 숨을 들이마셔 볼에 바람을 불어넣고는 컵 위에 보글보글 물거품을 만들어 낸다.

포트 부인 : (타이르며) 칩!
칩 : (미안해하며) 앗, 미안해요.
포트 부인 : (벨에게) 정말 용감한 행동을 했어요, 아가씨.
워로브 : 우리 모두 그렇게 생각해요.
벨 : 하지만 아빠를 잃었고, 제 꿈과 모든 것을…

방 안에 있는 모든 하인들이 벨이 슬퍼하자 미안해하며 그녀를 위로한다.

- **spill**
  쏟다
  If a liquid spills or if you spill it, it accidentally flows over the edge of a container
- **trick**
  묘기
  A trick is a clever or skilful action that someone does in order to entertain people
- **bubble**
  거품
  Bubbles are small balls of air or gas in a liquid
- **brave**
  용감한
  Someone who is brave is willing to do things which are dangerous, and does not show fear in difficult or dangerous situations

Wanna see me do a trick?
trick에는 속임수라는 뜻도 있지만, 여기서는 '묘기, 재주'라는 뜻으로 쓰였다. wanna는 want to(~하고 싶다)의 구어체 표현으로 실제 회화에서 많이 활용되므로 알아두자.

Zoom In

Wanna see me do a trick?
내 묘기 좀 볼래요?

MRS. POTTS : Cheer up, child. It'll turn out all right in the end. You'll see. (she looks up, startled.) Oops! Listen to me, jabbering on while there's a supper to get on the table. Chip!

CHIP : (hopping away) Bye!

Belle stands and the Wardrobe approaches her.

WARDROBE : Well now, what shall we dress you in for dinner? Let's see what I've got in my drawers.

The doors fly open and moths flutter out. She slams them shut.

WARDROBE : Oh! How embarrassing. Ho ho ho... Oh! Here we are.

One door opens the other serves as an arm. It pulls out a pink dress.

WARDROBE : You'll look ravishing in this one!

BELLE : That's very kind of you, but I'm not going to dinner.

WARDROBE : Oh, but you must!

Cogsworth waddles in.

COGSWORTH : Ahem, ahem, ahem. Dinner... is served.

Cut to Beast pacing back and forth in front of fire with Mrs. Potts and Lumiere looking on. Beast raises his voice in a rage.

포트 부인 : 기운 내요, 아가씨. 모든 것이 잘 될 거예요. 두고 봐요. (놀라면서) 이런! 내 정신 좀 봐. 저녁 준비는 안하고 수다만 떨었네. 칩!

칩 : (통통 뛰어가면서) 안녕.

벨이 일어서자 워로브가 그녀에게 다가간다.

워로브 : 자, 어디 보자. 저녁 식사엔 무엇을 입고 갈까요? 뭐가 있는지 찾아볼까요.

옷장 문이 갑자기 열리고 나방들이 쏟아져 나온다. 그녀는 옷장 문을 쾅 닫는다.

워로브 : 이런… 낭패가 있나. 호호호… 아! 여기 있군.

한 쪽 문이 열리고, 다른 쪽이 팔이 되어 옷을 꺼내준다. 분홍색 드레스를 꺼낸다.

워로브 : 오, 이게 좋겠군요. 잘 어울릴 거예요.

벨 : 호의는 감사하지만 저는 만찬에 가지 않을 거예요.

워로브 : 안 돼요, 가야 해요.

콕스워즈가 뒤뚱뒤뚱 걸어 들어온다.

콕스워즈 : 에헴, 에헴. 저녁식사 시간입니다.

야수가 벽난로 주변을 앞뒤로 어슬렁대고, 포트 부인과 루미에르가 위에서 내려다본다. 야수는 화가 나서 목소리를 높인다.

- **jabber**
  재잘거리다
  If you say that someone is jabbering, you mean that they are talking very quickly and excitedly, and you cannot understand them

- **approach**
  접근하다
  When you approach something, you get closer to it

- **drawer**
  서랍
  A drawer is part of a desk, chest, or other piece of furniture that is shaped like a box and is designed for putting things in. You pull it towards you to open it

- **embarrassing**
  당황스러운
  Something that is embarrassing makes you feel shy or ashamed

- **ravishing**
  아름다운
  If you describe someone or something as ravishing, you mean that they are very beautiful

That's very kind of you, but I'm not going to dinner.
상대방이 베푼 친절에 감사할 때 It's(That's) kind of you.라는 표현을 많이 쓴다. 또be going to 동사원형'은 가까운 미래에 예정된 계획을 나타낼 수 있다.
ex) I'm going to see a dentist tomorrow.

Zoom In

**That's very kind of you,
but I'm not going to dinner.**
호의는 감사하지만 저는 만찬에 가지 않을 거예요.

BEAST : What's taking so long? I told her to come down. Why isn't she here yet?

MRS. POTTS : Oh, try to be patient, sir. The girl has lost her father and her freedom all in one day.

LUMIERE : Uh, Master. Have you thought that, perhaps this girl could be the one to break the spell?

BEAST : (angrily) Of course I have. I'm not a fool.

LUMIERE : Good. So, you fall in love with her, she falls in love with you, and... Poof! The spell is broken! We'll be human again by midnight!

MRS. POTTS : Oh, it's not that easy, Lumiere. These things take time.

LUMIERE : But the rose has already begun to wilt.

BEAST : Oh, It's no use. She's so beautiful and... well, look at me!

Lumiere shrugs his shoulders and looks at Mrs. Potts.

MRS. POTTS : Oh, you must help her to see past all that.

BEAST : I don't know how.

Mrs. Potts stamps down from the fireplace and hops to the table. Lumiere also comes down to the floor and advises Beast to be gentle.

MRS. POTTS : Well, you can start by making yourself more presentable. Straighten up. Try to act like a gentleman.

Beast sits up then straightens his face very formally.

야 수 : 왜 이렇게 늦는 거지? 분명히 내려오라고 했는데. 왜 아직 안 오는 거지?

포트 부인 : 진정하세요, 주인님. 그녀는 하루 만에 아버지, 자유, 그리고 모든 것을 잃었어요.

루미에르 : 주인님. 그녀가 우리의 마법을 풀어 줄 수 있다고 생각해보셨어요?

야 수 : (화를 내며) 당연히 해봤지. 나는 바보가 아니야.

루미에르 : 좋아요. 주인님이 그녀를 사랑하고 그녀도 주인님을 사랑하게 되면, 마법이 풀릴 거예요! 오늘 밤 우리는 다시 인간이 될 수 있어요!

포트 부인 : 그건 쉽지 않아요. 시간도 걸리고.

루미에르 : 하지만 장미가 시들기 시작한다구요.

야 수 : 소용없어. 그녀는 너무 아름답지만 나는… 내 모습을 봐!

루미에르는 어깨를 움츠리고 포트 부인을 쳐다본다.

포트 부인 : 그녀가 모든 진실을 알 수 있게 보여줘야 해요.

야 수 : 어떻게 해야 할지 모르겠어.

포트 부인은 벽난로에서 뛰어 내려와 테이블 위로 올라간다. 루미에르 역시 바닥으로 내려와서 야수에게 부드럽게 행동하라고 충고한다.

포트 부인 : 우선, 교양 있게 행동하셔야 해요. 똑바로 서서, 신사답게 행동하세요.

야수는 자세를 바로 하고 딱딱한 표정을 짓는다.

- **patient**
  참을성 있는
  If you are patient, you stay calm and do not get annoyed, for example when something takes a long time, or when someone is not doing what you want them to do

- **wilt**
  시들다
  If a plant wilts, it gradually bends downwards and becomes weak because it needs more water or is dying

- **presentable**
  내놓을 만한
  If you say that someone looks presentable, you mean that they look fairly tidy or attractive

- **straighten**
  똑바르게 하다
  If you straighten something, you make it tidy or put it in its proper position

What's taking so long?
take라는 동사에는 많은 뜻이 있지만, 대표적인 의미 중 하나가 '시간이 걸리다'라는 뜻이다. 따라서 What's taking so long?은 무엇을 하기에 시간이 이렇게 오래걸리냐고 묻는 표현이 된다.

Zoom In

What's taking so long?

왜 이렇게 늦는 거지?

LUMIERE : (adding in) Ah yes, when she comes in give her a dashing debonair smile. Come, come. Show me the smile.

Beast bears his ragged fangs in a scary and yet funny grin.

MRS. POTTS : But don't frighten the poor girl.

LUMIERE : Impress her with your rapier wit.

MRS. POTTS : But be gentle.

LUMIERE : Shower her with compliments.

Beast looks back and forth at them. Mrs. Potts and Lumiere talk to him firmly.

MRS. POTTS : But be sincere

LUMIERE : And above all...

BOTH : You must control your temper!

The door creaks open. Beast wipes the silly face off, and looks to the door expectantly.

LUMIERE : Here she is!

Cogsworth enters.

COGSWORTH : Uh, good evening.

Beast goes from expectant to mad.

BEAST : (growling) Well, where is she?

COGSWORTH : (buying time) Who? Oh! Ha ha ha... The girl. Yes, the girl. Well, actually she's in the process of... ah... circumstances being what they are... ah... she's not coming.

루미에르 : (덧붙이며) 그래요, 그녀가 오면 멋지고 다정한 미소를 지으세요. 자, 한 번 웃어 보세요.

야수는 그의 고르지 못한 송곳니를 내 보이고는 우스꽝스럽게 미소 짓는다.

포트 부인 : 놀라게 하지 마시구요.
루미에르 : 번뜩이는 재치로 좋은 인상을 주셔야죠.
포트 부인 : 하지만 부드럽게요.
루미에르 : 그녀에게 칭찬을 퍼부으세요.

야수는 포트 부인과 루미에르를 번갈아가며 쳐다본다. 그들은 야수에게 강력하게 말한다.

포트 부인 : 하지만 진정으로
루미에르 : 그리고 가장 중요한 것은…
루미에르, 포트 부인 : 화를 내셔서는 안 돼요.

문이 끼익 소리를 내며 열린다. 야수는 바보 같은 표정을 지우고 기대에 차서 문 쪽을 바라본다.

루미에르 : 그녀예요.

콕스워즈가 들어온다.

콕스워즈 : 저… 저예요.

야수의 기대감은 분노로 변해간다.

야 수 : (으르렁대며) 그녀는 어디 있지?
콕스워즈 : (시간을 벌며) 누구요? 아, 그녀는… 저, 그러니까 사실, 그녀는 준비 중… 어… 사정이 생겨서, 어… 오지 않는답니다.

- **debonair**
  멋지고 당당한
  A man who is debonair is confident, charming, and well-dressed
- **grin**
  웃음
  A grin is a broad smile
- **compliment**
  칭찬
  A compliment is a polite remark that you say to someone to show that you like their appearance, appreciate their qualities, or approve of what they have done
- **expectant**
  기대하는
  If someone is expectant, they are excited because they think something interesting is about to happen

You must control your temper!
must는 '~해야 한다'는 의무를 나타내는 조동사이다. control one's temper는 '화를 참다, 감정을 자제하다'는 숙어이다. control대신에 keep을 써도 같다.

Zoom In

You must control your temper!
화를 내셔서는 안 돼요.

Cut to ext of den with door slightly ajar.
Cogsworth talks to Beast hesitatingly. Beast gets hopping mad.

BEAST : What!!!!!!!

Door bares open and Beast comes running out with Objects giving chase.

COGSWORTH : Your grace! Your eminence! Let's not be hasty!

Cut to ext of Belle's room. Beast runs up to it and bangs on the door.
Beast yells at her in front of the door. When he gets furious Lumiere and Cogsworth try to persuade him to calm down and be gentle.

BEAST : (yelling) I thought I told you to come down to dinner!

BELLE : (from behind the door) I'm not hungry.

BEAST : You'll come out or I'll...I'll ...I'll break down the door!

LUMIERE : (interrupting) Master, I could be wrong but that may not be the best way to win the girl's affections.

COGSWORTH : (pleading) Please! Attempt to be a gentleman.

BEAST : (growing angrier) But she is being so... difficult!

MRS. POTTS : Gently... gently.

BEAST : (very dejected) Will you come down to dinner?

BELLE : No!

Beast looks at the Objects very frustrated.

COGSWORTH : Suave. Genteel.

Trying to act formal, Beast bows at the door.

살짝 문틈이 보이는 야수의 방 바깥 장면 장면.
콕스워즈는 야수에게 망설이면서 말한다. 야수는 화가 나서 뛰쳐 나간다.

야 수 : 뭐라고?

문이 쾅 열리고 야수는 달려 나오자, 하인들이 쫓아간다.

콕스워즈 : 주인님! 왕자님! 참으셔야 합니다.

벨의 방 바깥 장면 장면. 야수는 뛰어 올라와 문을 두드린다.
야수는 문 앞에서 그녀에게 소리친다. 그가 격분하자, 루미에르와 콕스워즈는 그에게 진정하고 신사답게 행동하라며 설득한다.

야 수 : (소리치며) 내가 내려 와서 저녁 먹으라고 했을 텐데.
벨 : (문 뒤에서) 배고프지 않아요.
야 수 : 나오지 않으면 내가… 문을 부숴버리겠어!
루미에르 : (끼어들며) 주인님, 죄송하지만, 그런 식으로는 아가씨의 마음을 사로잡기 힘들어요.
콕스워즈 : (애원하며) 제발! 신사답게 구세요.
야 수 : (화나서 으르렁대며) 하지만 날 너무… 힘들게 해!
포트 부인 : 부드럽게. 부드럽게.
야 수 : (기가 죽은 목소리로) 식사하러 와 주겠소?
벨 : 싫어요.

야수가 절망한 얼굴로 하인들을 본다.

루미에르 : 친절하게, 상냥하게.

정중하게 행동하려고 노력하면서 야수는 문을 향해 인사한다.

- **eminence**
  명성
  Eminence is the quality of being very well-known and highly respected
- **hasty**
  서두르는
  A hasty movement, action, or statement is sudden, and often done in reaction to something that has just happened
- **affection**
  애정
  If you regard someone or something with affection, you like them and are fond of them
- **suave**
  정중한
  Someone who is suave is charming, polite, and elegant, but may be insincere

Will you come down to dinner?
상대방에게 제안을 할 때 'Will you 동사원형 ~?' 이렇게 물을 수 있다. 한편 'Would you 동사원형~?'이 더 정중한 표현이므로 꼭 기억해 둔다.
ex) Would you please join me for dinner?

Zoom In

Will you come down to dinner?
식사하러 와 주겠소?

BEAST : It would give me great pleasure if you would join me for dinner.

COGSWORTH : Ahem, ahem, we say 'please.'

BEAST : (once again dejected) ...please.

BELLE : (mad at Beast) No, thank you.

Beast gets angry and barks out. He crosses both arms and orders his servants not to give Belle any food.

BEAST : (furious) You can't stay in there forever!

BELLE : (provokingly) Yes I can!

BEAST : Fine! Then go ahead and starve!!!! (to Objects) If she doesn't eat with me, then she doesn't eat at all!

Beast runs back down the hall, slamming a door and causing a piece of the ceiling to fall on Lumiere.

MRS. POTTS : Oh, dear! That didn't go very well at all, did it?

COGSWORTH : Lumiere, stand watch at the door and inform me at once if there is the slightest change.

LUMIERE : (taking guard position next to door) You can count on me mon capitan.

COGSWORTH : Well, we might as well go downstairs and start cleaning up.

Cut to int of Beast's lair. Beast enters knocking over and destroying things in his path.

BEAST : I ask nicely, but she refuses. What a... what does she want me to do... beg?

야 수 : 함께 식사를 할 수 있다면 영광이겠습니다.
루미에르 : 에헴, 에헴, '부디'라고 말해요.
야 수 : (다시 가라앉은 목소리로) 부디…
벨 : (야수에게 화를 내며) 싫어요.

야수는 화가 나서 으르렁댄다. 그는 양 손을 엑스자로 만들어 보이며 벨에게 음식을 가져다주지 말라고 하인들에게 명령한다.

야 수 : (화가 나서) 그럼 그 안에 평생 있을 거요?
벨 : (약올리며) 그럴 거예요.
야 수 : 좋아! 그럼 쫄쫄 굶으라고!!! (하인들에게) 나와 같이 식사하기 전에는 아무 것도 주지 마!

야수는 다시 복도를 달려가서 문을 쾅 닫고, 천장 조각들이 루미에르 위로 떨어진다.

포트 부인 : 오, 이런! 완전히 일이 꼬이고 말았네.
콕스워즈 : 루미에르, 자네가 여기서 문을 지키고 있다가, 무슨 일이 생기면 당장 보고하도록.
루미에르 : (문 옆에 지켜 서서) 저만 믿으십시오, 집사님.
콕스워즈 : 자, 우린 내려가서 청소를 시작하는 게 좋겠소.

야수의 방 내부 장면. 야수가 들어와서 발에 닿는 물건들을 부순다.

야 수 : 부드럽게 요청했는데 거절당했어. 나보고… 나보고 도대체 어쩌라는 거야? 애걸복걸 하라는 거야?

- **starve**
  굶주리다
  If people starve, they suffer greatly from lack of food which sometimes leads to their death
- **ceiling**
  천장
  A ceiling is the horizontal surface that forms the top part or roof inside a room
- **slight**
  약간의
  Something that is slight is very small in degree or quantity
- **refuse**
  거절하다
  If you refuse to do something, you deliberately do not do it, or you say firmly that you will not do it
- **beg**
  간청하다
  If you beg someone to do something, you ask them very anxiously or eagerly to do it

You can count on me.
count on은 '믿다, 기대다, 의지하다, ~에 달려있다'라는 동사구이다. 같은 표현으로 depend on(upon), rely on, rest on등이 있으니 함께 기억해두자.

Zoom In

You can count on me.
저만 믿으십시오.

Beast picks up the Magic Mirror.

BEAST : Show me the girl.

The Magic Mirror shines then glows green and reveals Belle in her bedroom talking to the Wardrobe. Wardrobe talks to Belle softly and Belle listens to her words with her arms folded.

WARDROBE : (in mirror pleading) But the master's really not so bad once you get to know him. Why don't you give him a chance?

BELLE : (still disturbed by the attack) I don't want to get to know him. I don't want to have anything to do with him!

Beast sets down Magic Mirror, speaking tenderly.

BEAST : I'm just fooling myself. She'll never see me as anything... but a monster.

Another petal falls off the rose.

BEAST : It's hopeless.

Beast puts his head in his hands as in a depressed state. Fade to ext of Belle's room. Door creaks open. Belle silently emerges. We see her feet go by as three bright spots shine through a curtain at floor level. Behind it are Lumiere and Featherduster. Lumiere and Featherduster are having a good time behind the curtain and come out of the curtain.

FEATHERDUSTER : Oh, no!

LUMIERE : Oh, yes!

FEATHERDUSTER : Oh, no!

야수는 마법의 거울을 집어 든다.

야 수 : 그녀를 보여줘.

마법의 거울이 반짝이고 초록색 빛이 나면서 침실에 있는 벨의 모습이 나타난다. 벨은 워로브와 대화를 나누고 있다. 워로브는 벨에게 부드럽게 말을 걸고, 벨은 팔짱을 낀 채 그녀의 말을 듣는다.

워로브 : (거울 속에서 애원하듯이) 주인님도 알고 보면 좋은 분이에요. 한 번 기회를 주시지 그러세요.

벨 : (여전히 불안해하면서) 알고 싶지 않아요. 그와는 아무 것도 하고 싶지 않아요.

야수는 부드럽게 말하면서 마법의 거울을 내려 놓는다.

야 수 : 바보 같은 짓을 했어. 그녀의 눈에 비친 나는… 야수일 뿐이야.

또 다른 장미꽃잎이 떨어진다.

야 수 : 희망이 없어.

야수는 절망하며 손으로 머리를 감싸 쥔다. 야수의 모습이 점점 희미해지고, 벨의 방 바깥쪽이 점점 뚜렷해진다. 끼익 하고 문이 열린다. 벨이 조용히 나타난다. 그녀의 발이 지나가는 쪽으로 바닥 쪽에서 커튼을 뚫고 세 개의 불빛이 나타난다. 커튼 뒤에는 루미에르와 페더더스터가 있다. 루미에르와 페더더스터가 커튼 뒤에서 즐거운 시간을 보내다가 커튼 밖으로 나온다.

페더더스터 : 안 돼요.
루미에르 : 괜찮아.
페더더스터 : 안 돼요.

- **reveal**
  나타나다
  To reveal something means to make people aware of it
- **tenderly**
  부드럽게
  with tenderness
- **petal**
  꽃잎
  The petals of a flower are the thin coloured or white parts which together form the flower
- **hopeless**
  희망이 없는
  If you feel hopeless, you feel very unhappy because there seems to be no possibility of a better situation or success

I'm just fooling myself.
fool은 명사로 '바보, 멍청이'라는 뜻도 있지만, 동사로 쓰이면 '~를 우롱하다, 바보짓을 하다'라는 뜻을 가지게 된다. 여기서는 fooling myself라고 하였으므로 스스로를 우롱하여 바보짓을 한 상황을 탄식하며 쓸 수 있는 표현이 된다.

Zoom In

I'm just fooling myself.
바보 같은 짓을 했어.

LUMIERE : Oh, yes, yes, yes!

FEATHERDUSTER : I've been burnt by you before!

Lumiere and Featherduster have emerged and Lumiere takes her in his arms. Suddenly he looks up and sees Belle walking down the hall. He drops Featherduster.

FEATHERDUSTER : Oof!

LUMIERE : Zut alors! She has emerged!

루미에르 : 괜찮다니까.

페더더스터 : 당신에게 덴 적이 있다구요!

루미에르와 페더더스터가 등장하고 루미에르가 그를 팔로 지탱한다. 갑자기 그는 벨이 복도를 걸어내려가는 것을 보게 된다. 그는 페더더스터를 떨어뜨린다.

페더더스터 : 앗!

루미에르 : 맙소사. 그녀가 나왔네!

- **burn**
  타다
  To injure or oxidize with a fire or flame

- **emerge**
  나타나다
  To emerge means to come out from an enclosed or dark space such as a room or a vehicle, or from a position where you could not be seen

- **hall**
  복도
  The hall in a house is the long walkway through which you reach other rooms

Key Expressions

130 **It'll turn out all right in the end.** 결국 모두 괜찮아 질 거예요.

turn out은 '드러나다, 판명되다'라는 동사구이고, in the end는 '마침내, 결국'이라는 표현이다.

· It turned out to be true. 그것이 사실로 드러났다.

130 **Well now, what shall we dress you in for dinner?**
자. 어디 보자. 저녁 식사엔 무엇을 입고 갈까요?

조동사 shall은 의문문으로 쓰여 제안을 나타낼 수 있다. 'Shall we 동사원형~?'의 형태로 쓰면 '~할래요?'라는 의미가 된다.

· What time shall we meet? 몇 시에 만날까요?

132 **You fall in love with her, she falls in love with you, and the spell is broken!**
주인님이 그녀를 사랑하고 그녀도 주인님을 사랑하게 되면, 마법이 풀릴 거예요!

fall in love with는 '사랑에 빠지다'라는 숙어로, fall대신에 be동사를 써도 좋다. 뒤에 at first sight가 붙으면 '첫눈에 반하다'라는 표현이 된다.

· I fell in love with him at first sight. He is my Mr. Right.
나는 그와 첫눈에 사랑에 빠졌어. 그는 내 이상형이야.

132 Well, you can start by making yourself more presentable. 더 정중하게 하는 것부터 시작하세요.

by ~ing는 '~함으로써'라는 전치사구로 자주 사용된다. 또한 make뒤에는 목적어와 목적보어가 나올 수 있다.

· You can take the advantageous position by having your positive manner. 당신은 적극적인 자세를 가짐으로써 유리한 위치를 차지할 수 있다.

136 You'll come out or I'll... I'll break down the door!

당장 나오지 않으면 문을 부숴버리겠어!

or에는 '또는'이라는 선택의 의미도 있지만, '그렇지 않으면'이라는 뜻도 있다. 주로 '명령문+or'의 문형으로 쓰여 '~해라. 그렇지 않으면 ~하겠다.'는 의미를 나타낸다.

· Listen to my advice, or you'll regret it.
내 충고를 들어. 그렇지 않으면 후회하게 될 거야.

140 Why don't you give him a chance?

그에게 기회를 줘보지 그래요?

'Why don't you 동사원형 ~?'은 '~하는 게 어때?'라는 제안의 표현이다. How about ~ing?, What about ~ing?와 동일한 의미이다.

· Why don't you have dinner with me? 나랑 저녁 먹는 게 어때요?

Chapter 7

잊을 수 없는 저녁 만찬과 서쪽 탑의 비밀

An Unforgettable Dinner and the West Tower

시간 00:37:22 ~ 00:49:17

Belle goes down the stairs.
Cut to kitchen where we find Cogsworth, Mrs. Potts, Chip and the Stove.
Mrs. Potts puts Chip onto the cupboard.

MRS. POTTS : Come on, Chip. Into the cupboard with your brothers and sisters. (helping him in)

CHIP : But I'm not sleepy.

MRS. POTTS : Yes you are.

CHIP : No, I'm... not.

He falls asleep and Mrs. Potts shuts the cupboard door. A banging of pots and pans comes from the Stove. Stove gets angry outwardly while opening the pot lid. Cogsworth throws a cloth into the closet.

STOVE : I work and I slave all day long and for what? A culinary masterpiece gone to waste.

MRS. POTTS : Oh, stop your grousing. It's been a long night for all of us.

벨, 계단을 내려간다.
부엌 장면. 콕스워즈와 포트 부인, 칩, 그리고 화로가 보인다.
포트 부인은 칩을 찬장에 집어넣는다.

포트 부인 : 얘야, 칩. 형, 누나들과 찬장에 들어가야지. (그가 들어가도록 도와준다)

칩 : 하지만 안 졸린걸요.

포트 부인 : 곧 잠이 올 거야.

칩 : 안 졸려요.

칩은 잠이 들고 포트 부인은 찬장 문을 닫는다. 화로에서 냄비와 프라이팬이 쿵쾅거린다. 스토브는 냄비 뚜껑을 열어보며 화를 낸다. 콕스워즈는 찬장에 천 조각을 던져 넣는다.

스토브 : 도대체 뭘 위해서 하루 종일 열심히 음식을 만들었지? 훌륭한 음식들이 쓸모없게 되다니.

포트 부인 : 그만 불평하세요. 모두에게 힘든 밤일 테니.

- **cupboard**
  찬장
  A cupboard is a piece of furniture that has one or two doors, usually contains shelves, and is used to store things
- **outwardly**
  겉으로는
  You use outwardly to indicate the feelings or qualities that a person or situation may appear to have, rather than the ones that they actually have
- **culinary**
  요리의
  Culinary means concerned with cooking
- **masterpiece**
  걸작
  A masterpiece is an extremely good painting, novel, film, or other work of art
- **grouse**
  불평하다
  If you grouse, you complain

COGSWORTH : Well, if you ask me, she was just being stubborn. After all he did say 'please.'

MRS. POTTS : But if the master doesn't learn to control that temper he'll never break the...

Belle enters and Cogsworth cuts off Mrs. Potts before she can say 'spell.'

COGSWORTH : (interrupting) Splendid to see you out and about, Mademoiselle. (Lumiere comes running in) I am Cogsworth, head of the household.

He leans over to kiss her hand but Lumiere butts in front of him.

COGSWORTH : (hesitantly) This is Lumiere.

LUMIERE : Enchante, chérie.

Cogsworth tries to talk around Lumoere who is still kissing Belle's hand.

COGSWORTH : If there's... stop that... anything we... please (finally shoving him out of the way) ...can do to make your stay more comfortable.

Lumiere burns the hand of Cogsworth.

COGSWORTH : Ow!!!!

BELLE : I am a little hungry.

MRS. POTTS : (excited, to the other tea pots) You are? Hear that? She's hungry. Stoke the fire, break out the silver, wake the china.

콕스워즈 : 내 생각으로는 그녀가 너무 고집을 부렸어. 무엇보다 주인님이 '부디'라고까지 말했는데.

포트 부인 : 하지만 주인님이 참는 법을 배우지 못한다면, 절대…

벨이 들어오자, 콕스워즈는 포트 부인이 '주문'이라는 말을 하기 전에 그녀의 말을 자른다.

콕스워즈 : (끼어들며) 환영합니다. 아가씨. (루미에르가 뒤따라 뛰어 들어온다) 이 성의 집사 콕스워즈입니다.

그는 그녀의 손에 입 맞추려 몸을 숙이지만, 루미에르가 그의 몸을 들이민다.

콕스워즈 : (망설이며) 이쪽은 루미에르입니다.

루미에르 : 반갑습니다. 아가씨.

콕스워즈는 벨의 손에 입 맞추고 있는 루미에르의 주변에서 말을 하려고 애쓴다.

콕스워즈 : 만약 필요하신 게 있다면… (결국 그를 밀치고는) …편안하게 해드리겠습니다.

루미에르가 콕스워즈의 손에 불을 붙인다.

콕스워즈 : 아오!

벨 : 배가 좀 고파요.

포트 부인 : (신이 나서) 그래요? 다들 들었죠? 아가씨가 배가 고프대요. 불을 지피고, 은 식기와 접시들을 깨웁시다.

- **stubborn**
  완고한
  Someone who is stubborn or who behaves in a stubborn way is determined to do what they want and is very unwilling to change their mind
- **household**
  식구
  A household is all the people in a family or group who live together in a house
- **butt**
  들이밀다
  If a person or animal butts you, they hit you with the top of their head
- **china**
  자기
  China is a hard white substance made from clay. It is used to make things such as cups, bowls, plates, and ornaments

Splendid to see you out and about.
splendid는 정말 좋다는 뜻이다. 이렇게 감정을 나타내는 형용사 뒤에 to부정사가 오면 '~하게 되어 ~하다'라는 원인을 나타내는 뜻이 된다. 이 문장에서는 만나게 되어 정말 기쁘다는 의미이다.

Zoom In

Splendid to see you out and about.
환영합니다.

The fire on the Stove roars to life and drawers open to reveal silverware standing at attention.

COGSWORTH : (secretively) Remember what the master said.

MRS. POTTS : Oh, pish posh. I'm not about to let the poor child go hungry.

Dishes and tableware come out from the cupboard. Lumiere wants to give Belle some food, so he cuts off Cogsworth in the middle of what he's saying.

COGSWORTH : (thinking he is giving in to the ultimate demand) Oh, all right, fine. Glass of water, crust of bread, and then...

LUMIERE : Cogsworth, I am surprised at you. She's not a prisoner. She's our guest. We must make her feel welcome here. (to belle) Right this way, Mademoiselle.

COGSWORTH : Well keep it down. If the master finds out about this, it will be our necks!

LUMIERE : Of course, of course. But what is dinner without a little music?

Lumiere has started out the swinging door. He lets it close and the door hits Cogsworth and sends him across the room to land in a pan filled with pancake batter. He screams his line as he is in flight.

COGSWORTH : Music!?!

Cut to dining room where Belle is seated at the end of a long table. Lumiere is on the table and a spotlight shines on him. The chair approaches Belle automatically. Belle sits on the chair.

화로의 불이 되살아나고, 서랍들이 열려 은 식기가 차렷 자세로 서 있다.

콕스워즈 : (은밀하게) 주인님 말씀 잊지 말아요.

포트 부인 : 됐어요. 배고픈 사람을 그냥 놔둘 수 없지요.

접시들과 식기들이 찬장에서 나온다. 루미에르는 벨에게 음식을 주고 싶어서, 콕스워즈의 말을 중간에서 자른다.

콕스워즈 : (최후의 타협안을 제시하며) 좋아요. 물 한 컵과 빵이나 한 쪽…

루미에르 : 콕스워즈, 무슨 말을 그렇게 해. 아가씨는 죄수가 아니야 손님이라고. 우리는 그녀를 편히 모셔야 한다구. (벨에게) 이쪽으로 오시죠. 아가씨.

콕스워즈 : 소리 좀 내지 말게. 주인님이 아시면 우린 끝이야!

루미에르 : 물론이지. 하지만 저녁식사라면 당연히 음악이 있어야겠지?

루미에르는 여닫이문을 열었다가 닫자, 문짝이 콕스워즈의 얼굴에 부딪쳐서 그는 팬케이크 반죽으로 가득 찬 팬 속에 빠지고 만다. 그는 공중에서 소리친다.

콕스워즈 : 음악?

벨이 식탁 끝에 앉아 있는 식당 장면. 루미에르는 테이블 위에서 스포트라이트를 받고 있다. 의자는 자동으로 벨에게 다가온다. 벨은 의자에 앉는다.

- **silverware**
  은 식기
  You can use silverware to refer to all the things in a house that are made of silver, especially the cutlery and dishes

- **crust**
  빵 껍질
  The crust on a loaf of bread is the outside part

- **swing**
  흔들다
  If something swings or if you swing it, it moves repeatedly backwards and forwards or from side to side from a fixed point

- **batter**
  반죽
  Batter is a mixture of flour, eggs, and milk that is used in cooking

- **automatically**
  자동으로
  in a reflex manner

If the master finds out about this, it will be our necks!
'If+주어+동사'는 조건의 부사절로 '~한다면'이라는 뜻으로 해석된다. 주의할 점은 주절에는 will이 쓰였지만, 조건의 부사절에서는 현재형이 미래를 대신한다는 것이다. 또 여기서의 neck는 비유적인 의미의 '목'을 함축한다.

Zoom In

If the master finds out about this, it will be our necks!

주인님이 아시면 우린 끝이야!

LUMIERE : Ma chére, Mademoiselle. It is with deepest pride and greatest pleasure that we welcome you tonight. And now, we invite you to relax. Let us pull up a chair as the dining room proudly presents... your dinner.

Food in silver wares jumps on the table and a spotlight shines on them. The spotlight moves to Lumiere again and all the silver wares dance beating time to the music.

LUMIERE : (singing) *BE OUR GUEST, BE OUR GUEST*
PUT OUR SERVICE TO THE TEST
TIE YOUR NAPKIN 'ROUND YOUR NECK, CHÉRIE
AND WE PROVIDE THE REST!

The Chair has wrapped a napkin around the neck of Belle, who takes it off and places it on her lap. The Chair puts its arms on its waist as if it were mad. The pot comes in front of Belle and pours some soup into the dish automatically.

LUMIERE : (singing) *SOUP DU JOUR, HOT HORS D'OEUVRES*
WHY WE ONLY LIVE TO SERVE
TRY THE GREY STUFF, IT'S DELICIOUS
DON'T BELIEVE ME? ASK THE DISHES!

Lumiere offers Belle a plate of hors d'oeuvres. She dips her finger in one and tastes it.

LUMIERE : (singing) *THEY CAN SING, THEY CAN DANCE*
AFTER ALL, MISS, THIS IS FRANCE!
AND A DINNER HERE IS NEVER SECOND BEST!
GO ON UNFOLD YOUR MENU, TAKE A GLANCE AND THEN YOU'LL
BE OUR GUEST, OUI OUR GUEST, BE OUR GUEST!

루미에르 : 어서 오세요. 아가씨. 오늘 밤 아가씨를 모시게 된 것을 무한한 영광으로 생각합니다. 자 이제, 당신을 편안한 곳으로 초대하죠. 식당에서 자랑스러운 만찬이 펼쳐지는 동안 의자를 당겨 편히 앉으세요.

은 식기에 담긴 음식들이 테이블로 튀어 올라오자, 스포트라이트를 받는다. 스포트라이트는 다시 루미에르에게로 옮겨 가고, 은 식기들은 음악의 박자에 맞추어 춤을 춘다.

루미에르 : (노래하며) *손님이 되어 주세요. 손님이 되어 주세요*
우리의 서비스를 시험해 보세요
냅킨을 두르기만 하시면,
나머지는 우리가 다 갖다 드립니다

의자가 벨의 목에 냅킨을 둘러주고, 벨은 그것을 그녀의 무릎 위에 올려 둔다. 의자의 팔걸이는 화가 난 듯이 양 손을 허리 위에 올린다. 냄비가 벨의 앞에 와서는 수프를 접시에 저절로 따른다.

루미에르 : (노래하며) *수프는 어때요. 뜨거우니 조심해요*
저희는 대접하는 낙으로 살지요
한 번 맛 보세요. 훌륭해요
믿기 어려우세요? 접시에게 물어보세요!

루미에르는 벨에게 전채 요리를 가져다준다. 그녀는 손가락으로 하나를 찍어서 맛을 본다.

루미에르 : (노래하며) *노래를 부를 수도 있고 춤도 출 수 있어요*
무엇보다 프랑스풍이죠
이곳의 만찬은 이 세상 최고이지요
메뉴를 펴 보세요
우리의 손님이 되어 주세요, 손님이 되어 주세요. 손님이 되어 주세요!

- **relax**
  휴식을 취하다
  If you relax or if something relaxes you, you feel more calm and less worried or tense
- **mad**
  화가 난
  If you say that someone is mad, you mean that they are very angry
- **dip**
  살짝 담그다
  If you dip something in a liquid, you put it into the liquid for a short time, so that only part of it is covered, and take it out again
- **glance**
  흘끗 봄
  A glance is a quick look at someone or something

It is with deepest pleasure and greatest pride that we welcome you tonight.
형용사에 est가 붙어 '가장 ~한'이라는 최상급의 의미를 나타내고 있다. 여기서는 오늘 밤 당신을 모시게 되어 가장 기쁘고 영광스러운 순간이라는 뜻이 되겠다.

Zoom In

It is with deepest pride and greatest pleasure that we welcome you tonight.
오늘 밤 아가씨를 모시게 된 것을 무한한 영광으로 생각합니다.

A cabinet at the end of the table opens to reveal a large China Collection, which rolls out and begins to perform. Lumiere hands Belle a menu, which she begins to read.

LUMIERE : (singing) ***BEEF RAGOUT, CHEESE SOUFFLÉ***
PIE AND PUDDING EN FLAMBÉ!
WE'LL PREPARE AND SERVE WITH FLAIR
A CULINARY CABARET!

Plates of food go dancing by with Cogsworth in the pudding. Lumiere sets his torch to it and it explodes turning Cogsworth's face black with soot.

LUMIERE : (singing) ***YOU'RE ALONE AND YOU'RE SCARED***
BUT THE BANQUET'S ALL PREPARED!
NO ONE'S GLOOMY OR COMPLAINING
WHILE THE FLATWARE'S ENTERTAINING!

The Flatwares enters a swimming scene.

LUMIERE : (singing) ***WE TELL JOKES, I DO TRICKS***
WITH MY FELLOW CANDLESTICKS

Flatwares make a fountain spout.
Lumiere standing on a plate is elevated and begins to juggle his candles. Mugs enter the shot.

MUGS : (singing) ***AND IT'S ALL IN PERFECT TASTE***
THAT YOU CAN BET!!!

The Mugs begin a gymnastics routine hopping over one another and passing a beverage from one to the next.

테이블 끝의 찬장 문이 열리고 거대한 도자기 무리들이 모습을 드러낸다. 도자기들은 굴러 나와서 춤을 추기 시작한다. 루미에르는 벨에게 메뉴를 가져다주고, 그녀는 그것을 읽기 시작한다.

루미에르 : (노래하며) *맛있는 고기, 치즈 수플레,*
플랑베한 파이와 푸딩!
솜씨 좋게 준비해서 드립니다
음식들의 춤 잔치!

음식이 담긴 접시들이 춤을 추고, 콕스워즈는 푸딩 속에 빠져 있다. 루미에르가 불을 붙이자 펑 터지면서, 콕스워즈의 얼굴이 그을음으로 까맣게 된다.

루미에르 : (노래하며) *당신은 혼자라 무서울 지도 모르지만,*
만찬이 준비되어 있잖아요!
식기들이 즐거움을 주고,
아무도 우울해하거나 불평하지 않죠

식기들은 물에 빠지는 장면을 연출한다.

루미에르 : (노래하며) *우리는 정담을 나누고,*
저는 묘기를 부리죠
내 동료 촛대들과

식기들은 분수 물이 뿜어져 나오게 한다.
접시 위에 서있는 루미에르는 위로 올라가서 촛불로 저글링을 하기 시작한다. 머그잔들이 등장한다.

머그잔 : (노래하며) *모든 것이 완벽하죠*
틀림없어요!

머그잔들은 체조 식으로 뛰어서, 음료를 옆 잔들에게 전달한다.

- **banquet**
  연회
  A banquet is a grand formal dinner
- **prepare**
  준비하다
  If you prepare something, you make it ready for something that is going to happen
- **gloomy**
  우울한
  If a place is gloomy, it is almost dark so that you cannot see very well
- **gymnastics**
  체조
  Gymnastics consists of physical exercises that develop your strength, coordination, and ease of movement

We'll prepare and serve with flair.
serve with는 '대접하다, 모시다'라는 뜻이고, flair는 '솜씨, 재간'이라는 뜻이므로 "솜씨 좋게 대접하다"라는 의미가 된다. 특히 serve with는 손님에게 음식 등을 대접할 때 자주 쓰이는 숙어이므로 기억해두자.

Zoom In

We'll prepare and serve with flair.
솜씨 좋게 준비해서 드립니다.

ALL : (singing) *COME ON AND LIFT YOUR GLASS*
YOU'VE WON YOUR OWN FREE PASS
TO BE OUR GUEST, BE OUR GUEST, BE OUR GUEST!

LUMIERE : (singing) *IF YOU'RE STRESSED IT'S FINE DINING WE SUGGEST!*

ALL : (singing) *BE OUR GUEST, BE OUR GUEST, BE OUR GUEST!*

Cogsworth hisses at them to be quiet.
All leave except Cogsworth, who looks scared then begins to inch away. Lumiere enters and holds him there.

LUMIERE : (singing) *LIFE IS SO UNNERVING*
FOR A SERVANT WHO'S NOT SERVING!
HE'S NOT WHOLE WITHOUT A SOUL TO WAIT UPON

Cogsworth blows out Lumiere.

COGSWORTH : Get off!

LUMIERE : (singing) *AH, THOSE GOOD OLD DAYS WHEN WE WERE USEFUL*
SUDDENLY, THOSE GOOD OLD DAYS ARE GONE

Lumiere sings as if he were reminiscing. Salt becomes snow. Snow begins to fall. Cogsworth looks up and sees the salt and pepper shakers doing their thing.

LUMIERE : (singing) *TEN YEARS WE'VE BEEN RUSTING*
NEEDING SO MUCH MORE THAN DUSTING
NEEDING EXERCISE, A CHANCE TO USE OUR SKILLS!

Lumiere dusts the salt of the head of Cogsworth who tries to escape. He trips and falls into the gelatin mold.

다함께 : (노래하며) *이리 와서 잔을 들어요*
무료 입장입니다
우리의 손님이 되어 주세요.손님이 되어 주세요. 손님이 되어 주세요!

루미에르 : (노래하며) *제발, 우리의 만찬에 참석해주세요!*

다함께 : (노래하며) *우리의 손님이 되어 주세요, 손님이 되어 주세요, 손님이 되어 주세요!*

콕스워즈가 조용히 하라고 쉿 소리를 낸다.
무서워서 바들바들 떠는 콕스워즈를 제외하고 모두는 도망가기 시작한다. 루미에르가 들어와서 그를 붙잡는다.

루미에르 : (노래하며) *시중들 사람이 없는 하인의 삶은 너무나 슬픈 일이지!*
기다리는 동안 보람도 없고 따분했죠

콕스워즈가 루미에르의 불을 끈다.

콕스워즈 : 이거 놔!

루미에르 : (노래하며) *바쁘게 지내던 옛 시절*
좋은 나날들이 그리워져요

루미에르는 추억에 잠긴 듯이 노래한다. 소금이 눈이 되어 내린다. 콕스워즈는 위를 올려다보고는 소금통과 후추통이 그들의 역할을 하는 것을 본다.

루미에르 : (노래하며) *지난 10년 동안 우리는*
먼지만 뒤집어쓰며 살아왔죠
우리의 솜씨를 뽐낼 기회의 순간이 필요했죠

루미에르는 콕스워즈의 머리에 쌓인 소금을 털어주고, 콕스워즈는 빠져나가려 한다. 그는 빠져나가다가 젤라틴 틀에 빠져버린다.

■ **hiss**
쉿 소리를 내다
To hiss means to make a sound like a long 's'

■ **rust**
녹슬다
When a metal object rusts, it becomes covered in rust and often loses its strength

■ **dust**
먼지
Dust is very small dry particles of earth or sand

■ **escape**
탈출하다
If you escape from a place, you succeed in getting away from it

■ **mold**
틀
A mold is a hollow container that you pour liquid into. When the liquid becomes solid, it takes the same shape as the mold

You've won your own free pass.
free에는 자유라는 뜻 외에 '무료'라는 뜻이 있다. 따라서 위 문장은 '무료입장권을 획득하셨습니다.'라는 의미가 되어, 그냥 몸만 와서 드시면 된다는 의미를 함축한다.

Zoom In

You've won your own free pass.
무료입장입니다.

LUMIERE : (singing) ***MOST DAYS WE JUST LAY AROUND THE CASTLE***
FLABBY FAT AND LAZY
YOU WALKED IN, AND OOPS-A-DAISY!

Lumiere jumps on a spoon in the gelatin, which catapults Cogsworth out of the mold. Cut to kitchen, where Mrs. Potts is surrounded by soap bubbles. Kettles, pots, cups, and dishes are dancing. Wine bottles, napkins, and glasses are turning round and round.

MRS. POTTS : (singing) ***IT'S A GUEST, IT'S A GUEST!***
SAKES ALIVE, WELL I'LL BE BLESSED!
WINE'S BEEN POURED AND THANK THE LORD
I'VE HAD THE NAPKINS FRESHLY PRESSED!

Mrs. Potts continues to dance around the kitchen.

MRS. POTTS : (singing) ***WITH DESSERT, SHE'LL WANT TEA***
AND MY DEAR, THAT'S FINE WITH ME!
WHILE THE CUPS DO THEIR SOFT SHOEING
I'LL BE BUBBLING, I'LL BE BREWING!
I'LL GET WARM, PIPING HOT
HEAVEN SAKES IS THAT A SPOT?
CLEAN IT UP, WE WANT THE COMPANY IMPRESSED!
WE'VE GOT A LOT TO DO...
IS IT ONE LUMP OR TWO?
FOR YOU OUR GUEST!

Mrs. Potts is cleaned off by a napkin. She hops onto the tea cart and rolls into the dining room, where she offers tea to Belle. When Belle picks up the cup flowers come close to her.

ALL : (singing) ***SHE'S OUR GUEST!***

루미에르 : (노래하며) *수많은 나날들을 성에 누워서*
무기력하게 느릿느릿 살아왔는데
당신이 나타난 거예요. 생기 있게!

루미에르는 젤라틴에 든 숟가락 위로 뛰어 들고, 콕스워즈가 젤라틴 틀 밖으로 내던져진다. 부엌 장면. 포트 부인이 비누 거품으로 둘러싸여 있다.
주전자, 냄비, 컵, 접시들이 춤을 춘다. 와인 병, 냅킨, 유리잔들도 빙글빙글 돌고 있다.

포트 부인 : (노래하며) *손님이다. 손님이야*
놀라워, 축하합시다!
와인을 따라두고, 신께 감사드려요
냅킨도 잘 접어놓았죠

포트 부인은 계속 해서 부엌 주변을 돌며 춤을 춘다.

포트 부인 : (노래하며) *디저트와 차도 준비 했죠*
얘야, 난 괜찮아
컵들이 춤출 때 나는 물을 끓이죠
보글보글 끓을 거예요
따뜻해지고, 몹시 뜨거워질 거예요
세상에, 얼룩이 생겼다구?
깨끗이 닦자, 좋은 인상을 줄 수 있도록!
우리는 많은 것들을 준비했지요
설탕은 한 덩어리? 두 덩어리?
우리의 소중한 손님을 위해서!

냅킨이 포트 부인을 닦는다. 그녀는 티 카트에 올라타고 식당으로 가서 벨에게 차를 대접한다. 벨이 컵을 들자, 꽃들이 그녀 가까이로 온다.

다함께 : (노래하며) *우리의 손님이야!*

■ **flabby**
무기력한
If you describe something as flabby, you are criticizing it for being lazy and out of shape

■ **blessed**
축복받은
If someone is blessed with a particular good quality or skill, they have that good quality or skill

■ **brew**
끓이다
If you brew tea or coffee, you make it by pouring hot water over tea leaves or ground coffee

■ **impressed**
감명을 받은
deeply or markedly affected or influenced

We've got a lot to do.
have got은 have와 동일한 의미를 가지고 있다. 따라서 할 일이 많을 때 We have a lot to do.라고 해도 되지만, have 대신에 have got을 써도 같은 의미가 되는 것이다. 구어체에서는 have got을 더 많이 사용하니 연습해 보자.

Zoom In

We've got a lot to do.
할 일이 많아요.

MRS. POTTS : (singing) *SHE'S OUR GUEST!*

ALL : (singing) *BE OUR GUEST!*
BE OUR GUEST! BE OUR GUEST!
OUR COMMAND IS YOUR REQUEST!
IT'S TEN YEARS SINCE WE HAD ANYBODY HERE
AND WE'RE OBSESSED!
WITH YOUR MEAL, WITH YOUR EASE,
YES INDEED, WE AIM TO PLEASE
WHILE THE CANDLELIGHT'S STILL GLOWING
LET US HELP YOU, WE'LL KEEP GOING...

Wine glasses, dishes, and cups are dancing in a row. Candles cheer by doing waves.
The China and Candlesticks perform an elaborately choreographed dance sequence ending in a scene of Lumiere.
Lumiere puts on a hat and dances on the cake in the spotlight. A Chandelier hanging from the ceiling comes down to the table and dances with all food.

ALL : (singing) *COURSE BY COURSE*
ONE BY ONE
TILL YOU SHOUT "ENOUGH, I'M DONE!"
THEN WE'LL SING YOU OFF TO SLEEP AS YOU DIGEST
TONIGHT YOU'LL PROP YOUR FEET UP
BUT FOR NOW LET'S EAT UP
BE OUR GUEST! BE OUR GUEST! BE OUR GUEST!
PLEASE BE OUR GUEST!!

A fantastic ending comes of the song with Silverware flying through the air Plates and Featherdusters dancing. Cogsworth the focus of attention until Lumiere comes sliding in and sends him flying out of camera range.

BELLE : Bravo! That was wonderful!

포트 부인 : (노래하며) *우리의 손님이야!*

다함께 : (노래하며) *우리의 손님이야!*
우리의 손님이 되어 주세요. 손님이 되어 주세요
당신이 원하는 것은 무엇이든지!
누군가가 오기를 10년을 기다렸지요
편안하게 식사하세요
정말 행복하지요
촛불이 타는 동안 즐겁게 식사하세요

와인 잔, 접시, 컵들이 일렬로 서서 춤을 춘다. 촛불들은 파도타기 응원을 한다.
도자기와 촛대들은 정교한 연속된 안무동작을 하고, 루미에르 장면으로 끝난다.
루미에르는 모자를 쓰고 케이크 위에서 스포트라이트를 받으며 춤을 춘다. 천장에 매달린 샹들리에가 테이블로 내려오고, 음식들과 함께 춤을 춘다.

다함께 : (노래하며) *코스요리를*
하나씩 하나씩 맛보세요
식사를 마칠 때까지
소화가 되는 동안 노래를 불러드릴게요
오늘 밤 발을 굴러 봐요
자, 이제 드세요
우리의 손님이 되어 주세요. 손님이 되어 주세요. 부디 손님이 되어 주세요!

은 식기가 공중에서 날아오고, 접시들과 빗자루가 춤을 추는 훌륭한 엔딩이다. 콕스워즈는 루미에르가 미끄러져 와서 그를 카메라 밖으로 내보낼 때까지 주목을 받는다.

벨 : 브라보! 정말 훌륭해요.

- **obsessed**
  사로잡힌
  If someone is obsessed with a person or thing, they keep thinking about them and find it difficult to think about anything else

- **glow**
  빛나다
  If something glows, it produces a dull, steady light

- **elaborately**
  정교하게
  You use elaborately to describe something that is very complex because it has a lot of different parts

- **digest**
  소화하다
  When food digests or when you digest it, it passes through your body to your stomach

Our command is your request!
command는 '명령, 지시'라는 뜻이고, request는 '요구, 요청'이라는 뜻이다. 따라서 직역하면 위 문장은 '우리의 명령은 당신의 요구이다'라고 되므로, 당신이 요구한 것은 무엇이든 따르겠다는 의미를 내포한다.

Zoom In

Our command is your request!
당신이 원하는 것은 무엇이든지.

COGSWORTH : Thank you, thank you, Mademoiselle. Yes, good show wasn't it everyone. (looking at his own face) Oh, my goodness look at the time. Now, it's off to bed off to bed!

Lumiere comes up next to Cogsworth.

BELLE : Oh, I couldn't possibly go to bed now. It's my first time in an enchanted castle.

COGSWORTH : Enchanted? Who said anything about the castle being enchanted?

He tries to cover it up just as a Fork runs past.

COGSWORTH : (to Lumiere) It was you, wasn't it!

BELLE : I... figured it out for myself.

Cogsworth and Lumiere have been fighting. They both look at her then stop. Cogsworth dusts himself off and Lumiere fixes his wax nose.

BELLE : I'd like to look around, if that's all right.

Belle feels better after the dinner show. She becomes curious about the castle and asks to look around it. Cogsworth hesitates first but is taken easily by Belle's request.

LUMIERE : (excited) Oh! Would you like a tour?

COGSWORTH : Wait a second... wait a second. I'm not sure that's such a good idea. (confidentially, to Lumiere) We can't let her go poking around in certain places, if you know what I mean.

콕스워즈 : 감사합니다. 감사합니다. 아가씨. 모두 들 수고 했어요. (자신의 얼굴을 보면서) 오, 이런. 시간 좀 봐. 잘 시간이에요.

루미에르는 콕스워즈 옆으로 다가온다.

벨 : 지금은 잠들 수 없을 것 같아요. 마법의 성에 온 첫 날이잖아요.

콕스워즈 : 마법이라구요? 누가 마법에 걸렸다고 말해줬죠?

포크가 재빨리 지나가고, 그는 부인해보려고 한다.

콕스워즈 : (루미에르에게) 너지?

벨 : 음, 저 혼자서 알아냈어요.

콕스워즈와 루미에르는 다투고 있다가, 그녀를 바라보더니 싸움을 멈춘다. 콕스워즈는 먼지를 털어내고, 루미에르는 코를 다시 고친다.

벨 : 괜찮다면 성안을 구경하고 싶은데요.

벨은 디너쇼를 보고 기분이 좋다. 그녀는 이 성에 대해 호기심이 생겨서 구경하고 싶다고 부탁하나, 콕스워즈는 처음에는 망설이지만 벨의 부탁에 쉽게 넘어간다.

루미에르 : (신이 나서) 오! 구경사고 싶으세요?

콕스워즈 : 잠깐만… 잠깐만요. 좋은 생각인지 모르겠네요. (루미에르에게 은밀하게) 아가씨를 함부로 이곳저곳 다니게 할 수 없잖아. 무슨 말인지 알지.

- **enchanted**
  마법에 걸린
  influenced as by charms or incantations

- **curious**
  호기심 있는
  If you are curious about something, you are interested in it and want to know more about it

- **hesitate**
  망설이다
  If you hesitate, you do not speak or act for a short time, usually because you are uncertain, embarrassed, or worried about what you are going to say or do

- **confidentially**
  은밀히
  in a confidential manner

I'd like to look around, if that's all right.
'would like to 동사원형'은 '~하고 싶다'라는 뜻으로 'want to부정사'와 같은 표현이다. if that's all right(괜찮다면)과 같은 표현을 붙이면 보다 정중하게 허락을 구할 수 있다.

Zoom In

I'd like to look around, if that's all right.
괜찮다면 성 안을 구경하고 싶은데요.

Belle pokes Cogsworth in the belly.

BELLE : Perhaps you'd like to take me. I'm sure you know everything there is to know about the castle.

COGSWORTH : (flattered) Well, actually I... ah yes, I do!

INT. HALLWAY OF THE CASTLE

Fade to Cogsworth, Lumiere and Belle walking down a hall with Footstool. Cogsworth is lecturing. Suits of armor are standing in lines side by side.

COGSWORTH : As you can see, the pseudo facade was stripped away to reveal a minimalist Rococo design. Note the unusual inverted vaulted ceilings. This is yet another example of the late neoclassical Baroque period. And as I always say, if it's not baroque, don't fix it! Ha ha ha. Now then, where was I?

He turns to find the heads of the Suits of Armor have turned to follow Belle.

COGSWORTH : As you were!

They all snap back to face forward.

COGSWORTH : Now, then if I may draw your attention to the flying buttresses above the... Mademoiselle?

Cogsworth keeps lecturing alone with excitement but nobody pays attention. He turns back to the group and is one girl short. He sees her beginning to climb the grand staircase. He and Lumiere run up to her and jump in front of her, blocking her progress upstairs. Both of them try to keep Belle from going upstairs. They are embarrassed. However, Belle shows a special interest and wonders about upstairs.

벨은 콕스워즈의 배를 찌른다.

벨 : 당신이 안내 좀 해 주시겠어요? 당신이라면 성 안에 모든 곳을 잘 아실 것 같아요.

콕스워즈 : (으쓱하며) 네, 사실 그렇죠!

내부. 성의 복도

콕스워즈, 루미에르, 벨이 풋스툴과 함께 복도를 걷고 있는 장면이 점점 확대된다. 콕스워즈는 강의를 하고 있다. 갑옷을 입은 병사들이 한 줄로 나란히 서 있다.

콕스워즈 : 보시다시피 이 성은 로코코 양식을 돋보이게 하려고 가짜 표면을 벗겨냈지요. 독특한 반전이 돋보이는 아치형 천장을 보세요. 바로 후기 고전 바로크 양식이구요, 언제나 말하듯이, 바로크 양식이 아니라면 고집할 필요도 없지요. 하하하, 제가 어디까지 말했죠?

그는 갑옷 입은 병사들의 머리가 벨을 따라 돌아가 있는 것을 발견한다.

콕스워즈 : 원 위치!

병사들은 다시 얼굴을 앞으로 빠르게 돌린다.

콕스워즈 : 만약 벽장식에 관심이 있으시다면… 아가씨?

콕스워즈는 혼자 신나서 강의를 계속하지만, 아무도 집중해서 듣지 않는다. 그는 다시 무리로 돌아왔는데 한 명이 빠져 있다. 그는 그녀가 큰 계단을 오르려는 것을 본다. 콕스워즈와 루미에르는 그녀를 따라 뛰어 올라가서 그녀가 계단을 올라가지 못하도록 뛰어내려 앞을 막는다. 둘은 벨이 위쪽으로 올라가지 못하게 하려고 애를 쓴다. 그들은 당황했다. 그러나 벨은 위층에 대해 특별한 관심과 호기심을 보이고 있다.

- **actually**
  사실
  You use actually to indicate that a situation exists or happened, or to emphasize that it is true
- **minimalist**
  미니멀리스트
  Minimalist is used to describe ideas, artists, or designers that are influenced by minimalism
- **inverted**
  반전된
  being in such a position that top and bottom are reversed
- **buttress**
  지지대
  Buttresses are supports, usually made of stone or brick, that support a wall

Now then, where was I?
대화 도중에 Where was I?라는 말이 나오면 내가 어디있냐는 장소를 묻는 표현이 아니라 어디까지 말했는지를 묻는 표현이니 반드시 기억해둔다. 실제로 대화중에 자주 쓰이는 표현이니 활용해보자.

Zoom In

Now then, where was I?
제가 어디까지 말했죠?

BELLE : What's up there?

COGSWORTH : Where? Up there? Nothing. Absolutely nothing of interest at all in the West Wing. Dusty, dull, very boring.

Lumiere has been shaking his head but Cogsworth nudges him and he nods in agreement.

BELLE : Oh, so that's the West Wing.

LUMIERE : (to Cogsworth) Nice going!

BELLE : I wonder what he's hiding up there.

LUMIERE : Hiding? The master is hiding nothing!

BELLE : Then it wouldn't be forbidden.

She steps over them but they dash up and block her again.

COGSWORTH : Perhaps Mademoiselle would like to see something else. We have exquisite tapestries dating all the way back to...

BELLE : (again stepping over them) Maybe later.

LUMIERE : (with Cogsworth, again dashing and blocking) The gardens. Or the... library perhaps?

BELLE : (now, with incredible interest) You have a library?

COGSWORTH : (thrilled that he has found something to interest her) Oh yes! Indeed!

LUMIERE : With books!

COGSWORTH : Scads of books!

LUMIERE : Mountains of books!

COGSWORTH : Forests of books!

LUMIERE : Cascades...

벨 : 위에는 뭐가 있죠?

콕스워즈 : 어디요? 저 위쪽이요? 아무것도 없어요. 서쪽 탑에는 관심을 가질만한 게 먼지밖에 없답니다. 지루한 곳이죠.

루미에르는 고개를 흔들다가, 콕스워즈가 그를 쿡쿡 찌르자 고개를 끄덕인다.

벨 : 오, 저기가 서쪽 탑이군요.

루미에르 : (콕스워즈에게) 잘 한다!

벨 : 저 위에 뭘 숨겨 놓았을까?

콕스워즈 : 숨겨요? 아무것도 숨긴 것 없어요.

벨 : 그럼 가도 되겠네요.

벨은 그들을 넘어 올라가지만, 그들은 급하게 다시 그녀 앞을 막는다.

콕스워즈 : 아가씨. 다른 곳이 보고 싶으실 것 같은데. 고대 시대의 정교한 태피스트리라든지…

벨 : (다시 그들을 넘어가며) 나중에요.

루미에르 : (콕스워즈와 함께 다시 급히 막는다) 정원이나, 도서관은 어때요?

벨 : (드디어 놀라운 관심을 보이며) 도서관이 있다구요?

콕스워즈 : (그녀의 관심사를 찾아 신이 나서) 그럼요. 정말이에요!

루미에르 : 책들이 가득한!

콕스워즈 : 많은 책들이!

루미에르 : 산더미처럼!

콕스워즈 : 빽빽하게!

루미에르 : 쏟아질듯이…

- **dull**
  따분한
  If you describe someone or something as dull, you mean they are not interesting or exciting
- **hide**
  감추다
  If you hide something or someone, you put them in a place where they cannot easily be seen or found
- **exquisite**
  정교한
  Something that is exquisite is extremely beautiful or pleasant, especially in a delicate way
- **tapestry**
  태피스트리
  A tapestry is a large piece of heavy cloth with a picture sewn on it using coloured threads
- **cascade**
  풍성하게 늘어진 것
  If you refer to a cascade of something, you mean that there is a large amount of it

Nice going!
우리말에서도 반어법으로 상대방이 잘못을 하였을 때 '잘 한다'라고 말하곤 하는데, 영어에서도 마찬가지이다. 위 상황에서는 루미에르가 서쪽 탑에 대해 언급한 콕스워즈를 질책하며 비꼬듯이 '잘~한다'라고 말한 것이다.

Zoom In

Nice going!

잘 한다!

LUMIERE : Swamps of books!

COGSWORTH : More books than you'll ever be able to read in a lifetime! Books on every subject ever studied by every author who ever set pen to paper.

Lumiere and Cogsworth begin marching off and Belle begins to follow but her curiosity overtakes her and she turns back to the West Wing. Her excitement begins to dwindle though when she enters the hallway leading to Beast's lair. As she walks down the hall, she stops to look in a mirror that has been shattered into several pieces, each one reflecting her concerned look. She reaches the end of the hall and finds a closed door with gargoyle handles. She takes a deep breath then reaches out and opens the door.

INT. WEST TOWER

Cut to int of lair where Belle begins to explore. She is truly shocked by everything she sees. She wanders around looking and knocks over a table but she catches it before it crashes to the floor. She then turns her head and sees a shredded picture on the wall.
We can only see part of a portrait. It is the same portrait that was shredded in the opening. Belle reaches out and lifts the shreds of the picture to reveal the prince. We never see this, however, for then she turns her head and sees the rose under the bell jar. She walks over to it, her eyes transfixed. She reaches out then lifts off the jar leaving the rose unprotected. She reaches up, brushes back the strand of hair that has been repeatedly falling on her forehead then reaches out to touch the rose. As she nears it a shadow falls over her. Beast has been on the balcony, and sees her.
Beast snorts and growls toward Belle. Belle is astonished.
He jumps back into the room,then slams the jar back on the rose. He then turns his attention to Belle.
Belle is frightened and steps backwards. Beast feels anger and yells out.

BEAST : (growing angry) Why did you come here?

BELLE : (backing away, scared) I'm... I'm sorry,

BEAST : I warned you never to come here!

BELLE : I didn't mean any harm.

루미에르 : 넘쳐 날만큼!

콕스워즈 : 평생 읽어도 다 못 읽을 거예요. 세상 모든 것들에 대한 책이 다 있고, 어떤 작가의 책들이든지 다 있어요.

루미에르와 콕스워즈는 앞으로 걸어가고, 벨은 뒤따르기 시작하지만 그녀의 호기심이 그녀를 서쪽으로 발길을 돌리게 한다. 하지만 그녀의 흥분되는 마음은 야수의 방에 가는 복도에 들어서자 서서히 사라진다.
벨은 복도를 걷다가 조각조각 부서져 있는 거울을 보기 위해 멈추는데, 각 조각들이 그녀의 근심어린 표정을 비춘다. 그녀는 복도 끝에 다다르고 괴물 석상 손잡이가 달린 닫힌 문을 발견한다. 그녀는 심호흡을 하고 손을 뻗어 문을 연다.

내부. 서쪽 탑
야수의 방 내부 장면. 벨이 방 안을 돌아다니기 시작한다. 그녀는 보이는 모든 것들에 깜짝 놀란다. 그녀는 돌아다니다가 테이블을 넘어뜨리지만, 바닥에 떨어지기 전에 붙잡는다. 그러고 나서 그녀는 고개를 돌려 벽에 걸린 찢어진 그림을 본다.
초상화의 일부만이 보인다. 이야기가 시작할 때 등장했던 것과 같은 초상화이다. 벨은 손을 뻗어서 그림의 조각을 들어 올리니 왕자의 모습이 드러난다. 그녀가 장미꽃이 든 유리로 된 종으로 고개를 돌렸기 때문에 완전한 그림을 볼 수는 없다. 그녀는 손을 뻗어 유리 덮개를 들어 올리고, 장미는 무방비상태로 놓여 있다. 그녀는 손을 올려 이마에 자꾸 떨어지는 머리를 뒤로 빗어 넘기고는, 장미를 만져보기 위해 가까이 간다. 그녀가 장미에 가까워지는 순간 그림자가 드리워진다. 야수가 발코니에서 그녀를 보고 있다. 야수는 콧김을 내뿜으며 벨을 향해 으르렁댄다. 벨은 깜짝 놀란다.
그는 방 안으로 뛰어 들어와 유리덮개로 장미를 재빨리 덮는다. 그러고 나서 벨 쪽으로 몸을 돌린다.
벨은 매우 겁이 나서 뒷걸음질친다. 야수는 화가 나서 소리친다.

야 수 : (화가 나서) 왜 여기 온 거지?

벨 : (뒷걸음질 치며 겁에 질려) 죄송해요.

야 수 : 내가 이곳에 오지 말라고 경고했을 텐데!

벨 : 다른 나쁜 뜻은 없었어요.

- **author**
  작가
  The author of a piece of writing is the person who wrote it
- **dwindle**
  줄어들다
  If something dwindles, it becomes smaller, weaker, or less in number
- **shatter**
  산산조각나다
  If something shatters or is shattered, it breaks into a lot of small pieces
- **shredded**
  조각난
  prepared by cutting
- **astonished**
  깜짝 놀란
  If you are astonished by something, you are very surprised about it

I didn't mean any harm.
mean에는 '의도하다'라는 뜻이 있으므로, 해할 의도는 없었다는 표현이 된다. I mean~, I didn't mean~ 두 표현 모두 자주 쓰이므로 상대방의 오해를 풀거나 자신의 말과 행동을 설명할 때 활용해보도록 한다.

Zoom In

I didn't mean any harm.
다른 나쁜 뜻은 없었어요.

BEAST : (angrier) Do you realize what you could have done? (begins to thrash at the furniture)

Beast keeps smashing everything that attracts his notice.

BELLE : (pleading, but still scared) Please, stop!

BEAST : (screaming) Get out!!!!

BELLE : (still scared) No!

BEAST : (screaming) Get out!

Belle turns and flees the room. Beast calms down then falls into despair finally realizing that he may have destroyed his chances with Belle. Beast covers his face with both hands. He seems to be tortured.
Belle reaches the stairway and grabs her cloak. She rushes down the stairs wrapping the cloak around her and bursting past a confused Lumiere and Cogsworth.

LUMIERE : Wh- Where are you going?

Belle opens the door and tries to leave the castle.

BELLE : Promise or no promise, I can't stay here another minute!

COGSWORTH : Oh no, wait, please... please wait!

Lumiere tries to respond but Belle slams the door behind her. He and Cogsworth both bow their heads in sadness.

EXT. OUTSIDE THE CASTLE
Cut to Belle outside in the forest on Phillipe.
Flocks of birds fly away.
Belle begins to ride through the forest but Phillipe comes to a stop. She looks up and sees the Wolves. She gasps then pulls the reins and begins to flee. She runs from side to side making the Wolves hit the trees.

야 수 : (더 화가 나서) 당신이 얼마나 큰일을 저질렀는지 알고 있어? (가구를 부수기 시작한다.)

야수는 그의 눈에 띄는 모든 것들을 계속해서 부순다.

벨 : (애원하듯이, 하지만 여전히 겁에 질려서) 제발 그만해요. 안 돼요!
야 수 : (소리치며) 나가!!! 나가!!!
벨 : (여전히 겁에 질려서) 안 돼요!
야 수 : (소리치며) 나가!

벨은 방에서 도망치듯 달려 나온다. 진정이 된 야수는 다시 절망에 빠지고, 벨과의 기회를 망쳐버렸다는 사실을 깨닫는다. 야수는 두 손으로 얼굴을 움켜쥔다. 그는 괴로워 보인다.
벨은 계단으로 가서 망토를 집어 든다. 그녀는 서둘러 계단을 내려가면서 망토를 두르고는 당황하는 루미에르와 콕스워즈 옆을 쏜살같이 지나간다.

콕스워즈 : 어디, 어디가세요?

벨은 문을 열고 성을 떠나려 한다.

벨 : 약속이고 뭐고, 난 더 이상 여기 못 있겠어요.
콕스워즈 : 안 돼요, 기다려요… 제발 기다려요.

루미에르는 대답을 하려고 하지만, 벨은 문을 쾅 닫는다. 루미에르와 콕스워즈는 슬픔에 잠겨 고개를 숙인다.

외부. 성 밖
벨이 필립을 타고 숲으로 나오는 장면.
새 떼들이 날아간다.
벨은 말을 타고 숲으로 가기 시작하는데, 필립이 멈춘다. 그녀가 위를 올려다보니 늑대가 보인다. 그녀는 숨이 턱 막혀서 고삐를 당기고 도망가려고 한다. 그녀는 좌우로 달리면서 늑대들이 나무에 부딪치게 한다.

smash
박살내다
If you smash something or if it smashes, it breaks into many pieces, for example when it is hit or dropped

destroy
파괴하다
To destroy something means to cause so much damage to it that it is completely ruined or does not exist any more

confused
혼란스러운
If you are confused, you do not know exactly what is happening or what to do

respond
대답하다
When you respond to something that is done or said, you react to it by doing or saying something yourself

rein
고삐
Reins are the thin leather straps attached round a horse's neck which are used to control the horse

I can't stay here another minute!
a minute와 부정어가 함께 나오면 '한 시도 ~않다'라는 표현이 된다. 따라서 한 시도 이곳에 더 있지 못하겠다는 의미가 된다.
ex) I can't stand your chatter another minute!

Zoom In

I can't stay here another minute!
난 더 이상 여기 못 있겠어요!

Phillipe runs out on a frozen pond but his and Belle's weight collapse the ice. The Wolves chase her into the water. Some begin to drown but Phillipe is able to get out of the water before anything serious happens.
He runs into a clearing but becomes surrounded by Wolves. He bucks, throwing Belle off and wrapping the reins around a tree branch. The Wolves's begin their attack on Phillipe, but Belle comes to his rescue and beats them away with a stick. One Wolf grabs the stick in its mouth and breaks half of it off leaving Belle defenseless. Another leaps at her grabbing the corner of her cloak and dragging her to the ground.
She looks up and sees a Wolf about to jump on top of her.

BELLE : No!

Suddenly, Beast appears in front of Belle.
The Wolf leaps and is caught in mid-air by Beast. He throws the Wolf away then stands behind them and Belle. They lunge at each other. One rips a hole in Beast's shoulder and the others focus their attack on that spot.
Wolves keeps biting Beast and Beast shakes them off. Finally, Beast throws a Wolf against a tree knocking it out. The others turn and run in fear. However, he receives a wound and his arm is bleeding.
Beast turns back to Belle, looks at her despairingly then collapses. Belle, grateful to be alive, turns back to Phillipe and begins to get on but her conscience takes over and she walks over to the fallen Beast. Fade to Belle and Phillipe walking back to the castle with Beast on the horse's back.

필립은 얼음이 언 연못 위로 달리지만, 그와 벨의 무게 때문에 얼음이 부서진다. 늑대들은 그녀를 물속까지 쫓아간다. 몇 마리는 물에 빠져 죽고, 필립은 다른 심각한 일이 생기기 전에 물을 빠져나온다.
그는 빈 터로 달려가지만, 늑대들에게 포위당한다. 그가 껑충 뛰어 벨을 떨어뜨리고, 고삐는 나뭇가지에 말린다. 늑대들은 필립을 공격하기 시작하지만, 벨이 늑대들을 막대기로 때려서 구해준다. 한 마리의 늑대는 막대기를 입으로 잡아 채 반으로 부러뜨리고, 벨은 무방비상태가 된다. 또 한 마리는 그녀에게 뛰어 와 그녀의 망토 끝을 잡아 물고는 그녀를 땅으로 끌고 간다.
그녀가 위를 올려다보니 늑대가 그녀 위로 뛰어들려고 한다.

벨 : 안돼!

갑자기, 벨 앞에 야수가 나타난다.
늑대는 뛰어 올라 공중에서 야수에 의해 붙잡힌다. 그는 늑대를 던져버리고, 늑대들과 벨 뒤에 선다. 그들은 서로 돌진한다. 한 마리는 야수의 어깨에 상처를 내고, 다른 늑대들은 그 부위를 집중적으로 공격한다.
늑대들은 계속 야수를 깨물고, 야수는 그들을 떨쳐 낸다. 마침내, 야수가 한 늑대를 나무에 던져버리자, 그 늑대는 정신을 잃는다. 다른 늑대들은 겁에 질려 돌아서서 도망친다. 하지만 야수는 상처를 입어 그의 팔에 피가 흐르고 있다.
야수는 벨에게로 돌아가서 그녀를 절망적인 눈빛으로 바라보고 쓰러진다. 벨은 필립에게로 돌아가서 말을 타려고 하지만, 살려줘서 고마운 마음에 그녀의 양심에 가책을 느끼고, 쓰러진 야수에게로 걸어간다. 벨이 야수를 필립의 등에 싣고 함께 성으로 돌아가는 장면이 점점 희미해진다.

rescue
구하다
If you rescue someone, you get them out of a dangerous or unpleasant situation

defenseless
무방비의
lacking protection or support

leap
뛰다
If you leap, you jump high in the air or jump a long distance

lunge
달려들다
If you lunge in a particular direction, you move in that direction suddenly and clumsily

Key Expressions

154 **Remember what the master said.**
주인님 말씀 잊지 말아요.

what에는 '무엇'이라는 뜻 외에도 '~하는 것'이라는 의미가 있다. 또한 위와 같이 동사원형으로 시작하는 문장은 명령문이므로 '주인님이 말한 것을 잊지 말라'는 명령을 표현한다.

· I know what you mean. 네가 무슨 뜻으로 말하는지 알겠어.

158 **Lumiere hands Belle a menu, which she begins to read.** 루미에르는 벨에게 메뉴를 가져다주고, 그녀는 그것을 읽기 시작한다.

쉼표 뒤에 관계대명사(who, which)가 나오면 뒤에서 앞으로 해석하지 않고, 쉼표 앞과 뒤를 순차로 연결하여 해석한다.

· He told me his new phone number, which I wrote down on a piece of paper. 그는 나에게 그의 새 전화번호를 말해주었고, 나는 그것을 종이에 받아썼다.

158 **No one's gloomy or complaining, while the flatware's entertaining!** 식기들이 공연하는 동안 누구도 우울해하거나 불평하지 않는다.

while은 '~동안'이라는 뜻의 접속사로, 뒤에 절을 이끈다. 위 문장에서는 '~동안'이라는 시간의 부사절로 쓰였지만, '~한 반면에'라는 뜻도 있으니 주의한다.

· The phone rang while I was taking a shower.
내가 샤워하는 동안에 전화가 울렸다.

166 **I'm not sure that's such a good idea.**
좋은 생각인지 잘 모르겠네요.

I'm sure뒤에 절이 나오면 '~를 확신하다'는 뜻이므로, 이의 부정문인 I'm not sure~은 '~인지 확신이 없다, 잘 모르겠다'는 의미가 된다.

· I'm not sure he'll like my present. 그가 내 선물을 좋아할지 모르겠네요.

170 **I wonder what he's hiding up there.**
그가 저 위에 무엇을 숨겨놓았을지 궁금하네요.

I wonder~은 '~가 궁금하다, 알고 싶다'는 의미로 뒤에 주로 절이 많이 나온다. 한편, 여기서의 what은 위 문장과 달리 '무엇'이라는 뜻으로 쓰였다.

· I wonder where she is. I haven't seen her for weeks.
그녀가 어디에 있는지 궁금해. 몇 주 동안 그녀를 못 봤거든.

172 **More books than you'll ever be able to read in a lifetime!** 평생 읽어도 다 못 읽을 거예요.

more than은 '~보다 더 많다'는 의미로, 평생 동안 읽을 수 있는 책보다 더 많은 책이 있다는 의미이다. 'be able to 동사원형'은 '~할 수 있다', in a lifetime은 '평생'이라는 표현이니 함께 기억하도록 한다.

· A chance like this comes but once in a lifetime.
이런 기회는 평생에 다시없을 것이다.

Chapter 8

야수, 벨과 사랑에 빠지다

The Beast Falls in Love with Belle

시간 00:49:18 ~ 01:02:01

Zoom inside the castle

INT. IN THE CASTLE
Fade to int of den with Belle pouring hot water out of Mrs. Potts. She soaks a rag in the water then turns to Beast, who is licking his wounds.

BELLE : Here now. Oh, don't do that.

Beast growls at her as she tries to clean the wound with her rag.

BELLE : Just... hold still.

She touches the rag to the wound and Beast roars in pain. The Objects, who have been watching jump back into hiding from the outburst. Belle and Beast have an argument.

BEAST : That hurts!

BELLE : (in counterpoint) If you'd hold still, it wouldn't hurt as much.

성 안의 모습이 줌인된다.

내부. 성 안
방의 모습이 보인다. 벨은 포트부인에 담긴 따뜻한 물을 붓고 있다. 천 조각을 물에 담근 후 자신의 몸에 난 상처를 핥고 있는 야수 쪽을 향한다.

벨 : 이리 오세요. 그러지 말구요.

천 조각으로 상처부위를 씻으려 하는 벨을 향해 야수가 으르렁거린다.

벨 : 좀 참으세요.

벨은 천 조각을 상처 부위에 가져다 대고 야수는 고통으로 신음한다. 이것을 지켜보고 있던 하인들은 갑작스런 야수의 으르렁거리는 소리에 몸을 숨긴다. 벨과 야수는 말다툼을 한다.

야 수 : 악… 아파.

벨 : (지지 않고 대꾸하며) 가만히 있으면, 그다지 아프진 않을 거예요.

■ **den**
방, 소굴
A den is the home of certain types of wild animals such as lions or foxes

■ **wound**
상처
A wound is damage to part of your body, especially a cut or a hole in your flesh, which is caused by a gun, knife, or other weapon

■ **rag**
천 조각
A rag is a piece of old cloth which you can use to clean or wipe things

■ **argument**
말다툼
An argument is a statement or set of statements that you use in order to try to convince people that your opinion about something is correct

BEAST : Well if you hadn't have run away this wouldn't have happened!

BELLE : If you hadn't frightened me, I wouldn't have run away!

Beast opens his mouth to respond but has to stop and think of a good line.

BEAST : Well, you shouldn't have been in the West Wing!

BELLE : Well, you should learn to control your temper!

Beast raises his hand to bring out another point but finds he has none so he bows his head down again. The Objects emerge from their hiding as Belle has conquered the ferocious temper of Beast. Belle moves the rag closer to the wound.

BELLE : Now, hold still. This might sting a little.

Beast gives a surprised grunt then grits his teeth as the rag is applied. Belle speaks tenderly.

BELLE : By the way... thank you for saving my life.

Beast opens his eyes looking surprised.

BEAST : (also very tenderly) You're welcome.

Camera zooms out and we see the Objects looking on with interest.

INT. GASTON'S TAVERN

Fade to Gaston's tavern, which is empty except for Gaston, Lefou and Monsieur Doctor, who are all sitting at a table.

야 수 : 당신이 도망가지만 않았어도 이런 일은 없었을 거요.
벨 : 당신이 나를 겁먹게만 안했어도, 난 도망가지 않았을거에요.

야수는 뭐라고 대답하려 입을 열었지만 딱히 뭐라고 해야 좋을지 몰라 말문이 막힌다.

야 수 : 당신 서쪽 탑에 가지 말았어야지.
벨 : 당신은 성질 죽이는 법 좀 배워야 겠어요.

야수는 뭔가 또 꾸짖을 말을 꺼내려 손을 든다. 하지만 아무 말도 할 것이 없자 이내 고개를 다시 떨군다. 벨이 야수의 불같은 성질을 잠재우자 숨어있던 하인들이 나타난다. 벨은 천 조각을 야수의 상처 부위에 갖다 댄다.

벨 : 자, 가만히 있어요. 좀 아플거에요.

야수가 깜짝 놀라 신음한다. 천 조각이 닿자 이를 꽉 깨문다. 벨이 부드럽게 말한다.

벨 : 아참! 제 생명을 구해주셔서 감사해요.

야수는 깜짝 놀라 눈을 동그랗게 뜬다.

야 수 : (또한 아주 부드러운 목소리로) 천만에요.

카메라가 줌아웃 되고 신하들이 호기심을 가지고 바라보는 것이 보인다.

내부. 개스톤의 술집
개스톤의 술집이 보인다. 테이블에 앉아있는 개스톤, 르푸, 의사만이 술집에 있다.

- **frighten**
  겁먹게 하다
  If something or someone frightens you, they cause you to suddenly feel afraid, anxious, or nervous
- **temper**
  성질
  If you refer to someone's temper or say that they have a temper, you mean that they become angry very easily
- **sting**
  따끔거리다
  If a part of your body stings, or if a substance stings it, you feel a sharp pain there
- **empty**
  비어 있는
  An empty place, vehicle, or container is one that has no people or things in it

Well, you shouldn't have been in the West Wing!
should have p.p.는 '~했었어야 했다'는 과거에 하지 못한 일에 대한 후회를 나타내고, shouldn't have pp는 '~하지 말았어야 했다'는 과거에 했던 일에 대한 후회를 나타낸다.

Zoom In

Well, you shouldn't have been in the West Wing!
당신이 서쪽 탑에 가지 말았어야지!

DOCTOR : I don't usually leave the asylum in the middle of the night but he said you'd make it worth my while.

Gaston pulls out a sack of gold and tosses it in front of him. He takes out a piece, scrapes it on his chin and continues.

DOCTOR : Aah, I'm listening.

GASTON : It's like this. I've got my heart set on marrying Belle, but she needs a little persuasion.

LEFOU : (butting in) Turned him down flat!

Gaston slams a beer mug on Lefou's head.

GASTON : Everyone knows her father's a lunatic. He was in here tonight raving about a beast in a castle...

Lefou struggles to get his head out of the glass. Doctor picks up a gold coin from the purse filled with coins.

DOCTOR : Maurice is harmless.

GASTON : The point is, Belle would do anything to keep him from being locked up.

LEFOU : Yeah, even marry him!

Gaston gives him another threatening look, and he ducks back under the mug.

의 사 : 난 보통 이런 야밤에는 내 정신병원을 나오지 않지. 하지만 그가 말하길 네가 내 팔자를 펴게 해줄 무언가를 가지고 있다고 하더군.

개스톤은 금이 든 주머니를 꺼내 의사 앞에 던진다. 의사는 금 한 조각을 집어 들고 턱에 비벼보더니 말을 잇는다.

의 사 : 그래, 말해 보게.
개스톤 : 얘기는 이렇다네. 나는 벨과 꼭 결혼을 하고 싶다네. 하지만 그녀는 뭐랄까… 설득이 필요하지.
르 푸 : (끼어들며) 벨이 개스톤을 깔끔하게 거부했지 뭐에요.

개스톤은 술잔으로 르푸의 머리를 친다.

개스톤 : 그녀의 아버지가 미쳤다는 건 모든 사람이 다 안다네. 오늘 밤만 해도 그는 성에 사는 야수를 보았다고 했다네.

르푸는 잔에서 머리를 빼내려 몸부림친다. 의사는 금화로 가득 찬 주머니에서 금화 하나를 집는다.

의 사 : 모리스가 정상이네.
개스톤 : 내 말은, 벨은 아버지가 갇히지 않게 하기 위해 무슨 짓이든 할 거라는 거지.
르 푸 : 심지어는 그와 결혼할지도 모르지.

개스톤은 르푸를 다시 협박하는 눈으로 바라본다. 그러자 르푸는 술잔 밑에 다시 숨는다.

asylum
정신병원
An asylum is a psychiatric hospital

worth
가치
Someone's worth is the value, usefulness, or importance that they are considered to have

persuasion
설득
Persuasion is the act of persuading someone to do something or to believe that something is true

lunatic
미친
If you describe someone's behaviour or ideas as lunatic, you think they are very foolish and possibly dangerous

rave
헛소리하다
If someone raves, they talk in an excited and uncontrolled way

I've got my heart set on marrying Belle.
have one's heart set은 '마음을 확고하게 먹다, 결심하다'라는 숙어이다. make up one's mind, decide, determine과도 바꾸어 쓸 수 있다.

Zoom In

I've got my heart set on marrying Belle.
나는 벨과 꼭 결혼을 하고 싶다네.

DOCTOR : So you want me to throw her father into the asylum unless she agrees to marry you? (they both nod in agreement.) Oh, that is despicable. Umm ha ha... I love it!

He looks at Gaston shrewdly and laughs wickedly.

INT. BELLE'S COTTAGE
Cut to int of Belle's cottage. Maurice is packing to leave.

MAURICE : If no one will help me, then I'll go back alone. Yes, is that everything? I don't care what it takes. I'll find that castle and somehow I… I'll get her out of there.

Maurice puts on his hat and gets out of his house. Maurice leaves on his journey.
Seconds later, Gaston and Lefou arrive with Doctor. They enter the house looking for one of the residents.

GASTON : Belle! Maurice!

LEFOU : Oh, well, I guess it's not gonna work after all.

Gaston grabs him by the neck and walks outside.

GASTON : They have to come back sometime. And when they do, we'll be ready for them. (drops Lefou into a snowbank by the porch) Lefou, don't move from that spot until Belle and her father come home.

LEFOU : But, but I... aww... nuts!

He pounds the side of the house and a pile of snow falls on his head.

의 사 : 그러니까 벨이 자네와 결혼하지 않는다면 아버지를 정신병원에 넣어버리라 그 말인가? (개스톤과 르푸는 맞다는 의미로 고개를 끄덕인다) 오, 그건 야비한 방법이지만. 마음에 드는 걸?

그는 개스톤을 보며 악랄한 웃음을 짓는다.

내부. 벨의 집
벨의 집으로 장소가 바뀐다. 모리스는 떠날 준비를 하고 있다.

모리스 : 아무도 도와주지 않는다면 나 혼자라도 가겠어. 도와줄 사람이 아무도 없다는 거야? 무슨 일이든 하겠어. 성을 찾아서 어떻게 해서든 벨을 구해 와야 돼.

모리스는 모자를 쓰고 집을 나온다. 모리스는 여정을 떠난다. 잠시 후, 개스톤, 르푸 그리고 의사가 벨의 집 앞에 도착한다. 그들은 벨이나 모리스를 찾으러 집 안으로 들어온다.

개스톤 : 벨 ! 모리스 !
르 푸 : 이런. 우리의 작전이 전혀 통하지 않겠는걸?

개스톤은 그의 목을 잡고 바깥으로 나간다.

개스톤 : 언젠가는 돌아오겠지. 그 때를 대비해서 우린 모든 준비를 해놔야 돼. (르푸를 현관 옆에 쌓인 눈더미에 떨어뜨린다) 자. 벨과 모리스가 올 때까지 여기서 꼼짝 말고 지키고 있어.
르 푸 : 하지만… 하지만… 제길…

그가 집의 벽을 쿵 치자 눈더미가 그의 머리 위로 쏟아진다.

- **despicable**
  비열한
  If you say that a person or action is despicable, you are emphasizing that they are extremely nasty, cruel, or evil
- **shrewd**
  약삭빠른
  A shrewd person is able to understand and judge a situation quickly and to use this understanding to their own advantage
- **resident**
  거주자
  The residents of a house or area are the people who live there
- **pound**
  치다
  If you pound something or pound on it, you hit it with great force, usually loudly and repeatedly

I don't care what it takes.
I don't care은 '신경 쓰지 않아, 개의치 않아'라는 의미이다. 따라서 무슨 일을 해야 하더라도 개의치 않고 하겠다는 의미가 된다.
ex) I don't care what people say.

Zoom In

I don't care what it takes.
무슨 일이든 하겠어.

EXT. OUTSIDE THE CASTLE

Fade to ext of castle. Belle is playing in the snow with Phillipe and Footstool. Beast, Cogsworth and Lumiere watch from the balcony.
Beast speaks tenderly touching his arm cured by Belle.

BEAST : I've never felt this way about anyone. (looks excited) I want to do something for her. (looks discouraged) But what?

Cogsworth starts his lecture proudly.

COGSWORTH : Well, there's the usual things... flowers, chocolates, promises you don't intend to keep...

Lumiere taps Cogsworth on the shoulder and cuts him off. Both of them fold their arms and speak out their ideas.

LUMIERE : Ahh, no, no. It has to be something very special. Something that sparks her interest... wait a minute.

INT. HALLWAY

Cut to int hallway leading to library. Beast and Belle are alone.

BEAST : Belle, there's something I want to show you. (begins to open the door, then stops.) But first, you have to close your eyes. (she looks at him questioningly.) It's a surprise.

Belle closes her eyes and Beast waves his hand in front of her. They are walking hand in hand. Then he opens the door. He leads her in.

외부. 성 밖
성 밖의 모습이 보인다. 벨은 필립, 풋스툴(발받침)과 함께 눈 위에서 놀고 있다. 야수, 콕스워즈, 루미에르가 발코니에서 이 모습을 보고 있다.
야수는 벨이 치료해준 자신의 팔을 만지며 부드러운 목소리로 말한다.

야 수 : 누구에게도 이런 감정은 느껴 본 적이 없어. (신난 모습으로) 그녀를 위해 뭔가를 하고 싶어. (풀이 죽은 모습으로) 하지만, 뭘 하지?

콕스워즈가 자랑스럽게 또 연설을 늘어놓기 시작한다.

콕스워즈 : 에… 글쎄요. 보통하는 것들은 꽃이나 초코, 지킬 생각도 없는 약속 같은 것이 있죠.

루미에르는 콕스워즈의 어깨를 치며 그의 말을 자른다. 둘 다 팔짱을 끼고 자신의 생각을 말한다.

루미에르 : 아… 아니 아니야. 뭔가 매우 특별한 것이 있어야해. 벨의 흥미를 끌 수 있는 그런 것. 어, 잠깐! 바로 그거야!

내부. 성 안의 복도
성의 도서관으로 가는 복도의 모습. 야수와 벨은 단 둘이 있다.

야 수 : 벨. 당신에게 보여줄 것이 있소. (도서관의 문을 열려다가 멈추며) 먼저 눈을 감아요. (벨은 궁금한 듯 야수를 바라본다) 당신을 놀라게 해주고 싶으니까.

벨이 눈을 감자, 야수는 그녀의 눈 앞에서 팔을 저어본다. 손을 잡고 들어가는 두 사람. 야수는 문을 열고 그녀를 도서관 안으로 안내한다.

- **cure**
  치료하다
  If doctors or medical treatments cure an illness or injury, they cause it to end or disappear

- **usual**
  흔한
  Usual is used to describe what happens or what is done most often in a particular situation

- **intend**
  의도하다
  If you intend to do something, you have decided or planned to do it

- **wave**
  흔들다
  If you wave or wave your hand, you move your hand from side to side in the air, usually in order to say hello or goodbye to someone

It has to be something very special.
have to(has to)는 '~해야 한다'는 뜻의 조동사로, 뒤에 be동사가 나오면 '~가 있어야 한다'는 뜻이 된다. -thing으로 끝나는 명사는 형용사가 뒤에서 수식한다는 것은 이미 살펴보았다.

Zoom In

It has to be something very special.
뭔가 매우 특별한 것이 있어야 해.

INT, IN THE LIBRARY

BELLE : (just as she enters the room) Can I open them?

BEAST : No, no. Not yet. Wait here.

Beast walks away to draw back the curtains. He does and brilliant sunlight spills into the room. Belle flinches reflexively as the light hits her face.

BELLE : Now can I open them?

BEAST : All right. Now.

Belle opens her eyes and the camera pulls back to reveal the gigantic library filled with books.
There are book shelves all around. They are full of books from floor to ceiling.

BELLE : I can't believe it. I've never seen so many books in all my life!

BEAST : You... you like it?

BELLE : It's wonderful.

BEAST : Then it's yours.

Belle holds Beast's hands and feels grateful to him truly.

BEAST : Oh, thank you so much.

Objects including Chip are watching them.

MRS. POTTS : Oh, would you look at that?

LUMIERE : Ha ha! I knew it would work.

CHIP : What? What works?

COGSWORTH : It's very encouraging.

FEATHERDUSTER : Isn't this exciting!

내부. 도서관

벨 : (도서관에 들어오자 마자) 눈 떠도 될까요 ?
야 수 : 아니, 아니. 아직 아니요. 여기서 기다려요.

야수는 커튼을 젖히러 간다. 커튼을 젖히자 밝은 햇빛이 방안을 비춘다. 빛이 그녀의 얼굴을 비추자 벨은 반사적으로 움찔한다.

벨 : 이제 눈 떠도 돼요 ?
야 수 : 그렇게 해요.

벨이 눈을 뜬다. 책으로 가득한 도서관의 모습이 줌 아웃된 카메라에 담긴다.
사방에 책장이 있다. 바닥에서 천장까지 모두 책으로 가득하다.

벨 : 믿을 수 없어요. 이렇게 많은 책은 생전 처음 봐요.
야 수 : 당신… 마음에 들어요?
벨 : 그럼요.
야 수 : 그렇다면 모두 당신거요.

벨은 야수의 손을 잡고 진심으로 고맙게 생각한다.

벨 : 오, 너무 고마워요.

칩을 포함한 하인들이 그들을 지켜보고 있다.

포트 부인 : 저것 좀 봐요.
루미에르 : 하하. 그래 통할 줄 알았다니까!
칩 : 뭐가요? 뭐가 통해요?
콕스워즈 : 하하. 잘 될 거 같은데?
페더더스터 : 정말 멋지지 않아요?

- **brilliant**
  밝은
  You describe light, or something that reflects light, as brilliant when it shines very brightly

- **flinch**
  움찔하다
  If you flinch, you make a small sudden movement, especially when something surprises you or hurts you

- **gigantic**
  거대한
  If you describe something as gigantic, you are emphasizing that it is extremely large in size, amount, or degree

- **grateful**
  고마워하는
  If you are grateful for something that someone has given you or done for you, you have warm, friendly feelings towards them and wish to thank them

I can't believe it.
너무 놀라워서 믿을 수 없는 상황이 벌어졌을 때 아주 자주 쓰이는 표현이니 반드시 기억해두고 실생활에서 활용하도록 한다. It's impossible. Incredible!과도 같은 표현이다.

Zoom In

I can't believe it.

믿을 수 없어요.

CHIP : I didn't see anything.

MRS. POTTS : Come along, Chip. There's chores to be done in the kitchen.

CHIP : But what are they talking about? What's going on? Come on, Mom.

Objects walk away. Fade to breakfast table with Belle at one end and Beast at the other with Mrs. Potts between them.

INT. IN THE DINING ROOM

Belle is served breakfast and begins to eat. She looks at Beast gobbling up his food with no table manners whatsoever. Chip laughs but Mrs. Potts shoots him an admonishing look. Belle turns away and tries to ignore it but Chip comes to the rescue. He nudges the spoon with his nose and Beast reaches out for it. Belle looks at him in wonder as he tries to eat with the spoon but he has little success.

Finally, Belle puts down her spoon and lifts her bowl as if in a toast. Beast looks at the compromise and does the same. They both begin to sip their breakfast out of their bowls.

EXT. IN THE COURTYARD

Fade to courtyard where Belle and Beast are feeding the birds.

BELLE : (singing) *THERE'S SOMETHING SWEET*
AND ALMOST KIND
BUT HE WAS MEAN
AND HE WAS COARSE AND UNREFINED

Beast tries to feed birds but birds escape quickly.

BELLE : (singing) *AND NOW HE'S DEAR*
AND SO UNSURE
I WONDER WHY I DIDN'T SEE IT THERE BEFORE

칩 : 난 잘 모르겠는데요.

포트 부인 : 자 가자, 얘야. 부엌에 해야 할 일이 있어.

칩 : 하지만 무슨 얘길 하시는 거에요? 무슨 일이 일어난 거죠? 어서요, 엄마!

신하들이 물러난다. 테이블 양 쪽 끝에 앉아 아침식사를 하는 벨과 야수의 모습이 보인다. 그들 사이에 포트 부인이 있다.

내부. 식당
아침식사가 준비되었다. 식사를 하려는 차에 벨은 테이블 매너라고는 전혀 없이 게걸스럽게 음식을 먹어치우는 야수를 보게된다. 칩이 웃자, 포트부인이 꾸짖는 눈빛으로 그를 바라본다. 벨은 고개를 돌려 못 본 채 하려하는데 칩이 야수에게 도움을 주려한다. 칩은 코로 야수에게 스푼을 밀어주고 야수가 그것을 집는다. 벨은 스푼으로 먹으려고 노력하는 야수를 호기심 어린 눈으로 바라보지만, 야수에게 스푼으로 먹기란 어려운 모습이다.
마침내, 벨이 자신의 스푼을 내려놓고 건배를 하듯이 그녀의 그릇을 집어든다. 야수도 이에 응하듯 벨과 같이 그릇을 들어 건배하는 모습을 보인다. 둘 다 음식을 홀짝거리며 먹기 시작한다.

외부. 성의 뜰
뜰에서 벨과 야수가 새에게 모이를 주고 있다.

벨 : (노래하며) *뭔가 다정한 모습이 있는 그*
그리고 친절한 듯도 한 그
하지만 전에는 못되고
거칠고, 세련되지도 않았지

야수가 새들에게 모이를 주려고 하지만 새들이 빠르게 달아난다.

벨 : (노래하며) *하지만 이제 그는 사랑스럽네*
그리고 잘 모르겠어
왜 전에는 이런 걸 몰랐을까?

- **chore**
  일
  A chore is a task that you must do but that you find unpleasant or boring
- **gobble**
  게걸스럽게 먹다
  If you gobble food, you eat it quickly and greedily
- **admonish**
  타이르다
  If you admonish someone, you tell them very seriously that they have done something wrong
- **nudge**
  쿡 찌르다
  If you nudge someone, you push them gently, usually with your elbow, in order to draw their attention to something
- **compromise**
  타협
  A compromise is a situation in which people accept something slightly different from what they really want, because of circumstances or because they are considering the wishes of other people

I wonder why I didn't see it there before.
see에는 보다라는 뜻 외에 '알다, 깨닫다'는 의미도 있다. I wonder~은 '~가 궁금하다'는 의미이다. 따라서 왜 전에 이것을 알지 못했는지 궁금하다는 의미가 된다.

Zoom In

I wonder why I didn't see it there before.
왜 전에는 이런 걸 몰랐을까?

Beast is disappointed because birds are stepping back again and again.
Belle is trying to attract some birds to Beast who shoves a handful of seed at them. Finally, she takes a handful and gently spreads it out creating a trail.
One lands in his hands, and he looks up thrilled.
Birds peck at the food on his hands. Belle and Beast are surrounded by flocks of birds.

BEAST : (singing) *SHE GLANCED THIS WAY*
I THOUGHT I SAW
AND WHEN WE TOUCHED
SHE DIDN'T SHUDDER AT MY PAW
NO IT CAN'T BE
I'LL JUST IGNORE
BUT THEN SHE'S NEVER LOOKED AT ME
THAT WAY BEFORE

Belle has ducked around a tree, leaving Beast with the birds. She begins to look doubtful again but turns her head around the tree and laughs. Beast is covered with birds.
Belle stares at Beast surrounded by birds.

BELLE : (singing) *NEW AND A BIT ALARMING*
WHO'D HAVE EVER THOUGHT THAT THIS COULD BE?
TRUE, THAT HE'S NO PRINCE CHARMING
BUT THERE'S SOMETHING IN HIM THAT I SIMPLY DIDN'T SEE

Belle throws a snowball at Beast. He begins to gather a large pile of snow. We cut to the Objects looking out of a window at the two. In the background Belle throws another snowball at Beast, who drops his huge pile of snow on his head. He chases her around a tree but she ducks around the other side and sneaks up on him from behind.

새들이 계속해서 뒷걸음치자 야수는 실망한 모습이다.
벨이 새들을 야수에게 모이도록 도와주고, 야수는 새들을 위한 모이 한 웅큼을 손에 펼쳐 놓고 있다. 결국 벨이 그의 손에서 모이를 한 웅큼 쥐어 부드럽게 바닥에 쫙 뿌린다. 모이를 따라가면 그의 손으로 가게 만들었다.
그러자 새 한 마리가 그의 손에 앉고 야수는 좋아서 어쩔 줄 몰라한다.
새들이 야수의 손에 놓인 모이를 먹는다. 어느 덧 벨과 야수는 여러 마리의 새들에 둘러쌓여 있다.

야 수 : (노래하며) *그녀가 이쪽을 보았네*
그런 것 같단 말이야
그리고 우리가 손을 잡았을 때
그녀는 나의 거친 손에 놀라지 않았어
아니야. 그럴 리가 없어
그냥 무시해야지
하지만 또 생각해 보니 전에는 그녀가 나를 그런 눈으로 본적이 없었단 말이야

벨이 야수를 새들과 함께 둔 채, 나무 뒤로 숨는다. 그녀는 다시 확신에 차지 않은 표정이다. 하지만 나무 옆으로 고개를 돌려 야수를 본 후 웃는다. 야수의 몸이 새들로 덮혀있다.
벨은 그런 야수를 물끄러미 바라보고 있다.

벨 : (노래하며) *새롭고, 조금은 놀라워*
누가 이런 일이 가능하다고 생각이나 했을까?
그가 백마 탄 왕자님은 아닌 것은 사실이야
하지만 내가 알지 못했던 무언가가 그에겐 있네

벨이 야수에게 눈뭉치를 던진다. 야수는 큰 눈더미를 뭉치기 시작한다. 창문에서 이 둘을 바라보고 있는 하인들의 모습이 나타난다. 뒤에 있던 벨은 야수에게 또 눈뭉치를 던진다. 야수가 뭉친 어마어마한 눈덩이가 자신의 머리 위에 떨어진다. 야수가 나무 주위를 돌며 벨을 잡으려 한다. 하지만 벨은 반대 쪽으로 재빨리 몸을 옮기며 야수를 피하고 있다.

shove
아무렇게나 놓다
If you shove something somewhere, you push it there quickly and carelessly

thrilled
황홀해하는
If someone is thrilled, they are extremely pleased about something

ignore
무시하다
If you ignore someone or something, you pay no attention to them

charming
매력적인
If you say that something is charming, you mean that it is very pleasant or attractive

Who'd have ever thought that this could be?
have p.p.는 특히 ever과 같은 부사와 쓰이면 '~해본 적이 있다'는 경험을 나타낸다. 따라서 위 문장은 '누가 이런 일이 일어날 거라고 생각해본 적이 있을까?'라는 의미가 된다.

Zoom In

Who'd have ever thought that this could be?
누가 이런 일이 가능하다고 생각이나 했을까?

Objects are looking at them out of the window and start to sing a song.

LUMIERE : (singing) *WELL, WHO'D HAVE THOUGHT?*

MRS. POTTS : (singing) *WELL, BLESS MY SOUL*

COGSWORTH : (singing) *WELL, WHO'D HAVE KNOWN?*

MRS. POTTS : (singing) *WELL WHO INDEED?*

LUMIERE : (singing) *AND WHO'D HAVE GUESSED THEY'D COME TOGETHER ON THEIR OWN?*

MRS. POTTS : (singing) *IT'S SO PECULIAR*

ALL : (singing) *WE'LL WAIT AND SEE*
A FEW DAYS MORE
THERE MAY BE SOMETHING
THERE THAT WASN'T THERE BEFORE

Fade to den where Belle sits in front of a roaring fire and reads to Beast. Beast and Belle sit on the rug side by side. They are reading a book together. Objects including Chip watch from doorway.

COGSWORTH : (singing) *YOU KNOW, PERHAPS THERE IS SOMETHING THERE THAT WASN'T THERE BEFORE*

Chip keeps asking curiously what is going on.

CHIP : What?

MRS. POTTS : (singing) *THERE MAY BE SOMETHING THERE THAT WASN'T THERE BEFORE*

CHIP : What's there, Mama?

MRS. POTTS : Shh. I'll tell you when you're older.

The door closes and Objects are standing on stairs. Cogsworth holds a baton and gives directions to all the other Objects.

하인들이 창밖의 그들을 보며 노래를 부르기 시작한다.

루미에르 : (노래하며) *누가 생각이나 했을까?*
콕스워즈 : (노래하며) *이런 기쁜 일이 있다니!*
루미에르 : (노래하며) *누가 알았을까?*
콕스워즈 : (노래하며) *정말 몰랐어*
루미에르 : (노래하며) *그들이 알아서 서로를 좋아하게 될 줄 누가 생각이나 했겠어?*
포트 부인 : (노래하며) *아주 특별한 일이지*
모 두 : (노래하며) *기다려 봐요*
얼마 있으면
전엔 상상도 못했던 무언가가 일어날지도 몰라요

불타는 벽난로 앞에서 벨이 야수에게 책을 읽어주는 모습이 보인다.
야수와 벨은 카펫 위에 나란히 앉아 있다. 함께 책을 읽고 있는 두 사람.
칩을 포함한 하인들이 문가에서 그들을 보고 있다.

콕스워즈 : (노래하며) *아마도 상상도 못 한 일이 일어날 거에요*

칩이 호기심어린 눈으로 무슨 일인지 묻는다.

칩 : 뭐가요?
포트 부인 : (노래하며) 상상도 못 한 일이 일어날 꺼야
칩 : 뭐가요 ? 엄마.
포트 부인 : 나중에 더 크면 얘기해 주마.

문이 닫히고 하인들이 계단이 서 있다. 콕스워즈는 지휘봉을 들고 다른 하인들에게 지침사항을 일러주고 있다.

- **peculiar**
  이상한
  If you describe someone or something as peculiar, you think that they are strange or unusual, sometimes in an unpleasant way

- **rug**
  카펫
  A rug is a piece of thick material that you put on a floor. It is like a carpet but covers a smaller area

- **side by side**
  나란히
  nearest in space or position

- **including**
  비롯한, 포함하여
  You use including to introduce examples of people or things that are part of the group of people or things that you are talking about

There may be something there that wasn't there before.
may는 약한 추측을 나타내는 조동사이다. 따라서 지금까지 일어나지 않았던 일이 일어날지도 모른다는 의미이므로, '상상도 못할 일이 일어날 거야.'라는 뜻의 표현이 된다.

Zoom In

There may be something there that wasn't there before.

상상도 못할 일이 일어날 거야.

COGSWORTH : Right then. You all know why we're here. We have exactly 12 hours, 36 minutes and 15 seconds to create the most magical, spontaneous, romantic atmosphere known to man or beast.

He puts a hand over his mouth and laughs.

COGSWORTH : Or Beast...

All the Objects lift up their eyes and look at Cogsworth.

COGSWORTH : Right. Need I remind you that if the last petal falls from this rose the spell will never be broken.

The table holding the glass runs away. Footstool turns full circle under Cogsworth. Cogsworth is surprised.

COGSWORTH : Very well. You all know your assignments. Half of you to the West Wing. Half of you to the East Wing. The rest of you come with me.

LUMIERE : Oh, lighten up, Cogsworth and let nature take its course.

MRS. POTTS : It's obvious there's a spark between them.

COGSWORTH : Yes, but there's no harm in fanning the flames.

Cogsworth inserts the clockwork in his body and keeps talking.

COGSWORTH : You know... a little. Besides, they must fall in love tonight if we ever expect to be human again.

LUMIERE : Ah, human again...

콕스워즈 : 자, 왜 우리가 여기 모였는지 다들 알거요. 사람이 본, 음 아니면 야수가 본 것 중 가장 마법스러운 예상치 못한 로맨틱한 분위기를 만들어 낼 시간이 정확히 12시간 36분 15초가 남았단 말이지.

콕스워즈는 입에 손을 갖다 댄 후 웃는다.

콕스워즈 : 아니면 야수…

다른 하인들이 눈을 치켜뜨고는 콕스워즈를 쳐다본다.

콕스워즈 : 좋아. 다시 한번 말하지만, 마지막 꽃잎이 떨어지면 영원히 마법을 풀 수 없다.

꽃이 든 병이 놓인 테이블이 도망간다. 풋스툴이 콕스워즈의 발밑에서 휙하고 돈다. 콕스워즈는 깜짝 놀란다.

콕스워즈 : 좋아. 모두 자기가 할 일은 알고 있겠지. 반은 서쪽 탑으로, 다른 반은 동쪽 탑으로 간다. 나머지는 나를 따르라.

루미에르 : 긴장 좀 풀어, 콕스워즈. 자연의 섭리를 따라야지.

포트 부인 : 그 둘 사이에 불꽃이 튄 게 확실하다구.

루미에르 : 그래, 하지만 확실하게 불이 붙어도 나쁠 건 없잖아.

콕스워즈는 자신의 몸에 태엽을 넣고 계속해서 말을 한다.

콕스워즈 : 조금 밖에 모르는군. 게다가, 우리가 다시 사람이 되려면 저 둘이 오늘 밤 확실히 사랑에 빠져야해.

루미에르 : 아, 다시 사람이라…

- **spontaneous**
  자발적인
  Spontaneous acts are not planned or arranged, but are done because someone suddenly wants to do them

- **atmosphere**
  분위기
  The atmosphere of a place is the general impression that you get of it

- **assignment**
  임무
  You can refer to someone being given a particular task or job as their assignment to the task or job

- **obvious**
  명백한
  If something is obvious, it is easy to see or understand

Let nature take its course.
'let+목적어+목적격 보어(동사원형)'는 '~가 ~하는 것을 허락하다, 하게 하다'라는 표현이다. take its course는 '자연스럽게 되어 가다, 전개되다'라는 숙어로 run its course와도 바꾸어 쓸 수 있다.

Zoom In

Let nature take its course.

자연의 섭리를 따라야지.

MRS. POTTS : Human again.

LUMIERE : Yes, think what that means.

Objects start to sing and dance.

LUMIERE : (singing) *I'LL BE COOKING AGAIN*
BE GOOD LOOKING AGAIN
WITH A MADEMOISELLE ON EACH ARM
WHEN I'M HUMAN AGAIN
ONLY HUMAN AGAIN
POISED AND POLISHED AND GLEAMING WITH CHARM
I'LL BE COURTING AGAIN
CHIC AND SPORTING AGAIN

MRS. POTTS : (singing) *WHICH SHOULD CAUSE SEVERAL HUSBANDS ALARM*

LUMIERE : (singing) *HA, HA!*
I'LL HOP DOWN OFF THIS SHELF
AND TOUT DE SUITE BE MYSELF

BOTH : (singing) *I CAN'T WAIT TO BE HUMAN AGAIN*

OBJECTS : (singing) *WHEN WE'RE HUMAN AGAIN*
ONLY HUMAN AGAIN
WHEN WE'RE KNICKKNACKS AND WHAT-NOTS NO MORE
WHEN WE'RE HUMAN AGAIN, GOOD AND HUMAN AGAIN

WARDROBE : (singing) *OH, CHÉRIE, WON'T IT ALL BE TOP DRAWER?*
I'LL WEAR LIPSTICK AND ROUGE
AND I WON'T BE SO HUGE
WHY, I'LL EASILY FIT THROUGH THAT DOOR

포트 부인 : 다시 사람.
루미에르 : 그래, 그게 무슨 의미인지 생각해봐.

하인들이 노래하며 춤추기 시작한다.

루미에르 : (노래하며) *나는 다시 요리를 하겠지*
다시 잘생긴 사람이 되는 거야
양팔에 아가씨를 끼고
내가 다시 사람이 되면
사람이 되기만 한다면
때 빼고 광내서 매력이 철철 넘치게 해서
사랑을 구애하는
시크하게 멋진 사람이 되겠지
포트 부인 : (노래하며) *여러 남편들 긴장하게 말이야*
루미에르 : (노래하며) *하하!*
이 선반에서 풀려나
내 마음대로 살 수 있어
포트 부인, 루미에르 : (노래하며) *빨리 다시 사람이 되고 싶어*
하인들 : (노래하며) *다시 사람이 된다면*
사람이 되기만 한다면
더 이상 장난감 신세 되지 않겠지
다시 사람이 된다면, 멋진 사람이 된다면 말이야
워로브 : (노래하며) *나도 옷장 신세에서 벗어나*
립스틱과 루즈를 바를거야
그리고 이렇게 덩치도 크지 않고 날씬한 몸이 되어서
저 문을 쉽게 통과하겠지

poised
준비된
If someone is poised to do something, they are ready to take action at any moment

polish
광 내다
If you polish something, you put polish on it or rub it with a cloth to make it shine

knickknack
장신구
a small inexpensive mass-produced article

rouge
연지, 루주
Rouge is a red powder or cream which women and actors can put on their cheeks in order to give them more colour

I can't wait to be human again.
'can't wait to 동사원형'은 ~하는 것을 기다릴 수 없다는 뜻이므로, '빨리 ~하고 싶다'는 소망을 나타내는 표현으로 자주 사용된다.
ex) I can't wait to meet her.

Zoom In

I can't wait to be human again.
빨리 사람이 되고 싶어.

I'LL EXUDE SAVOIR FAIRE
I'LL WEAR GOWNS, I'LL HAVE HAIR
IT'S MY PRAYER TO BE HUMAN AGAIN

Wardrobe rolls up her body with a curtain and disappears. Fragments of bricks are flying.

MRS. POTTS, LUMIERE : (singing) *WHEN WE'RE HUMAN AGAIN*
ONLY HUMAN AGAIN
WHEN THE WORLD ONCE MORE STARTS MAKING SENSE

Cogsworth rides on a rake and enters the house. The rake pounds and finally he falls into the water bucket.

COGSWORTH : (singing) *I'LL UNWIND FOR A CHANGE*
LUMIERE : (singing) *REALLY? THAT'D BE STRANGE*

Lumoere pulls out Cogsworth from the bucket.

COGSWORTH : (singing) *CAN I HELP IF IT I'M T-T-TENSE?*
IN A SHACK BY THE SEA
I'LL SIT BACK, SIPPING TEA
LET MY EARLY RETIREMENT COMMENCE
FAR FROM FOOLS MADE OF WAX
I'LL GET DOWN TO BRASS TACKS AND RELAX!
OBJECTS : (singing) *WHEN I'M HUMAN AGAIN*

Brooms are sweeping the floor and making a cloud of dust. Footstool runs amok and jumps for joy.

재치 넘치는 화술을 보여주고
가운도 입고, 머리도 하는
다시 사람이 되는 게 나의 바램이야

워로브가 커튼으로 자신의 몸을 감싸고 사라진다. 벽돌 조각들이 튀어 나온다.

포트 부인, 루미에르 : (노래하며) *우리가 다시 사람이 된다면*
사람이 되기만 한다면
그럼 진짜 살맛 나는 세상이 될텐데

콕스워즈가 갈퀴를 타고 집안으로 들어온다. 갈퀴가 튀는 바람에 결국 콕스워즈는 물양동이에 떨어진다.

콕스워즈 : (노래하며) *나도 기분 전환 겸 긴장을 풀고*
루미에르 : (노래하며) *정말? 그거 진짜 이상하겠다*

루미에르가 콕스워즈를 양동이에서 꺼내준다.

콕스워즈 : (노래하며) *긴장하고 살 수 만은 없잖아*
바닷가에 오두막을 짓고
한가로이 차를 마시며
일찍 은퇴한 여유로운 삶을 시작하고 싶어
양초로 만든 바보 곁을 떠나
조용히 살고 싶어
하인들 : (노래하며) *내가 다시 사람이 된다면*

빗자루가 바닥을 쓸고 먼지를 일으킨다. 풋스툴이 기쁨에 차 마구 날뛴다.

- **exude**
  풍기다
  If someone exudes a quality or feeling, or if it exudes, they show that they have it to a great extent
- **savoir faire**
  재치
  Savoir-faire is the confidence and ability to do the appropriate thing in a social situation
- **unwind**
  긴장을 풀다
  When you unwind, you relax after you have done something that makes you tense or tired
- **retirement**
  은퇴
  Retirement is the time when a worker retires

It's my prayer to be human again.
prayer은 '기도'라는 뜻이므로 누군가의 간절한 소망을 나타낼 때 'It's one's prayer to 동사원형'의 형태로 쓸 수 있다.
ex) It's my prayer to enter the university.

Zoom In

It's my prayer to be human again.
다시 사람이 되는 게 나의 바람이야.

OBJECTS : (singing) *SO SWEEP THAT DUST FROM THE FLOOR*
LET'S LET SOME LIGHT IN THE ROOM
I CAN FEEL, I CAN TELL
SOMEONE MIGHT BREAK THE SPELL ANY DAY NOW
SHINE UP THE BRASS ON THE DOOR
ALERT THE DUSTBIN AND BROOM
IF IT ALL GOES AS PLANNED
OUR TIME MAY BE AT HAND ANY DAY NOW
OPEN THE SHUTTERS AND LET IN SOME AIR

MRS. POTTS : (singing) *PUT THESE HERE AND PUT THOSE OVER THERE*

OBJECTS : (singing) *SWEEP UP THE YEARS OF SADNESS AND TEARS*
AND THROW THEM AWAY
WE'LL BE HUMAN AGAIN
ONLY HUMAN AGAIN
WHEN THE GIRL FINALLY SETS US ALL FREE
CHEEKS A-BLOOMING AGAIN
WE'RE ASSUMING AGAIN
WE'LL RESUME OUR LONG LOST JOIE DE VIVRE
WE'LL BE PLAYING AGAIN
HOLIDAYING AGAIN
AND WE'RE PRAYING IT'S ASAP
WE WILL PUSH, WE WILL SHOVE
THEY WILL BOTH FALL IN LOVE
AND WE'LL FINALLY BE HUMAN AGAIN...

INT. BEAST'S ROOM

Beast and Belle are reading books. There are several books on the table. Beast gazes at Belle's face.

BELLE : For never was a story of more woe than this of Juliet and her Romeo.

하인들 : (노래하며) *바닥의 먼지를 쓸고*
방을 환하게 밝혀봐
난 느낄 수 있어, 알 수 있다구
누군가 마법을 풀어 줄지도 모른다는 걸
문고리를 반짝반짝 닦아놔
빗자루와 쓰레받이를 불어와
계획한 대로만 된다면
이제 우리의 마법이 풀리는 건 시간문제라구
창문을 열고 신선한 공기가 들어오게 해

포트 부인 : (노래하며) *이것들은 여기에, 저것들은 저기에 둬*

하인들 : (노래하며) *길었던 슬픔의 세월을 씻어내고*
모두 떨쳐버려
다시 사람이 된다면
사람이 된다면
벨 아가씨가 우리를 자유롭게 해주면
우린 다시 태어나
새 인생을 살게 될거야
다시 즐겁게 뛰어 놀 수 있고
잔치를 벌일 수 있겠지
어서 그날이 찾아왔으면
우리 모두 힘을 합쳐
둘이 사랑에 빠지게 합시다
그럼 우린 마침내 다시 사람이 되겠지

내부. 야수의 방
야수와 벨이 책을 읽고 있다. 테이블에 책이 여러권 놓여있다. 야수가 벨의 얼굴을 빤히 쳐다보고 있다.

벨 : 이 로미오와 줄리엣 이야기보다 더 가슴 아픈 이야기는 없었습니다.

- **dustbin**
  쓰레받기
  A dustbin is a small flat container made of metal or plastic. You hold it flat on the floor and put dirt and dust into it using a brush

- **sweep**
  쓸다
  If you sweep things off something, you push them off with a quick smooth movement of your arm

- **assume**
  가정하다
  If you assume that something is true, you imagine that it is true, sometimes wrongly

- **resume**
  다시 시작하다
  If you resume an activity or if it resumes, it begins again.

Let's let some light in the room.
'Let's 동사원형'은 '~하자'라는 청유와 제안의 표현이다. How about ~ing? What about ~ing? Why don't you ~ing?와도 바꾸어 쓸 수 있다.
ex) Let's go shopping tomorrow.

Zoom In

Let's let some light in the room.
방을 환하게 밝혀 봐.

BEAST : Could you read it again?

Belle hands over the book to Beast.

BELLE : Well, here, why don't you read it to me?

BEAST : Uh, all right. (hesitatingly)Uh... Uh... I can't.

BELLE : You mean, you never learned?

BEAST : I learned... a little. It's just been so long.

Belle puts a book on the center of the table. She tries to teach Beast how to read.

BELLE : Well, here, I'll help you. Let's start here.

BEAST : Here. Okay, "Twoe..."

BELLE : Two.

BEAST : Two... I knew that. Two households...

Sponges make a heart shape on the window. We can see the wide front yard of the castle.

OBJECTS : (singing) *WE'LL BE DANCING AGAIN*
WE'LL BE TWIRLING AGAIN
WE'LL BE WHIRLING AROUND WITH SUCH EASE
WHEN WE'RE HUMAN AGAIN
ONLY HUMAN AGAIN
WE'LL GO WALTZING THOSE OLD ONE, TWO, THREES
WE'LL BE FLOATING AGAIN

야 수 : 또 한번 읽어주겠소?

벨은 야수에게 책을 건낸다.

벨 : 자, 여기요, 이번엔 당신이 나한테 읽어 주지 그래요?

야 수 : 어, 그러죠. (망설이며) 어… 어… 나 실은 못해요.

벨 : 그러니까 당신 말은… 글 읽는 건 안 배웠다는 말인가요?

야 수 : 배우긴 했죠, 조금… 그냥 너무 오래 전이라서.

벨은 책을 테이블 가운데에 놓는다. 야수에게 책 읽는 법을 가르쳐주려고 한다.

벨 : 자, 내가 도와줄게요. 여기서부터 시작하죠.

야 수 : 여기요? 좋아요.

벨 : 두.

야 수 : 두! 알고 있었어요. 두 집안이…

스폰지가 창문에 하트모양을 그린다. 성의 넓은 앞 마당의 모습이 보인다.

하인들 : (노래하며) *다시 춤도 출 수 있어*
빙글빙글 돌며
가벼운 발걸음으로
다시 사람이 되면
사람이 되기만 한다면
옛날처럼 왈츠를 출수도 있어. 하나, 둘, 셋
공중을 나르고

- **center**
  가운데
  The center of something is the middle of it

- **yard**
  마당, 뜰
  A yard is a piece of land next to someone's house, with grass and plants growing in it

- **twirl**
  빙글빙글 돌다
  If you twirl something or if it twirls, it turns around and around with a smooth, fairly fast movement

- **float**
  떠가다
  Something that floats in or through the air hangs in it or moves slowly and gently through it

It's just been so long.
여기서 It's는 It has의 줄임말로, 현재완료가 쓰인 문장이다. 즉 과거에서부터 지금까지 글을 읽은 지가 오래 되었음을 의미한다. It's just been so long.은 오랜만이라는 말을 하고 싶을 때 유용하게 쓸 수 있는 표현이므로 통째로 기억해두자.

Zoom In

It's just been so long.
그냥 너무 오래전이라서.

WE'LL BE GLIDING AGAIN
STEPPING, STRIDING, AS FINE AS YOU PLEASE
LIKE A REAL HUMAN DOES
I'LL BE ALL THAT I WAS
ON THAT GLORIOUS MORN WHEN WE'RE FINALLY REBORN
AND WE'RE ALL OF US HUMAN

Wardrobe opens the window and jumps out from the window. Wardrobe dives into the fountain and water splashes all over.

WARDROBE : (singing) *AGAIN!*

바닥을 미끄러지지
최대한 우아하게 스텝을 밟고
진짜 사람이 하듯이 말이야
옛날의 나처럼
새 세상이 열리는 그 영광스런 날에
우리 모두 사람이 될거야

워르브가 창문을 열고 창 밖으로 뛰어 내린다. 분수대에 다이빙을 해서 물이 사방에 튄다.

옷 장 : (노래하며) *다시 사람!*

glide
미끄러지듯 가다
If you glide somewhere, you move silently and in a smooth and effortless way

stride
성큼성큼 걷다
If you stride somewhere, you walk there with quick, long steps

glorious
영광스러운
Something that is glorious is very beautiful and impressive

reborn
다시 태어난, 거듭난
If you say that someone or something has been reborn, you mean that they have become active again after a period of being inactive

Key Expressions

186 **Well if you hadn't have run away this wouldn't have happened!** 당신이 도망가지만 않았어도 이런 일은 없었을 거요.

과거 사실의 반대를 가정할 때는 가정법 과거완료 문장을 만든다. 가정법 과거완료는 if절에 had p.p.를, 주절에는 조동사 have p.p.를 써주면 된다.

· If I had studied harder, I could have earned a lot of money.
내가 더 열심히 공부했었더라면 돈을 많이 벌 수 있었을 텐데.

188 **Belle would do anything to keep him from being locked up.** 벨은 아버지가 갇히지 않게 하기 위해 무슨 짓이든 할 거라는 거지.

'keep 목적어 from ~ing'는 '목적어가 ~하는 것을 막다, 예방하다'라는 의미이다. keep 대신 stop, prevent, prohibit, ban을 써도 좋다. keep ~ing와 혼동하지 않도록 주의한다.

· He kept me from going out alone. 그는 나 혼자 밖에 나가지 못하게 하였다.

190 **So you want me to throw her father into the asylum unless she agrees to marry you?**
그러니까 벨이 자네와 결혼하지 않는다면 아버지를 정신병원에 넣어버리라 그 말인가?

unless는 '만약 ~하지 않는다면'이라는 부정의 조건을 이끄는 접속사로, if ~not과 같은 의미이다.

· Unless I'm mistaken, she left Korea last year.
내가 잘못 알고 있지 않는 한, 그녀는 작년에 한국을 떠났다.

192 I've never felt this way about anyone.
누구에게도 이런 감정은 느껴본 적이 없어.

현재완료(have/has+p.p.) 시제는 경험을 나타내는 용법으로 쓰일 수 있다. 즉 '~해본 적이 있다, ~해본 적이 없다'는 과거에서 현재에 이르기까지의 경험을 나타내준다. 특히 ever, never는 경험을 나타내는 표현과 함께 쓰이는 경우가 많다.

· I've never had Mexican food. 나는 멕시코 음식을 먹어본 적이 없어.

202 Yes, but there's no harm in fanning the flames.
그래, 하지만 확실하게 불이 붙어도 나쁠 건 없잖아.

There's no harm이라고 하면 해로울 것은 없다, 나쁠 건 없다는 의미이다. in ~ing는 '~하는 데 있어서'라는 전치사구로 자주 사용된다.

· There's no harm in asking. Don't hesitate.
물어봐서 나쁠 건 없어. 망설이지 마.

210 She tries to teach Beast how to read.
그녀는 야수에게 책 읽는 법을 가르쳐주려고 한다.

'try to동사원형'은 '~하기 위해 노력하다, 애쓰다'라는 의미이다. 'how to 동사원형'의 경우 '어떻게 ~하는지'라는 의미이므로, '~하는 방법'이라고 해석된다.

· I'm computer-illiterate. I don't even know how to search on the Internet.
저는 컴맹이에요. 인터넷 검색하는 방법조차 모른다니까요.

Chapter 9

성을 떠나며

Leaving the Castle

시간 01:02:02 ~ 01:14:18

INT. BEAST'S LAIR

Cut to int. of Beast's lair. He is in the tub getting washed up for the big night with Belle. Lumiere is there with him.

LUMIERE : Tonight is the night!

BEAST : (hesitantly) I'm not sure I can do this.

LUMIERE : You don't have time to be timid. You must be bold, daring.

BEAST : Bold. Daring.

Beast has emerged from the tub and shakes himself dry.

LUMIERE : There will be music, romantic candlelight, provided by myself. And when the moment is right, you confess your love.

Beast looks at himself in a mirror.

내부. 야수의 방
야수의 방의 모습. 벨과 멋진 시간을 보내기 위해 야수는 욕조에서 목욕을 하고 있다. 루미에르가 그와 함께 있다.

루미에르 : 오늘 밤이 그 중요한 밤입니다.

야 수 : (망설이며) 내가 잘 할 수 있을지 모르겠어.

루미에르 : 소심해할 시간이 없어요. 용감하고 대담해져야 해요.

야 수 : 용감하고 대담해져라…

야수가 욕조에서 나와 몸을 흔들어 물이 마른다.

루미에르 : 음악이 있고, 제가 직접 준비한 로멘틱한 촛불이 있을 겁니다. 그리고 적절한 타이밍에 사랑을 고백하세요.

야수는 거울에 비친 자신의 모습을 본다.

- **bold**
  용감한
  Someone who is bold is not afraid to do things which involve risk or danger

- **daring**
  대담한
  People who are daring are willing to do or say things which are new or which might shock or anger other people

- **tub**
  욕조
  A tub is a long, usually rectangular container which you fill with water and sit in to wash your body

- **confess**
  고백하다
  If someone confesses to doing something wrong, they admit that they did it

BEAST : (inspired) Yes, I... I con... No, I can't.

LUMIERE : You care for the girl, don't you?

BEAST : More than anything.

LUMIERE : Well, then you must tell her.

Coatrack has been cutting Beast's hair. It finishes and steps back.

LUMIERE : Voilà! You look so... so...

Cut to shot of Beast in pig-tails and bows.

BEAST : Stupid.

LUMIERE : Not quite the word I was looking for. Perhaps a little more off the top.

Coatrack begins to cut and chop again. Cogsworth enters.
Cogsworth points at the door and clears his throat.

COGSWORTH : Ahem ahem ahem. Your lady awaits.

Cut to grand staircase where Belle descends from the West Wing side in a glittering gold ball gown.
She reaches the landing and looks up at Beast, who is standing at the top of the stairs in his dress clothes. He is nudged on by Lumiere from behind the curtain and he descends and meets Belle at the landing. Beast and Belle exchange greetings politely. Arm in arm, they descend the last section of stairs and continue on their way to dinner. Mrs. Potts sings from her cart with Chip on board.

MRS. POTTS : (singing) *TALE AS OLD AS TIME*
TRUE AS IT CAN BE

야 수 : (힘을 얻어) 그래! 나는 할 수… 아니야. 난 못해.

루미에르 : 벨을 사랑하잖아요. 그렇죠?

야 수 : 무엇보다도 사랑하지.

루미에르 : 그럼 말해야죠.

옷걸이가 야수의 머리를 이발하고 있다. 이발이 끝난 후, 한걸음 물러난다.

루미에르 : 짜잔! 주인님… 모습이 아주… 아주…

야수의 모습이 보인다. 돼지꼬리 머리에 리본을 한 모습.

야 수 : 바보 같지.

루미에르 : 제가 하려던 말은 그게 아니구요. 윗 부분을 약간 고치시면 좀 나아질 것 같은데.

옷걸이가 다시 머리를 자르고 다듬기 시작한다. 콕스워즈가 들어온다.
콕스워즈가 문 쪽을 가리키며 목소리를 가다듬는다.

콕스워즈 : 에헴. 에헴. 에헴. 아가씨가 기다리고 계십니다.

웅장한 계단의 모습이 보인다. 벨이 눈부신 금색 드레스를 입고 왼편에서 내려온다.
벨은 계단을 내려와서 고개를 들어 멋진 옷을 입고 계단 위에 있는 야수를 바라본다. 루미에르가 커튼 뒤에서 야수를 민다. 야수는 계단을 내려와 벨과 만난다. 그들은 정중하게 서로에게 인사를 하고, 팔짱을 낀 채 계단의 마지막 부분을 내려와 저녁식사를 하러 간다. 차 받침대 위에 칩과 서 있는 포트 부인이 노래한다.

포트 부인 : (노래하며) *옛날 이야기*
아주 진실된 이야기

- **coatrack**
  옷걸이
  a rack with hooks for temporarily holding coats and hats

- **pig-tail**
  땋은 머리
  If someone has a pigtail or pigtails, their hair is plaited or braided into one or two lengths

- **bow**
  나비넥타이
  A bow is a knot with two loops and two loose ends that is used in tying shoelaces and ribbons

- **glittering**
  눈부신
  You use glittering to indicate that something sparkles

Not quite the word I was looking for.
I was looking for이 the word를 수식해주는 문장구조이다. look for은 '찾다'라는 의미로, 직역하면 내가 찾는 단어는 그것이 아니었다는 뜻이 되기 때문에, 결국 자신이 하려던 말이 아니었음을 해명하는 표현이 된다.

Zoom In

Not quite the word I was looking for.
제가 하려던 말은 그게 아니구요.

Footstool walks around Belle and comes down the stairs.

MRS. POTTS : (singing) *BARELY EVEN FRIENDS*
THEN SOMEBODY BENDS UNEXPECTEDLY
JUST A LITTLE CHANGE
SMALL TO SAY THE LEAST
BOTH A LITTLE SCARED
NEITHER ONE PREPARED, BEAUTY AND THE BEAST

INT. IN THE DINING ROOM

Beast struggles to have food with a spoon. Belle smiles at the sight. Listening to the violin music, she stands up. She comes up to Beast and takes his hand. Belle and Beast have moved into the ballroom, where they move through a computer-perfect dance sequence. Beast occasionally looks over at Lumiere and Cogsworth for their approval. Mrs. Potts and Chip are in the ballroom on their cart.

MRS. POTTS : (singing) *EVER JUST THE SAME*
EVER A SURPRISE
EVER AS BEFORE
EVER JUST AS SURE AS THE SUN WILL RISE

Beast and Belle dance a waltz. We can see the picture on the ceiling that looks like "The Creation of Adam". Seen from above, the view is spectacular.

MRS. POTTS : (singing) *TALE AS OLD AS TIME*
TUNE AS OLD AS SONG
BITTERSWEET AND STRANGE
FINDING YOU CAN CHANGE
LEARNING YOU WERE WRONG
CERTAIN AS THE SUN
RISING IN THE EAST

풋스툴이 벨 주위를 돌아다니다 계단을 내려온다.

포트 부인 : (노래하며) *친구라고도 할 수 없었던 사이*
그러다 뜻하지 않게 누군가 마음을 풀었죠
아주 작은 변화였어요
아주 작은 변화
둘다 조금은 겁이 났고
준비되지 않았죠. 미녀와 야수

내부 .식당
야수는 스푼으로 음식을 먹으려 한다. 벨은 그 장면을 보고 미소를 짓는다. 바이올린 음악을 들으며 그녀는 자리에서 일어난다. 야수에게 다가가 그의 손을 잡는다.
벨과 야수는 무도회장에서 완벽한 동작으로 춤을 춘다. 야수는 간간히 루미에르와 콕스워즈를 바라보며 자신이 잘하고 있는건지를 살핀다. 포트부인과 칩은 받침대 위에 서있다.

포트 부인 : (노래하며) *예전과 같은 느낌이면서도*
아주 놀라운 이 느낌
예전처럼 여전하면서
태양이 떠오르는 것처럼 확실한

야수와 벨은 왈츠를 춘다. 천장에 "아담의 창조"처럼 보이는 그림이 있다. 위에서 보는 모습이 웅장하다.

포트 부인 : (노래하며) *시간 속에 흘러온 오래된 이야기*
노래 속에 녹아온 선율같은 사랑
쓰면서도 달콤하고 신비한 사랑
그대가 변할 수 있음을 발견하고
그대가 과거에 잘못했음을 깨달을 수 있고
태양처럼 분명한
동쪽하늘에서 떠오르는

- **unexpected**
  예기치 못한
  If an event or someone's behaviour is unexpected, it surprises you because you did not think that it was likely to happen

- **sequence**
  장면
  A sequence of events or things is a number of events or things that come one after another in a particular order

- **spectacular**
  극적인
  Something that is spectacular is very impressive or dramatic

- **bittersweet**
  씁쓸하면서도 달콤한
  If you describe an experience as bittersweet, you mean that it has some happy aspects and some sad ones

Ever just as sure as the sun will rise.
'as 형용사/부사 as'는 '~만큼 ~하다'라는 원급 비교 표현이다. just등이 쓰이면 더욱 문장을 강조해 줄 수 있다. 위에서는 해가 뜨는 것만큼 확실한 일이라는 의미를 나타낸다.

Zoom In

Ever just as sure as the sun will rise.
태양이 떠오르는 것처럼 확실한.

TALE AS OLD AS TIME
SONG AS OLD AS RHYME
BEAUTY AND THE BEAST

Belle leans on Beast's chest. They seem to be happy.

MRS. POTTS : (singing) *TALE AS OLD AS TIME*
SONG AS OLD AS RHYME, BEAUTY AND THE BEAST
(to Chip) Off to the cupboard with you now, Chip. It's past your bedtime. Good night, love.

Chip slides off the end of the cart, and hops out of the room, but comes back for one last look.
The door opens. Beast and Belle go out to balcony.
Belle and Beast have adjourned to the balcony under a starry night.
Both of them perch on a railing. Beast goes near Belle and gives a bashful smile. He holds Belle's hand.

BEAST : Belle? Are you happy here with me?

BELLE : Yes.

She looks off into the distance.

BEAST : What is it?

BELLE : (looks at him desperately) If only I could see my father again, just for a moment. I miss him so much.

Beast looks disappointed for a moment then excited.

BEAST : There is a way.

The pair adjourn to Beast's lair where Beast hands Belle the Magic Mirror. Belle's face is reflected in the mirror.

시간 속에 흘러온 오래된 이야기
노래 속에 녹아온 선율같은 사랑
미녀와 야수

벨이 야수의 가슴에 몸을 기댄다. 행복해 보이는 두 사람.

포트 부인 : (노래하며) *시간 속에 흘러온 오래된 이야기 노래 속에 녹아온 선율같은 사랑, 미녀와 야수*
(칩에게) 이제 들어가 자렴, 얘야. 잠잘 시간이 이미 지났네. 잘 자거라.

칩이 받침대 밖으로 내려와 이내 방을 나간다. 하지만 한번 이라도 더 보려고 다시 돌아온다.
문이 열리고 야수와 벨이 발코니로 나온다.
둘은 별이 쏟아지는 밤 하늘 아래 발코니 쪽으로 간다.
발코니 난간에 걸터앉은 두 사람. 야수는 벨에게 가까이 다가가며 수줍은 미소를 짓는다. 벨의 손을 잡는 야수.

야 수 : 벨, 여기서 나와 있는 게 행복하오?
벨 : 그럼요.

그녀는 이내 고개를 저만치 돌린다.

야 수 : 왜 그러오?
벨 : (절박한 눈으로 야수를 보며) 아빠를 다시 볼 수 있다면 좋겠어요, 잠시만이라도. 아빠가 너무 보고 싶어요.

야수는 잠시 실망한 모습을 보이다 이내 들뜬 목소리로 말한다.

야 수 : 방법이 있소.

둘은 야수의 방으로 자리를 옮긴다. 야수는 벨의 손에 마법의 거울을 쥐어준다. 벨의 얼굴이 거울에 반사되어 보인다.

- **rhyme**
  각운
  If one word rhymes with another or if two words rhyme, they have a very similar sound. Words that rhyme with each other are often used in poems

- **adjourn to**
  자리를 옮기다
  If someone adjourn to somewhere, they move to a different place

- **starry**
  별이 총총한
  A starry night or sky is one in which a lot of stars are visible

- **bashful**
  수줍은
  Someone who is bashful is shy and easily embarrassed

It's past your bedtime.
past는 시간이 지났음을 나타내는 전치사의 역할도 할 수 있다.
ex) It's ten past eleven.

Zoom In

It's past your bedtime.
잠잘 시간이 이미 지났네.

BEAST : This mirror will show you anything. Anything you wish to see.

BELLE : (hesitantly) I'd like to see my father, please.

The Magic Mirror shines into life, and Belle turns her head away as it flashes. Then it reveals Maurice fallen in the woods, coughing and lost. Belle is shocked. Beast looks at her with concern.

BELLE : Papa. Oh, no. He's sick. He may be dying. And he's all alone.

Beast turns, then looks at the rose, deep in thought.

BEAST : Then... you... you must go to him.

BELLE : What did you say?

BEAST : I release you. You are no longer my prisoner.

BELLE : (in amazement) You mean... I'm free?

BEAST : Yes.

BELLE : Oh, thank you. (to Magic Mirror) Hold on, Papa. I'm on my way.

Belle turns to leave, then turns back and pushes the Magic Mirror back to Beast.
Beast doesn't receive the mirror. He says sadly, smoothing Belle's hair...

BEAST : Take it with you, so you'll always have a way to look back and remember me.

BELLE : Thank you for understanding how much he needs me.

Belle turns to leave and Beast looks down in depression. We see Belle's skirt fly past Cogsworth who has entered the room.

야 수 : 이 거울로 그 어떤 것도 볼 수 있소. 보고 싶은 것은 무엇이든 다.

벨 : (망설이며) 아빠가 보고 싶어요.

마법의 거울이 살아나며 번쩍이자 벨은 눈이 부셔 고개를 돌린다. 그런 다음 거울이 숲에서 헤매고 있는 모리스의 모습을 보여준다. 모리스는 기침을 하며 길을 잃은 모습이다. 벨은 충격을 받고 야수는 걱정스런 눈빛으로 그녀를 바라본다.

벨 : 아빠, 이런. 아빠가 아파요. 돌아가실지도 몰라요. 지금 혼자계시단 말이에요.

야수는 고개를 돌려 장미를 바라본다. 생각에 잠긴 야수.

야 수 : 그렇다면, 그에게 돌아가야죠.

벨 : 뭐라구요?

야 수 : 당신을 풀어주는 거요. 더 이상 나의 성에 갇혀 있지 않아도 되요.

벨 : (놀라며) 제가 자유로운 몸이라구요?

야 수 : 그렇소.

벨 : 오, 고마워요. (마법의 거울을 보며) 기다리세요, 아빠. 내가 지금 가요.

벨은 떠나려 하다 다시 몸을 돌려 마법의 거울을 야수에게 주려 한다.
야수는 거울을 받지 않는다. 벨의 머리를 어루만지며 슬프게 말한다.

야 수 : 그 거울 가져가시오. 있었던 일을 언제든지 되돌아보며 나를 기억할 수 있도록.

벨 : 아빠를 나를 얼마나 필요로 하는지 이해해줘서 고마워요.

벨은 떠나려 몸을 돌리고 야수는 절망에 고개를 떨군다. 벨의 치마가 막 방으로 들어온 콕스워즈를 스치며 지나간다.

- **concern**
  걱정
  Concern is worry about a situation

- **release**
  놓아주다
  If a person or animal is released from somewhere where they have been locked up or looked after, they are set free or allowed to go

- **smooth**
  어루만지다
  If you smooth something, you move your hands over its surface to make it smooth and flat

- **depression**
  절망
  Depression is a mental state in which you are sad and feel that you cannot enjoy anything, because your situation is so difficult and unpleasant

Hold on, Papa. I'm on my way.
Hold on.은 기다려달라는 뜻으로, 전화상으로도 자주 사용되는 표현이니 기억해두자. on one's way는 '~하는 도중이다, 가까워지다'라는 뜻의 숙어이다.

Zoom In

Hold on, Papa. I'm on my way.

기다리세요, 아빠. 내가 지금 가요.

COGSWORTH : Well, your Highness, I must say everything is going just swimmingly. I knew you had it in you.

BEAST : (very sad) I let her go.

COGSWORTH : Ha ha ha ...yes yes. Splend...

Cogsworth stops in the middle of his sentence.

COGSWORTH : You what? How could you do that?

BEAST : I had to.

COGSWORTH : (still amazed) Yes, but why?

BEAST : Because... I love her.

Cut to Cogsworth telling the rest of the Objects about Beast's decision. All the objects are disappointed.

ALL (EX. COGSWORTH) : He did what?!?!

COGSWORTH : Yes, I'm afraid it's true.

CHIP : She's going away?

LUMIERE : But he was so close.

MRS. POTTS : After all this time, he's finally learned to love.

LUMIERE : That's it then. That should break the spell.

MRS. POTTS : But it's not enough. She has to love him in return.

COGSWORTH : And now it's too late.

Belle rides on Phillipe and gets out of the castle.
Cut to Beast watching Belle leave from above. He roars in sorrow and anger. His roar turns into the sound of the wind. Belle is out in the snow calling out "Papa?" Finally, she finds him face down in a snowbank. They return home Lefou is still waiting disguised as a snowman.
Belle and Maurice enter their cottage. Lefou shakes the snow off his face.

콕스워즈: 주인님! 모든 것이 순조롭게 돌아가는 것 같군요. 잘 하실 줄 알았다구요.
야 수: (아주 슬프게) 그녀를 보내줬어.
콕스워즈: 하하하, 그래요. 아주 잘…

콕스워즈는 하던 말을 멈춘다.

콕스워즈: 어떻게 하셨다구요? 어떻게 그러실 수 있죠?
야 수: 그럴 수 밖에 없었어.
콕스워즈: (여전히 놀란 목소리로) 그래요, 하지만 왜요?
야 수: 왜냐하면… 그녀를 사랑하니까.

콕스워즈가 다른 신하들 모두에게 야수의 결심을 말하는 모습이 보인다. 모두가 실망한다.

모두(콕스워즈를 제외하고) : 주인님이 뭘 하셨다고?
콕스워즈: 안타깝지만 사실이라구.
칩 : 아가씨가 떠나는 거에요?
루미에르 : 하지만 거의 다 됐는데…
포트 부인 : 이제야 사랑을 알게 되었는데.
루미에르 : 그렇다면 마법이 풀려야죠.
포트 부인 : 하지만 그걸로는 충분하지 않지. 그녀 또한 그를 사랑해야지.
콕스워즈: 이젠 너무 늦어버렸네.

벨은 필립을 타고 성 밖으로 나온다.
저 위에서 야수는 벨이 떠나는 것을 지켜보고 있다. 슬픔과 분통함에 울부짖는다.
그의 울음소리가 바람소리가 된다. 벨은 아빠를 찾으며 눈 위를 가다가, 마침내 눈더미 위에 쓰러진 그를 발견한다. 그들은 집으로 돌아온다. 르푸가 눈사람으로 가장한 채 그들을 기다리고 있다.
벨과 모리스는 집으로 들어간다. 르푸는 얼굴을 덮고 있는 눈을 털어낸다.

- **Highness**
  주인님, 전하
  Expressions such as 'Your Highness' or 'His Highness' are used to address or refer to a member of the royal family
- **decision**
  결정
  When you make a decision, you choose what should be done or which is the best of various possible actions
- **sorrow**
  슬픔
  Sorrow is a feeling of deep sadness or regret

How could you do that?
How could you do that?은 어떻게 그럴 수가 있냐며 상대방을 원망할 때 쓰는 표현이다. How could you?, How is that possible?, How can you do it?과도 바꾸어 쓸 수 있다.

Zoom In

How could you do that?
어떻게 그러실 수 있죠?

LEFOU : Oh, they're back.

EXT. BELLE'S COTTAGE
Cut to black. Maurice sees Belle as his eyes open.

MAURICE : Belle?

BELLE : It's all right, Papa. I'm home.

Belle flings her arms around her father.

MAURICE : I thought I'd never see you again.

BELLE : I missed you so much.

MAURICE : But the Beast. Did you... How did you escape?

BELLE : I didn't escape, Papa. He let me go.

MAURICE : That horrible beast?

BELLE : But he's different, now. Papa! He's changed somehow.

There is sound coming from Belle's pack. The flap opens and the Magic Mirror falls out with Chip rolling to a stop on it.

CHIP : Hi!

BELLE : Oh, a stowaway.

Chip jumps on Maurice's blanket. Maurice puts Chip on his palm and grins at him.

MAURICE : Why hello there, little fella. Didn't think I'd see you again.

Chip turns to Belle with a look of question on his face.

르 푸 : 돌아왔군.

외부. 벨의 집
화면이 어두워졌다가 밝아진다. 모리스의 눈이 떠지면서 벨이 보인다.

모리스 : 벨.
벨 : 괜찮아요. 아빠. 저 집에 왔어요.

벨은 아빠를 안는다.

모리스 : 다시는 너를 못 보는 줄 알았어.
벨 : 아빠가 너무 보고 싶었어요.
모리스 : 하지만 야수는… 너… 어떻게 탈출한거냐?
벨 : 탈출한게 아니에요. 아빠. 저를 가도록 해줬어요.
모리스 : 그 끔찍한 야수가?
벨 : 하지만 지금은 그렇지 않아요. 이젠 달라졌다구요.

벨의 짐가방에서 어떤 소리가 들린다. 가방이 열리자 마법의 거울과 칩이 굴러나오며, 칩이 거울 위에 멈춘다.

칩 : 안녕!
벨 : 오, 너도 몰래 따라 왔구나.

칩이 모리스의 이불 위로 올라온다. 모리스는 손 위에 칩을 놓고 그를 보며 방긋 웃는다.

모리스 : 안녕, 꼬마야. 너를 다시 보게 될 줄은 몰랐는걸.

칩은 궁금한 표정으로 벨을 바라본다.

- **escape**
  탈출하다
  If you escape from a place, you succeed in getting away from it
- **horrible**
  끔찍한
  If you describe something or someone as horrible, you do not like them at all
- **flap**
  덮개
  A flap of cloth or skin, for example, is a flat piece of it that can move freely up and down or from side to side because it is held or attached by only one edge
- **blanket**
  담요
  A blanket is a large square or rectangular piece of thick cloth, especially one which you put on a bed to keep yourself warm
- **fella**
  남자
  You can refer to a man as a fellow or fella

I thought I'd never see you again.
자신의 생각을 이야기 할 때에는 I think(though)~로 문장을 시작한다. see one again은 '~를 다시 보다'라는 뜻의 숙어이다.

Zoom In

I thought I'd never see you again.
다시는 너를 못 보는 줄 알았어.

CHIP : Belle, why'd you go away? Don't you like us anymore?

BELLE : Oh, Chip. Of course I do. It's just that...

There is a knocking at the door. Belle opens it and Monsieur Doctor stands on the porch.

BELLE : May I help you?

DOCTOR : I've come to collect your father.

He steps aside to show the Asylum D'Loons wagon behind him.

BELLE : My father?

D'ARQUE : Don't worry, Mademoiselle. We'll take good care of him.

Belle gets shocked and angry. She comes out of the cottage.

BELLE : My father's not crazy.

Lefou swings a torch and stirs up the crowd.

LEFOU : (emerging from the crowd) He was raving like a lunatic. We all heard him, didn't we!

BYSTANDERS : Yeah!

Gaston folds his arms and gives a twisted smile. A man comes out of the wagon.

BELLE : No, I won't let you.

Maurice has emerged from the home.

칩 : 벨, 왜 성을 떠나 온 거죠? 우리가 싫어진거에요?
벨 : 오, 칩! 물론 그런게 아니지. 그건 단지…

문에서 노크하는 소리가 들린다. 벨이 문을 열자 의사가 서 있다.

벨 : 무슨 일이죠?
의 사 : 아버님을 모시러 왔소이다.

그는 옆으로 비껴서서 뒤에 서 있는 정신병원의 마차를 보여준다.

벨 : 우리 아빠를요?
의 사 : 걱정마요. 아가씨. 아버지를 잘 보살피겠소이다.

벨은 충격을 받아서 화가 났다. 그녀는 집 밖으로 나갔다.

벨 : 우리 아빠는 미치지 않았어요.

르푸는 횃불을 휘저으며 사람들을 선동한다.

르 푸 : (사람들 속에서 나오며) 미치광이처럼 지껄이는 걸. 우리는 다 들었다구. 그렇지 않나?
구경꾼 : 맞아!

개스톤은 팔짱을 끼고 야릇한 미소를 짓는다. 한 남자가 마차 밖으로 나온다.

벨 : 안 돼, 그러도록 내버려 두지 않을 거야.

모리스가 집 밖으로 나온다.

- **collect**
  데리러 가다
  When you collect someone or something, you go and get them from the place where they are waiting for you or have been left for you

- **stir up**
  선동하다
  to cause trouble, especially by making people feel strong emotions

- **crowd**
  사람들, 군중
  A crowd is a large group of people who have gathered together, for example to watch or listen to something interesting, or to protest about something

- **twisted**
  뒤틀린
  Something that is twisted is curled up and not straight

We'll take good care of him.
take care of는 '돌보다, 보살피다'라는 뜻의 동사구로 care for, look after와도 같은 의미이다.
ex) He really doesn't look after his health.

Zoom In

We'll take good care of him.
아버지를 잘 보살피겠소이다.

MAURICE : Belle?

LEFOU : Ah, Maurice. Tell us again, old man, just how big was the Beast?

Maurice tries to explain Beast.

MAURICE : (struggling) Well, he was... I mean, he was... he was... enormous. I'd I'd... say at least eight... no, more like ten feet.

Crowd laughs at him.

LEFOU : Well, you don't get much crazier than that.

Maurice comes down the stairs and says it's unjust.

MAURICE : It's true, I tell you!

Doctor waves his arms and Orderlies move in and pick up Maurice.

LEFOU : Get him out of here!

MAURICE : Let go of me!

Gaston has been watching from the sides, standing near Doctor.

BELLE : (to Doctor) No, you can't do this!

Doctor shakes her off and walks away.
Gaston puts his arms around Belle.

GASTON : Tsk, tsk, tsk. Poor Belle. It's a shame about your father.

BELLE : You know he's not crazy, Gaston.

모리스 : 벨?
르 푸 : 아, 모리스! 자, 그 야수가 얼마나 컸는지 다시 한번 얘기해 보겠나, 이 양반아?

모리스는 야수에 대해 설명하려고 한다.

모리스 : (설명하려 애쓰며) 그게 말이지, 야수는 어마어마하게 컸지. 적어도 8피트, 아니지 10피트는 될거야.

사람들이 그를 향해 웃는다.

르 푸 : 이렇게 미친 양반은 처음보네.

모리스는 계단을 내려와 불공평한 처사라고 말한다.

모리스 : 사실이라구. 진짜야.

의사가 손짓을 하자, 똘마니들이 모리스를 데리고 간다.

르 푸 : 데리고 가!
모리스 : 날 놔줘!

개스톤은 의사의 옆에 서서 이 장면을 지켜보고 있다

벨 : (의사에게) 안돼요. 이럴 순 없어요.

의사는 벨을 밀쳐낸 후, 멀어져간다.
개스톤은 팔로 벨을 감싼다.

개스톤 : 쯧쯧쯧. 가엾은 벨. 당신 아버지 일은 안됐어.
벨 : 우리 아빠가 미치지 않았다는 걸 당신은 알잖아요, 개스톤.

- **explain**
  설명하다
  If you explain something, you give details about it or describe it so that it can be understood

- **enormous**
  거대한
  Something that is enormous is extremely large in size or amount

- **feet**
  피트
  A foot is a unit for measuring length, height, or depth, and is equal to 12 inches or 30.48 centimetres. When you are giving measurements, the form 'foot' is often used as the plural instead of the plural form 'feet'

- **unjust**
  부당한
  If you describe an action, system, or law as unjust, you think that it treats a person or group badly in a way that they do not deserve

It's a shame about your father.
It's a shame은 '유감이다'라는 뜻을 나타낸다. 그밖에도 유감을 표하는 말로 I'm afraid~, I'm sorry~, It's a pity~, I regret~등이 있다.

Zoom In

It's a shame about your father.
당신 아버지 일은 안 됐어.

Gaston scratches his face idly and says archly.

GASTON : I might be able to clear up this little misunderstanding if...

BELLE : If what?

GASTON : If you marry me.

BELLE : What?

Gaston brings his face close to Belle's and talks to Belle in low voice.

GASTON : One little word, Belle. That's all it takes.

BELLE : Never!

GASTON : Have it your way. (turns and walks away slowly)

People try to put Maurice into the wagon. Maurice struggles not to get into the wagon.

MAURICE : (being thrown into the wagon) Belle? (she runs back into the house) Let go of me!

Belle comes back out with Magic Mirror. She yells to the crowd.

BELLE : My father's not crazy and I can prove it! (to mirror) Show me the Beast!

Magic Mirror again shines then produces the image of the still-depressed Beast. The crowd oohs and aahs at it. Gaston seems to be astonished.

WOMAN 1 : Is it dangerous?

개스톤은 자신의 얼굴을 멋쩍은 듯 긁으며 능글맞게 말한다.

개스톤 : 내가 이 오해를 풀수도 있을 것 같은데… 만약…

벨 : 만약에 뭐요?

개스톤 : 만약 당신이 나와 결혼을 한다면 말이오.

벨 : 뭐라구요?

개스톤은 자신의 얼굴을 벨의 얼굴에 가까이 가져다 대고 낮은 목소리로 말한다.

개스톤 : 한 마디만 하면 돼, 벨. 결혼하겠다고. 그게 전부라고.

벨 : 절대 그러진 않을거에요.

개스톤 : 마음대로 하시지. (몸을 돌려 유유히 멀어진다)

사람들이 모리스를 마차에 태우려 한다. 모리스는 들어가지 않으려 몸부림친다.

모리스 : (마차에 던져지며) 벨? (벨이 급하게 집안으로 뛰어 들어간다) 날 놔줘!

벨이 마법의 거울을 손에 들고 돌아온다. 사람들을 향해 소리치는 벨.

벨 : 우리 아빠는 미치지 않았어요. 내가 증명할 수 있다구요. (거울을 보며) 야수를 보여줘.

마법의 거울이 다시 한번 반짝이자, 아직도 풀이 죽어있는 야수의 모습이 보인다. 그것을 본 사람들이 놀란다. 개스톤도 아주 놀란 듯한 모습이다.

여성 1 : 위험한 야수 아니에요?

- **archly**
  능글맞게
  in an arch manner

- **misunderstand**
  오해하다
  If you misunderstand someone or something, you do not understand them properly

- **prove**
  증명하다
  If something proves to be true or to have a particular quality, it becomes clear after a period of time that it is true or has that quality

- **produce**
  보여주다
  If you produce an object from somewhere, you show it or bring it out so that it can be seen

Have it your way.
have one's way는 '마음대로 하다'라는 숙어이므로, Have it your way.는 좋을 대로, 네 맘대로 하라는 표현이 된다. Do as you please. Suit yourself. See if I care.등과 바꾸어 쓸 수 있다.

Zoom In

Have it your way.
마음대로 하시지.

BELLE : (trying to reassure her) Oh, no. He'd never hurt anyone. Please, I know he looks vicious but he's really kind and gentle. He's my friend.

Gaston catches Belle by the shoulder and turns her around.

GASTON : If I didn't know better I'd think you had feelings for this monster.

BELLE : He's no monster, Gaston. You are!

GASTON : She's as crazy as the old man.

He grabs the Mirror from her hand.
Gaston threatens villagers with the mirror. Women seem to be frightened.

GASTON : The Beast will make off with your children! He'll come after them in the night.

BELLE : No!

Gaston swings the Mirror and leads villagers.

GASTON : We're not safe 'til his head is mounted on my wall! I say we kill the Beast!

Mob cheers him and repeats the words "kill him".
All villagers agree with Gaston's idea.

MAN 1 : We're not safe until he's dead.

MAN 2 : He'll come stalking us at night!

WOMAN 1 : Set to sacrifice our children to his monstrous appetite!

벨 : (안심 시키며) 아니요. 절대 누구를 해친 적이 없어요. 무섭게 보이지만, 매우 친절하고 신사다워요. 제 친구에요.

개스톤이 그녀의 어깨를 잡고 그녀의 몸을 자신을 향해 돌린다.

개스톤 : 내가 잘은 모르지만, 내 생각엔 그 괴물을 좋아한다는 의미로 들리는군.

벨 : 그는 괴물이 아니에요. 개스톤. 바로 당신이 괴물이지!

개스톤 : 자기 아빠처럼 미쳤군.

그는 마법의 거울을 손에 쥔다.
그 거울을 가지고 마을 사람들을 겁주는 개스톤. 여성들이 겁을 먹는 모습이다.

개스톤 : 야수가 당신의 아이들을 해칠지 몰라. 한밤중에 쫓아와서 말이야.

벨 : 아니에요.

개스톤은 거울을 흔들며 마을 사람들을 선동한다.

개스톤 : 야수를 죽이기 전엔 우린 안전하지 않아. 야수를 죽여버리자.

사람들이 개스톤을 응원하며 "야수를 죽이자"라는 말을 반복한다.
모든 마을 사람들이 개스톤의 생각에 동의를 하고 있다.

남자 1 : 야수가 죽기전까지 우린 안전하지 않아.

남자 2 : 밤에 우리를 몰래 따라 올지도 몰라.

여자 1 : 우리 아이들로 그 괴물같은 식욕을 채우려들지도 몰라.

- **vicious**
  포악한
  A vicious person or a vicious blow is violent and cruel
- **villager**
  마을 사람
  You refer to the people who live in a village, especially the people who have lived there for most or all of their lives, as the villagers
- **sacrifice**
  희생하다
  If you sacrifice something that is valuable or important, you give it up, usually to obtain something else for yourself or for other people
- **appetite**
  식욕
  Your appetite is your desire to eat

We're not safe until he's dead.
not ~ until~은 '~하기까지는 ~하지 않다'는 의미이므로, 곧 '~하고 나서야 비로소 ~하다'라는 의미를 함축한다. 즉 위 문장은 야수가 죽어야 우리가 안전할 수 있다는 의미이다.

Zoom In

We're not safe until he's dead.
야수가 죽기 전까지 우린 안전하지 않아.

MAN 3 : He'll wreak havoc on our village if we let him wander free.

Gaston takes away someone's torch and lifts it up.

GASTON : (singing) *SO IT'S TIME TO TAKE SOME ACTION, BOYS!*
IT'S TIME TO FOLLOW ME!

Gaston throws a torch into a haystack creating an instant bonfire. He begins to prance around it warning of the dangers of the horrible Beast.

GASTON : (singing) *THROUGH THE MIST, THROUGH THE WOODS*
THROUGH THE DARKNESS AND THE SHADOWS
IT'S A NIGHTMARE BUT IT'S ONE EXCITING RIDE
SAY A PRAYER, THEN WE'RE THERE
AT THE DRAWBRIDGE OF A CASTLE
AND THERE'S SOMETHING TRULY TERRIBLE INSIDE

Gaston chases Lefou around mimicking a monster.

GASTON : (singing) *IT'S A BEAST*
HE'S GOT FANGS, RAZOR SHARP ONES
MASSIVE PAWS
KILLER CLAWS FOR THE FEAST

Magic Mirror shows the face of Beast to Lefou which Gaston exaggerates about.

GASTON : (singing) *HEAR HIM ROAR, SEE HIM FOAM*
BUT WE'RE NOT COMING HOME
TILL HE'S DEAD, GOOD AND DEAD, KILL THE BEAST!
KILL THE BEAST!

남자 3 : 야수가 활개치게 내버려 두면 우리 마을에 큰 피해를 가져올거야.

개스톤은 누군가의 횃불을 빼앗아 높이 든다.

개스톤 : (노래하며) *자, 이제 행동으로 보여줘야 할 때다*
나를 따르라!

개스톤이 횃불을 건초더미 위에 던지자, 곧바로 모닥불이 지펴진다. 개스톤은 그 주의를 활보하며 끔찍한 야수의 위험함을 사람들에게 경고하는 노래를 부른다.

개스톤 : (노래하며) *안개를 헤치고, 숲을 따라*
어둠속을 걷는 것은
무서운 일이긴 하지만 흥분되는 일이라네
기도를 한 다음, 그 성에 도착하겠지
성의 다리 앞에 말이야
바로 그 성 안에 진짜 무서운 것이 있지

개스톤은 괴물 흉내를 내며 르푸를 쫓는다.

개스톤 : (노래하며) *바로 그 야수라네*
야수의 이빨은 아주 날카로워
어마어마한 손을 가졌고
만찬을 위한 날카로운 발톱이 있지

마법의 거울이 르푸에게 야수의 얼굴을 보여준다. 개스톤이 과장하여 설명하고 있는 그 얼굴이다.

개스톤 : (노래하며) *포효하는 소리를 들어봐. 입에 거품 무는 모습 좀 봐*
하지만 우린 마을로 돌아오지 않을거야
저 야수를 죽이기 전에는. 야수를 죽이자!

- **havoc**
  대 파괴
  Havoc is great disorder, and confusion

- **wander**
  돌아다니다
  If you wander in a place, you walk around there in a casual way, often without intending to go in any particular direction

- **nightmare**
  악몽
  A nightmare is a very frightening dream

- **massive**
  거대한
  Something that is massive is very large in size, quantity, or extent

- **claw**
  발톱
  The claws of a bird or animal are the thin, hard, curved nails at the end of its feet

So it's time to take some action, boys!
'It's time to 동사원형'은 '~할 시간이다'라는 숙어라는 점은 살펴보았다. take action은 "조치를 취하다, 행동하다"라는 숙어이며, take measures 와도 같은 의미이므로 둘 다 기억해 두자.

Zoom In

So it's time to take some action, boys!
자, 이제 행동으로 보여줘야 할 때다.

Belle tries to stop him clinging to his sleeve.

BELLE : (interjecting) No, I won't let you do this.

GASTON : If you're not with us you're against us. Bring the old man.

MAURICE : Get your hands off me!

Gaston throws them into the basement and bolts the door.

GASTON : We can't have them running off to warn the creature!

BELLE : Let us out!

GASTON : (to the crowd) We'll rid the village of this Beast. Who's with me?

A chorus of "I am"s comes from the Crowd.

MOB : (singing) *LIGHT YOUR TORCH, MOUNT YOUR HORSE!*

Gaston hops onto the horse and leads the crowd. Villagers are following Gaston.

GASTON : (singing) *SCREW YOUR COURAGE TO THE STICKING PLACE*

MOB : (singing) *WE'RE COUNTING ON GASTON TO LEAD THE WAY!*
THROUGH A MIST, TO A WOOD
WHERE WITHIN A HAUNTED CASTLE
SOMETHING'S LURKING THAT YOU DON'T SEE EVERY DAY!

Gaston leads the Mob through the town and out into the forest. They start chopping trees in preparation for their assault on the castle.

벨이 개스톤에게 매달려 그를 막으려 한다.

벨 : (말을 가로채며) 안 돼. 이럴 순 없어.
개스톤 : 당신이 우리를 따르지 않는다면, 우리 적이지. 그 영감을 데려와.
모리스 : 날 건들지 말게.

개스톤은 모리스와 벨을 지하실에 넣고 빗장을 걸어 잠근다.

개스톤 : 저들이 야수에게 알리지 못하게 해야 돼.
벨 : 우릴 내보내 줘요.
개스톤 : (군중에게) 야수로부터 마을을 지키자. 누가 나와 함께 할건가?

군중에서 "내가 함께 하겠소" 라는 들린다.

군 중 : (노래하며) *횃불을 밝히고, 말을 타고 나가자*

개스톤은 말을 타고 군중을 이끈다. 마을 사람들이 개스톤을 따라간다.

개스톤 : (노래하며) *용기 단단히 내시고*
군 중 : (노래하며) *우린 개스톤이 길을 잘 안내해 줄 것을 믿는다네*
안개를 헤치고, 숲을 따라
유령의 성이 있는 곳으로
평소에는 보지 못하는 무언가가 도사리고 있는 곳으로

개스톤은 군중을 이끌고 마을을 빠져나와 숲으로 간다. 그 숲에서 성을 공격하기 위한 준비로 나무를 자르기 시작한다.

- **creature**
  생물
  You can refer to any living thing that is not a plant as a creature, especially when it is of an unknown or unfamiliar kind
- **rid**
  제거하다
  If you rid a place or person of something undesirable or unwanted, you succeed in removing it completely from that place or person
- **courage**
  용기
  Courage is the quality shown by someone who decides to do something difficult or dangerous, even though they may be afraid
- **lurk**
  숨어있다
  If someone lurks somewhere, they wait there secretly so that they cannot be seen, usually because they intend to do something bad

Who's with me?
Who's with me?는 누가 나와 함께 하겠냐고 묻는 표현이므로, 자신의 편에 서겠는지, 자신을 따르겠는지를 묻는 의미를 가지고 있다.

Zoom In

Who's with me?

누가 나와 함께 할 건가?

MOB : (singing) *IT'S A BEAST*
ONE AS TALL AS A MOUNTAIN!
WE WON'T REST
TILL HE'S GOOD AND DECEASED!
SALLY FORTH, TALLY HO
GRAB YOUR SWORD, GRAB YOUR BOW
PRAISE THE LORD AND HERE WE GO!

GASTON : We'll lay siege to the castle and bring back his head!

INT. IN THE BASEMENT

Cut to int of basement where Belle is prying at the window with a stick.

BELLE : I have to warn the Beast. This is all my fault. Oh, Papa. What are we going to do?

MAURICE : (comforting her) Now, now. We'll think of something.

We see Chip looking in through the window. He turns around, thinking and then he sees Maurice's contraption with the axe on the end of it.
Chip is excited to find the axe and cries "Oh!".
Villagers march through the forest. They keep singing and marching.

MOB : (singing) *WE DON'T LIKE-WHAT WE DON'T UNDERSTAND*
IN FACT, IT SCARES US
AND THIS MONSTER IS MYSTERIOUS AT LEAST!

Gaston and villagers cut down trees with axes. They carry logs on their shoulders and march in a line.

MOB : (singing) *BRING YOUR GUNS, BRING YOUR KNIVES*
SAVE YOUR CHILDREN AND YOUR WIVES
WE'LL SAVE OUR VILLAGE AND OUR LIVES
WE'LL KILL THE BEAST!

군 중 : (노래하며) *괴물이야*
산처럼 거대한
우린 안심할 수 없어
그가 죽기 전까지는
빠르게 공격해, 위험을 알리는 신호를 줘
칼을 잡고 활을 쥐고
신이시여, 우리가 갑니다!

개스톤 : 성을 포위해 야수의 머리를 가져오자!

내부. 지하실
벨이 막대기로 창 밖을 엿보고 있는 지하실의 모습

벨 : 야수에게 알려야 해. 이게 모두 다 내 잘못이야. 오, 아빠. 우리 어쩌면 좋죠?

모리스 : (딸을 위로하며) 자, 생각 좀 해보자.

칩이 창문을 통해 그들을 보고 있다. 생각을 하며 뒤를 돌았다가 모리스가 발명한 기계를 보게 된다. 그 기계의 끝에는 도끼가 달려 있다.
칩은 그 도끼를 발견해 신이 나서 "오!" 하고 외친다.
마을 사람들이 숲을 가로질러 전진한다. 노래를 부르며 나아가는 사람들.

군 중 : (노래하며) *우린 우리가 이해하지 못하는*
건 딱 질색이지
그런 건 우릴 두렵게 한단 말이야
이 야수는 좋게 말해서 미스테리하지

개스톤과 마을 사람들은 도끼로 나무를 자른다. 어깨에 통나무를 매고 줄을 지어 전진한다.

군 중 : (노래하며) *총을 가져와, 칼을 가져와*
아이들과 아내를 지키자
우리 마을과 우리 목숨을 지키자
야수를 죽이자!

- **decease**
  죽다
  a more formal word for die
- **praise**
  찬송하다
  If you praise God, you express your respect, honour, and thanks to God
- **siege**
  포위
  A siege is a military or police operation in which soldiers or police surround a place in order to force the people there to come out or give up control of the place
- **warn**
  경고하다
  If you warn someone about something such as a possible danger or problem, you tell them about it so that they are aware of it
- **mysterious**
  기이한
  Someone or something that is mysterious is strange and is not known or understood

This is all my fault.
fault는 잘못이라는 뜻으로, It's (This is) all my fault.는 모두 내 잘못이라며 자책할 때 자주 쓰이는 표현이다. My bad. I was in error. I did wrong.과도 같은 의미이다.

Zoom In

This is all my fault.
이게 모두 내 잘못이야.

INT. IN THE CASTLE

COGSWORTH : I knew it! I knew it was foolish to get our hopes up.

LUMIERE : Maybe it would have been better if she had never come at all.

Footstool comes in barking. They rush over to the window expecting the return of Belle.

LUMIERE : Could it be?

MRS. POTTS : Is it she?

Gaston and villagers are striding ahead and coming into the castle.

LUMIERE : (realizing the Mob is not Belle) Sacrebleu! I invaders!

COGSWORTH : Encroachers!

MRS. POTTS : (seeing Gaston) And they have the mirror!

COGSWORTH : (issuing orders) Warn the master. If it's a fight they want, we'll be ready for them.

Cogsworth turns around from window.

COGSWORTH : Who's with me? Aahh!

The door is slammed as the rest of the Objects leave Cogsworth behind.

GASTON : Take whatever booty you can find but remember the Beast is mine!

Cut to stairway where Objects are marching down to do battle with the Mob.

내부. 성 안

콕스워즈 : 내 이럴 줄 알았다구. 희망을 갖는 것 자체가 바보같은 일인 걸 알았어.

루미에르 : 벨이 아예 오지 않았더라면 좋았을텐데.

풋스툴이 짖으며 창 쪽으로 간다. 모두들 벨이 돌아왔나 기대하며 창밖을 내다본다.

루미에르 : 과연?

포트 부인 : 벨인가?

개스톤과 마을 사람들이 성큼성큼 성으로 오고있다.

루미에르 : (벨이 아닌 것을 알고는) 제기랄, 침입자야!

콕스워즈 : 침입자들!

포트 부인 : (개스톤을 보고) 그리고 저들이 마법의 거울을 가지고 있네.

콕스워즈 : (명령을 내리며) 주인님께 알려. 저들이 싸우려고 하는 거라면, 우리도 준비를 해야지.

콕스워즈는 고개를 돌린다.

콕스워즈 : 누가 나와 함께 할 건가? 아!

다른 하인들이 콕스워즈만 남겨두고 모두 떠나고 문이 닫힌다.

개스톤 : 가져가고 싶은 것은 다 가져가라. 하지만 야수는 내가 처리할거라는 걸 기억해.

군중과의 전투를 하러 하인들이 계단을 내려오는 모습이 보인다.

▪ **foolish**
바보 같은
If someone's behaviour or action is foolish, it is not sensible and shows a lack of good judgment

▪ **bark**
짖다
When a dog barks, it makes a short, loud noise, once or several times

▪ **invader**
침입자
Invaders are soldiers who are invading a country

▪ **encroacher**
침입자
someone who enters by force in order to conquer

▪ **booty**
전리품
Booty is a collection of valuable things stolen from a place, especially by soldiers after a battle

I knew it was foolish to get our hopes up.
it was foolish to~에서 'to 동사원형'이 진주어이고, it은 그것을 대신하는 가주어이다. 따라서 to부정사 이하가 foolish(어리석다)고 해석을 해주어야 한다.

Zoom In

I knew it was foolish to get our hopes up.
희망을 갖는 것 자체가 바보 같은 일이었어.

OBJECTS : (singing) *LIGHTS ABLAZE, BANNERS HIGH!*
WE GO MARCHING INTO BATTLE
UNAFRAID, ALTHOUGH THE DANGER JUST INCREASED!

Mob is trying to break open the door with a thick log.

MOB : (singing) *RAISE THE FLAG, SING THE SONG*
HERE WE COME, WE'RE FIFTY STRONG
AND FIFTY FRENCHMEN CAN'T BE WRONG
LET'S KILL THE BEAST!

하인들 : (노래하며) *심장이 뜨겁게 타오르네, 용기를 내라*
우리는 전투를 하러 가네
위험하지만 우리는 두려운 줄 모르네!

사람들이 두꺼운 통나무로 문을 부수려고 한다.

군 중 : (노래하며) *깃발을 높이 올려라, 노래를 부르라*
힘센 50명의 남자들이 간다
우리가 틀릴 리가 없어
야수를 죽이자!

- **ablaze**
  불타는 듯
  Something that is ablaze is burning very fiercely

- **march**
  행진하다
  When soldiers march somewhere, or when a commanding officer marches them somewhere, they walk there with very regular steps, as a group

- **unafraid**
  두려워하지 않는
  If you are unafraid to do something, you are confident and not at all nervous about doing it

- **flag**
  깃발
  A flag is a piece of cloth which can be attached to a pole and which is used as a sign, signal, or symbol of something, especially of a particular country

Key Expressions

220 **You don't have time to be timid.** 소심하게 굴 시간 없어요.

'time to 동사원형'은 '~할 시간'이라는 뜻이므로, 'don't have time to 동사원형'은 '~할 시간이 없다'는 부정의 의미가 된다. timid는 '소심한, 용기 없는'이라는 뜻이다.

· We don't have time to relax. The movie starts soon.
여유부릴 시간 없어요. 영화가 곧 시작한다구요.

226 **If only I could see my father again, just for a moment.**
아빠를 다시 볼 수만 있다면 좋겠어요, 잠시만이라도.

if절에 동사의 과거형이 쓰인 가정법 과거 문장이다. just for a moment는 '잠시만'이라는 숙어로, just for a while과도 같은 의미이다.

· Could you wait just for a moment, please? 잠시만 기다려주시겠습니까?

228 **I'd like to see my father, please.** 아빠가 보고 싶어요.

'would like to 동사원형'은 '~하고 싶다'는 희망을 나타내는 표현이다. 'want to 동사원형'과 같은 뜻을 나타낸다.

· I'd like to have a sound sleep. 한 숨 푹 자고 싶다.

228 Thank you for understanding how much he needs me. 아빠가 나를 얼마나 필요로 하는지 이해해줘서 고마워요.

thank for~은 '~해줘서 고맙다'는 의미로 for뒤에 명사 또는 동명사가 온다. 또한 'how much 주어+동사'는 '얼마나 ~한지'라는 의미의 의문사절이다.

· Thank you for inviting me. I'm honored to be here.
초대해주셔서 감사합니다. 이곳에 오게 되어 영광이에요.

244 We're counting on Gaston to lead the way!
우린 개스톤이 길을 잘 안내해줄 것이라고 믿는다!

count on은 '의지하다, 기대다'라는 숙어이다. 이외에도 depend on, rely on도 같은 뜻을 가진 동사구이다.

· You can count on me when in trouble. 어려운 일이 생기면 나에게 의지하렴.

248 Take whatever booty you can find but remember the Beast is mine!
가져가고 싶은 것은 다 가져가라. 하지만 야수는 내가 처리할거라는 걸 기억해.

whatever은 '~한 어떤 것, ~한 무엇'이라는 복합관계대명사이다. no matter what~으로 바꾸어 쓸 수도 있다.

· Whatever decision you made I would support it.
네가 어떤 결정을 내려도 나는 그것을 지지한다.

Chapter 10

야수, 벨의 사랑을 통해 왕자가 되다

The Beast Becomes a Prince Through Belle's Love

시간 01:14:19 ~ 01:25:51

INT. BEAST'S LAIR

Cut to int of Beast's lair, where Mrs. Potts is briefing him.

MRS. POTTS : Pardon me, Master.

BEAST : Leave me in peace.

MRS. POTTS : But Sir, the castle is under attack!

MOB : (singing) *KILL THE BEAST, KILL THE BEAST!*

People keep beating the door with the log.
The Objects have tried to block off the door, but it is being bashed in by the Mob.

LUMIERE : This isn't working!

FEATHERDUSTER : Oh, Lumiere! We must do something!

LUMIERE : Wait! I know!

MOB : (singing) *KILL THE BEAST, KILL THE BEAST!*

Cut to Beast's lair.

내부. 야수의 방
야수의 방 장면. 포트 부인이 야수에게 상황 설명을 하고 있다.

포트 부인 : 죄송합니다, 주인님.
야 수 : 날 그냥 내버려두게.
포트 부인 : 하지만 주인님, 성이 공격당하고 있어요.
사람들 : (노래하며) *야수를 죽이자. 야수를 죽이자!*

사람들은 계속해서 통나무로 문을 세게 친다.
하인들은 문을 막기 위해 노력해 보지만, 사람들은 문을 강타한다.

루미에르 : 이걸로는 안 되겠어.
빗자루: 오, 루미에르, 어떻게 좀 해봐야겠어요.
루미에르 : 잠깐, 그렇지!
사람들 : (노래하며) *야수를 죽이자. 야수를 죽이자*

야수의 방 장면.

- **brief**
보고하다
If someone briefs you, especially about a piece of work or a serious matter, they give you information that you need before you do it or consider it

- **attack**
공격
An attack is when opposing forces advance aggressively

- **log**
통나무
A log is a piece of a thick branch or of the trunk of a tree that has been cut so that it can be used for fuel or for making things

- **bash**
세게 치다
If someone bashes you, they attack you by hitting or punching you hard

MRS. POTTS : What shall we do, Master?

BEAST : (still very sad) It doesn't matter now. Just let them come.

MOB : (singing) *KILL THE BEAST, KILL THE BEAST, KILL THE BEAST!!*

The mob succeeds in breaking in and finds a grand entrance filled with assorted pieces of Furniture, Teacups, Candlesticks, Featherdusters and Clocks. They tiptoe in and Lefou unknowingly picks up Lumiere.

LUMIERE : Now!!!

All the objects spring into life attacking their human enemies.

INT. BELLE'S COTTAGE

Cut back to Belle's home, where Chip has readied the invention.

CHIP : Yes! Here we go!

Maurice looks out from the window and sees the advancing axe.

MAURICE : What the devil? Belle, look out!

The invention crashes into the door and a red cloud of smoke poofs out of the basement. Belle and Maurice emerge from the wreckage to find Chip swinging on a loose spring.

CHIP : You guys gotta try this thing.

INT. IN THE CASTLE

Cut back to the castle where the attack continues.

MRS. POTTS : Up here, you scurvy scum. Now!

포트 부인 : 어떻게 하죠? 주인님.

야 수 : (여전히 실의에 찬 목소리로) 이젠 상관없어. 그냥 내버려둬.

사람들 : (노래하며) *야수를 죽이자. 야수를 죽이자. 야수를 죽이자!*

사람들은 침입하는데 성공한다. 가구, 찻잔, 촛대, 빗자루, 시계가 넓은 출입구에 조화롭게 배치되어 있다. 사람들은 발끝으로 살금살금 걸어가고, 르푸는 모르고 루미에르를 집어 든다.

루미에르 : 지금이야!

모든 성 안의 물건들이 튀어 나와 인간 적들을 공격한다.

내부. 벨의 오두막집
벨의 오두막집 장면. 칩은 발명품을 가동시킨다.

칩 : 좋았어. 자, 간다!

모리스가 창문 밖을 내다보니 앞으로 전진 하는 도끼가 보인다.

모리스 : 저럴 수가! 벨, 피해!

발명품은 문을 부수고, 붉은 색 연기가 지하실 밖으로 날아간다. 벨과 모리스는 기계의 잔해로부터 모습을 드러내고, 칩이 느슨한 스프링에 매달려 노는 것을 본다.

칩 : 한 번 해봐요, 재밌어요.

내부. 성 안
공격이 계속되는 성 안의 장면.

포트 부인 : 여기다, 혼내줘라. 지금이다!

- **succeed**
  성공하다
  If you succeed in doing something, you manage to do it

- **assorted**
  여러 가지의, 조화로운
  A group of assorted things is a group of similar things that are of different sizes or colours or have different qualities

- **unknowingly**
  모르고
  If someone does something unknowingly, they do it without being aware of it

- **wreckage**
  잔해
  When something such as a plane, car, or building has been destroyed, you can refer to what remains as wreckage or the wreckage

It doesn't matter now.
matter에는 '중요하다'라는 의미가 있다. 따라서 It doesn't matter.라고 하면 중요하지 않다, 상관없다는 의미로 쓰인다. I don't care, It is none of my business, It has nothing to do with me.등도 같은 표현이다.

Zoom In

It doesn't matter now.
이젠 상관없어.

Meanwhile, Gaston has broken off from the mob and is searching for Beast. Belle, Maurice, Phillipe and Chip are making their way to the castle.
Gaston is looking for Beast carrying a bow and arrow. He kicks the door and looks inside.
Wardrobe puts a man in the closet and makes him change into girl's clothes. The man wearing girl's dresses screams and runs away.
Lefou threatens Lumiere with a torch. Lumiere is melting and the melted wax flows down. Cogsworth thrusts Lefou's hip with scissors. When a man pulls out Featherduster's feathers, Lumiere burns a man's hip and saves Featherduster.
Villagers are chasing after Footstool with rakes. When Footstool opens the door and enters the room villagers follow after it.

INT. IN THE KITCHEN
Knives and forks pop up from the drawers. Stove belches forth fire. Villagers hurry out and flee helter-skelter.
Finally, the invaders are chased out and the objects celebrate their victory.

COGSWORTH : And stay out!

Lumiere pulls over Cogsworth and kisses him once on each cheek. Cogsworth shakes it off.

INT. BEAST'S LAIR
Cut to Gaston, who finds Beast's lair. He raises his crossbow and takes aim. Beast looks up at him then looks back down in sadness again.
Gaston releases the arrow and it strikes Beast in the shoulder. He screams in pain and stands. Gaston rushes him and they fly out the window onto the balcony, where it has begun to rain.

GASTON : Ha ha ha ha ha!

Gaston corners Beast on the edge of the roof. Beast simply sits there in despair.

GASTON : Get up! Get up! What's the matter, Beast? Too kind and gentle to fight back?

그러는 동안 개스톤은 사람들로부터 빠져나와 야수를 찾아 나선다. 벨, 모리스, 필립과 칩은 성으로 출발한다.
개스톤은 활과 화살을 든 채 야수를 찾는다. 그는 문을 걷어차고 속안을 들여다본다.
워르브는 한 남자를 옷장에 가두고 그 안에서 그를 여자 옷으로 갈아입힌다. 여자로 변장된 남자는 소리를 지르며 도망간다.
르푸는 루미에르를 횃불로 위협한다. 루미에르가 녹으면서 촛농이 흘러내린다. 콕스워즈는 르푸의 엉덩이를 가위로 찌른다. 이번에는 한 남자가 페더더스터의 깃털을 뽑자, 루미에르는 남자의 엉덩이에 불을 지펴 페더더스터를 구해낸다.
마을 사람들은 괭이를 들고 풋스툴을 쫓아간다. 풋스툴이 문을 열고 방에 들어가자, 마을 사람들은 그 안으로 따라 들어간다.

내부. 부엌에서
칼들과 포크가 서랍에서 벌떡 일어난다. 화로는 불을 내뿜는다. 마을 사람들은 허둥지둥 도망친다.
마침내 침입자들은 쫓겨나고 성 안의 물건들은 그들의 승리를 환호한다.

콕스워즈 : 꺼져 버려라!

루미에르는 콕스워즈를 끌어 당겨 그의 양 볼에 입을 맞춘다. 콕스워즈는 그를 뿌리친다.

내부. 야수의 방
개스톤이 야수의 방을 찾는 장면. 그는 활을 들어 올려 겨눈다. 야수는 그를 올려보더니 다시 슬픔에 잠겨 뒤돌아 본다.
개스톤은 화살을 쏘고, 그 화살은 야수의 어깨에 맞는다. 그는 고통스러워서 소리를 지르며 일어선다. 개스톤이 야수에게 달려가서는, 함께 발코니 창문 밖으로 뛰쳐나간다. 비가 오기 시작한다.

개스톤 : 하하하하하!

개스톤은 야수를 지붕 끝까지 몰아세운다. 야수는 실의에 차 가만히 앉아 있다.

개스톤 : 일어나. 일어나. 일어나! 야수가 어떻게 된 거야? 친절하고 신사다워서 못 싸우나?

- **melt**
  녹다
  When a solid substance melts or when you melt it, it changes to a liquid, usually because it has been heated
- **rake**
  갈퀴
  A rake is a garden tool consisting of a row of metal or wooden teeth attached to a long handle
- **belch**
  내뿜다
  If a machine or chimney belches something such as smoke or fire or if smoke or fire belches from it, large amounts of smoke or fire come from it
- **helter-skelter**
  허둥지둥한
  You use helter-skelter to describe something that is hurried and disorganized, especially when things happen very quickly, one after the other

Too kind and gentle to fight back?
'too 형용사/부사 to 동사원형'은 ~하기에 너무 ~하다는 의미이므로, '너무 ~해서 ~할 수 없다'라는 의미를 내포한다.
ex) I'm too tired to go further.

Zoom In

Too kind and gentle to fight back?
친절하고 신사다워서 못 싸우나?

Beast looks down ignoring him. Gaston walks into the foreground and breaks off a piece of the roof. He is about to smash it on Beast's head when Belle's voice drifts up. She is on the bridge and is yelling to Gaston telling him to stop.

BELLE : No!

BEAST : (hearing her voice and giving him new life) Belle.

BELLE : No, Gaston, don't!

Gaston swings down at Beast but he catches the weapon in his hand. Beast rises up and roars in Gaston's face. They proceed through a fight on the rooftop. Finally, Beast takes a hiding place among the gargoyles in the darkness. Meanwhile, Belle enters the castle on the ground.

BELLE : Let's go, Phillipe!

It lightens and thunders. Beast and Gaston keep fighting. Belle ascends the stairs. When Gaston can't look for Beast he shouts out loudly.

GASTON : Come on out and fight! Were you in love with her, Beast? Did you honestly think she'd want you when she had someone like me?

Beast has been provoked enough. He emerges and they fight again.

GASTON : It's over, Beast! Belle is mine!

This time, however, Beast picks up Gaston by the neck and holds him out over the edge of the roof. Gaston pleads with Beast.

GASTON : Let me go. Let me go. Please, don't hurt me! I'll do anything! Anything!

Beast's anger slowly melts off his face and the look of compassion returns. He pulls Gaston back onto the roof.

야수는 그를 무시하며 땅을 내려다본다. 개스톤은 앞으로 가서 지붕 조각을 떼어 낸다. 그는 그것으로 야수의 머리를 내려치려고 할 때, 벨의 목소리가 들려온다. 그녀는 다리 위에서 개스톤에게 멈추라고 소리친다.

벨 : 안 돼요!

야 수 : (그녀의 목소리를 듣자 활기를 띠며) 벨.

벨 : 개스톤, 안 돼요!

개스톤은 야수를 내려치려 하지만, 야수는 그의 손에 있는 흉기를 잡아낸다. 야수는 일어나 개스톤의 얼굴을 향해 으르렁댄다. 그들은 옥상에서 싸움을 계속한다. 마침내 야수는 어둠 속에서 괴물 석상 뒤에 숨는다. 그러는 동안 벨은 성 안으로 들어온다.

벨 : 어서 가자, 필립!

천둥번개가 친다. 야수와 개스톤은 계속 싸움을 한다. 벨은 계단을 오른다. 개스톤은 야수를 찾을 수 없자 큰 소리로 외친다.

개스톤 : 나와서 싸우자. 야수 주제에 그녀를 사랑한다고? 정말로 그녀가 나같은 사람을 두고 널 사랑한다고 생각해?

야수는 화가 머리 끝까지 난다. 야수가 나타나고 그들은 다시 싸움을 시작한다.

개스톤 : 이제 끝이다, 야수야! 벨은 내 꺼야.

하지만 이번에 야수는 개스톤의 멱살을 잡고 들어 올려, 지붕 너머 바깥쪽으로 그를 잡아들고 있다. 개스톤은 야수에게 애원한다.

개스톤 : 내려줘, 내려줘. 제발 날 해치지 마. 뭐든지 다 할게, 뭐든!

야수의 화가 서서히 풀리고, 연민의 눈빛이 되돌아온다. 그는 개스톤을 다시 지붕 위로 끌고 들어온다.

- **foreground**
  전경
  The foreground of a picture or scene you are looking at is the part or area of it that appears nearest to you

- **weapon**
  무기
  A weapon is an object such as a gun, a knife, or a missile, which is used to kill or hurt people in a fight or a war

- **honestly**
  솔직히
  You use honestly to emphasize that you are referring to your, or someone else's, true beliefs or feelings

- **compassion**
  동정
  Compassion is a feeling of pity, sympathy, and understanding for someone who is suffering

Were you in love with her, Beast?
be in love with는 '~를 사랑하다, ~와 사랑에 빠지다'는 숙어이다. fall in love with도 자주 사용되니 함께 기억해두자.

Zoom In

Were you in love with her, Beast?
야수 주제에 그녀를 사랑한다고?

BEAST : Get out!

He shoves Gaston to the ground. Above, Belle comes out on a balcony.

BELLE : Beast!

BEAST : Belle!

Beast begins to climb the tower until he reaches the balcony. He hangs over the side.

BEAST : Belle? You came back!

Beast and Belle stare passionately at each other, but the moment is interrupted when Gaston sneaks up and stabs Beast in the back. Beast roars in pain, and Belle is helpless. Gaston pulls the knife out and swings back for another shot. Beast starts to fall knocking Gaston off his balance. Belle reaches forward and pulls Beast back, while Gaston falls off never to be seen again. Belle helps the injured Beast up onto the balcony, where he lies down on the floor. The Objects come rushing out, but stay out of sight.
Beast lies on the floor and stares at Belle. He smiles weakly. Belle strokes his face.

BEAST : Belle! You... you came back.

BELLE : Of course I came back. I couldn't let them... Oh this is all my fault. If only I'd gotten here sooner.

BEAST : Maybe it's better… it's better this way.

BELLE : Don't talk like that. You'll be all right. We're together now. Everything's going to be fine. You'll see.

BEAST : At... at least I got to see you one... last... time.

Belle pulls Beast's paw up to her cheek. He holds it there for a second then drops it. His head falls back and his eyes close. She can't believe this has happened.

야 수 : 꺼져!

그는 개스톤을 땅으로 밀친다. 위에서 벨이 발코니로 나온다.

벨 : 야수!

야 수 : 벨!

야수는 발코니에 도착할 때까지 탑을 올라간다. 그는 옆면에 매달려있다.

야 수 : 벨… 돌아왔군요.

야수와 벨은 서로를 열렬히 쳐다보지만, 개스톤이 몰래 다가와 야수를 뒤에서 찌르자 그 순간은 끝이 난다. 야수는 고통스러워서 포효하고, 벨은 어쩔 줄을 모른다. 개스톤은 칼을 빼내서 다시 한 번 찌르려고 칼을 휙 돌린다.
야수가 떨어지려고 하자, 개스톤은 균형을 잃고 떨어진다. 벨은 손을 내밀어 야수를 붙잡고, 개스톤은 땅으로 떨어져 다시는 볼 수 없게 된다. 하인들이 달려 나오지만, 먼 발치에서만 바라본다. 야수는 바닥에 누워서 벨을 바라본다. 그가 희미하게 웃는다. 벨은 그의 얼굴을 쓰다듬는다.

야 수 : 벨… 당신… 돌아왔군요.

벨 : 그래요, 돌아왔어요. 막으려 했지만… 모두 내 잘못이에요. 제가 조금만 더 일찍 왔더라면.

야 수 : 오히려 잘 된 것 같소.

벨 : 그런 말 말아요. 괜찮을 거예요. 함께 있잖아요. 이제 모두 잘 될 거예요. 두고 보세요.

야 수 : 마지막으로 당신을 이렇게 만나보게 되다니…

벨은 야수의 손을 자신의 볼에 가져다 댄다. 그는 잠시 대고 있더니, 이내 손을 떨어뜨리고 만다. 그의 머리가 땅에 떨어지고 눈이 감긴다. 그녀는 이 상황을 믿을 수 없다.

- **passionate**
  열정적인
  A passionate person has very strong feelings about something or a strong belief in something

- **interrupt**
  방해하다
  If you interrupt someone who is speaking, you say or do something that causes them to stop

- **stroke**
  쓰다듬다
  If you stroke someone or something, you move your hand slowly and gently over them

- **paw**
  손, 발
  The paws of an animal such as a cat, dog, or bear are its feet, which have claws for gripping things and soft pads for walking on

If only I'd gotten here sooner.
if절에 과거완료(had pp)가 쓰였으므로, 과거사실의 반대를 가정한 것이다. 여기서는 일찍 오지 못해서 야수가 다쳤으므로 일찍 왔더라면 그렇지 않았을 상황을 가정하는 것이다.

Zoom In

If only I'd gotten here sooner.

제가 조금만 더 일찍 왔더라면.

BELLE : (crying) No, no! Please! Please! Please don't leave me! I love you!

Cut to Objects, who watch the last petal fall off the rose. They all look down at the floor and Cogsworth puts his arm around Mrs. Potts.
Cut back to Belle and Beast. The rain continues to fall. But one beam of light falls like a shooting star. Then another comes. And another and another. Belle finally notices what is happening. She stops crying for a second, then starts to back away. A fog begins to enshroud Beast. We see the Objects looking on in extreme anticipation. Beast rises up into the air magically and begins to turn.
He is enveloped in a cloud of light and becomes wrapped in his cloak.
Underneath, we can see Beast's body shifting and forming. A fore paw comes out and the claws turn into fingers. A hind paw emerges and develops into a foot.
Finally, a wind blows across his face and the fur melts away to reveal a young prince. He gradually descends and is laid on the floor again. The fog disappears and Belle reaches out to touch him. She jerks her hand back, however, when the figure begins to move. It stands then looks at its hands then turns to face Belle.
It is a human with the same blue eyes as Beast. It is obviously Beast transformed.
Belle gives him a mysterious look.

PRINCE : Belle! It's me!

She continues to look at him skeptically. But then she sees the blue eyes and instantly knows it is him.

BELLE : It is you!

They kiss. A fireworks display explodes around them. The gloom surrounding the castle disappears, revealing a blue sky. The castle is transformed with the gargoyles changing into cherubs. Finally, we return to the balcony where the Objects hop out to meet the Prince and Belle. One by one they are transformed back to their original human conditions.

PRINCE : Lumiere! Cogsworth! Oh, Mrs. Potts! Look at us!

벨 : (울면서) 안 돼요. 안 돼요. 제발. 날 떠나지 말아요! 사랑해요!

하인들 장면. 마지막 장미꽃이 떨어지는 것을 보고 있다. 그들은 모두 고개를 숙여 바닥만 쳐다보고, 콕스워즈는 포트 부인에게 어깨동무를 한다.
벨과 야수 장면. 비는 계속해서 쏟아진다. 하지만 별똥별 같은 한 줄기의 빛이 떨어진다. 그러고 나서 또 다른 빛이 떨어지고, 또 하나 더, 하나 더 떨어진다. 벨은 마침내 무슨 일이 벌어지는지 알게 된다. 그녀는 잠시 울음을 멈추고 뒷걸음질 친다. 안개가 야수를 완전히 감싼다. 하인들은 부푼 기대감을 품고 있다. 야수가 마법처럼 공중에 떠서 돌기 시작한다.
그는 많은 빛줄기로 둘러싸이고, 그의 망토가 둘러진다.
야수의 몸이 바뀌고 있다. 앞발이 빠져나와 발톱이 손으로 바뀐다. 야수의 뒷발은 발이 된다.
마침내, 그의 얼굴에 바람이 불더니 털이 사라지고 젊은 왕자의 얼굴이 드러난다. 그는 점점 아래로 내려와서 다시 바닥에 눕혀진다. 안개가 사라지고 벨은 그를 만져보려 가까이 다가간다. 그러나 사람이 움직이기 시작하자 그녀는 갑자기 손을 뒤로 뺀다. 그는 일어나서 그의 양 손을 바라보고는 벨 쪽으로 고개를 돌린다.
야수와 같은 푸른 눈을 가진 사람이다. 야수가 변한 것이 분명하다. 벨은 그를 신기하게 바라본다.

왕 자 : 벨! 나예요!

그녀는 의심스럽게 계속 지켜본다. 그러나 곧 그녀는 푸른 눈을 보고 그라는 것을 알게된다.

벨 : 당신이군요.

왕자와 벨은 키스한다. 그들 주위로 폭죽이 터진다. 성을 둘러싸고 있던 어둠이 사라지고 푸른 하늘이 나타난다. 괴물석상이 천사로 바뀌고 성의 모습도 변한다. 마침내, 하인들이 왕자와 벨을 만나기 위해 발코니로 뛰어 들어온다. 하나씩 그들은 원래 사람의 모습으로 돌아온다.

왕 자 : 루미에르! 콕스워즈! 포트 부인! 마법이 풀렸어!

shooting star
별똥별
A shooting star is a piece of rock or metal that burns very brightly when it enters the earth's atmosphere from space, and is seen from earth as a bright star travelling very fast across the sky

enshroud
(보이지 않게) 싸다
To enshroud something means to cover it completely so that it can no longer be seen

anticipation
기대
Anticipation is a feeling of excitement about something pleasant or exciting that you know is going to happen

skeptical
회의적인, 의심하는
If you are skeptical about something, you have doubts about it

cherub
천사
A cherub is a kind of angel that is represented in art as a naked child with wings

Please don't leave me!
부탁이나 명령을 하는 문장 앞뒤에 please를 붙이면 '제발, 부디'라는 의미가 더해져 더욱 간절함을 표현할 수 있다.

Zoom In

Please don't leave me!
제발 날 떠나지 말아요!

Chip comes riding in on Footstool.

CHIP : Mama! Mama!

The pair transforms back into a boy and dog.

MRS. POTTS : (picking up her boy) Oh my goodness!

LUMIERE : It is a miracle!

INT. IN THE BALLROOM

The Prince picks up Belle and swings her around. The ruffles of her skirt wipe to the ballroom, where all are gathered to celebrate. The Prince and Belle dance around the room as the rest of the characters get in their last lines.

LUMIERE : Ah, l'amour.

He says this and a Maid, obviously the former featherduster, walks by brushing him on the chin.

LUMIERE : Heh heh!

He starts to chase after her, but Cogsworth stops him.

COGSWORTH : Well, Lumiere, old friend. Shall we let bygones be bygones?

LUMIERE : Of course, mon ami. I told you she would break the spell.

COGSWORTH : I beg your pardon, old friend, but I believe I told you.

LUMIERE : No you didn't. I told you.

COGSWORTH : You most certainly did not, you pompous parrafin-headed pea-brain!

칩이 풋스툴을 타고 온다.

칩 : 엄마! 엄마!

그 둘은 각각 남자아이와 강아지로 바뀐다.

포트 부인 : (아들을 안아 들며) 오, 하느님!

루미에르 : 이건 기적이야!

내부. 무도회장에서

왕자는 벨을 들어 올려 그녀를 안고 빙글빙글 돈다. 치맛자락이 무도회장에 끌리고, 모든 사람들이 모여서 함께 축하한다. 왕자와 벨은 무도회장을 돌며 춤을 춘다.

루미에르 : 오, 사랑!

그가 말하자, 빗자루에서 변신한 것이 분명한 가정부가 걸어와서 붓으로 그의 턱을 간질인다.

루미에르 : 흐흐흐.

그는 그녀를 쫓아가려고 하지만, 콕스워즈가 그를 막는다.

콕스워즈 : 잠깐 루미에르. 우리 지난 일은 잊자구!

루미에르 : 물론이지, 친구. 그녀가 마법을 풀어 줄 거라고 했지?

콕스워즈 : 미안하지만, 친구, 그거 내가 한 말 같은데.

루미에르 : 무슨 소리, 내가 말했어.

콕스워즈 : 네가 언제 그랬어, 이 바보 멍청아!

- **miracle**
  기적
  If you say that a good event is a miracle, you mean that it is very surprising and unexpected
- **ruffle**
  주름 장식
  Ruffles are folds of cloth at the neck or the ends of the arms of a piece of clothing, or are sometimes sewn on things as a decoration
- **pompous**
  거만한
  If you describe someone as pompous, you mean that they behave or speak in a very serious way because they think they are more important than they really are
- **pea-brain**
  바보
  If you call someone a pea-brain, you are showing that you think they are very stupid or have done something very stupid

Shall we let bygones be bygones?
bygones는 지나간 일, 옛날 일이라는 뜻이므로, let bygones be bygones는 '지난 일은 잊어버리다, 덮어두다'라는 숙어가 된다. 'Shall we 동사원형~?'은 제안하는 표현이므로 지난 일은 잊고 다시 잘 지내보자는 제안의 표현으로 쓰였다.

Zoom In

Shall we let bygones be bygones?

우리 지난날은 잊자구!

LUMIERE : En garde, you overgrown pocket watch!

COGSWORTH : Take that.

LUMIERE : Stop shoving.

He takes off his glove and slaps Cogsworth across the face with it. They begin to fight.
Cut to Belle and the Prince who continue to dance around the floor. The camera stops on Mrs. Potts, Chip and Maurice, who is beginning to cry.

CHIP : Are they gonna live happily ever after, mama?

MRS. POTTS : Of course, my dear. Of course.

CHIP : (looks happy for a moment, then puzzled) Do I still have to sleep in the cupboard?

Maurice laughs and Mrs. Potts hugs her child and laughs. Cut to a camera looking over the entire ballroom with all in the shot. It slowly zooms out with Belle and the Prince dancing around the room, and fades into the final stained glass window. This one with Belle and the Prince in the center, surrounded by the rest of the characters.

CHORUS : (singing) *CERTAIN AS THE SUN*
RISING IN THE EAST
TALE AS OLD AS TIME, SONG AS OLD AS RHYME
BEAUTY AND THE BEAST!
TALE AS OLD AS TIME, SONG AS OLD AS RHYME
BEAUTY AND THE BEAST!

Fade out into credits.

The end.

루미에르 : 덤벼, 이 회중시계같은 뚱보야!
콕스워즈 : 인정해.
루미에르 : 그만 고집피워.

그는 장갑을 벗어 콕스워즈의 얼굴을 친다. 그들은 싸우기 시작한다.
왕자와 벨이 계속해서 춤을 추는 장면. 카메라는 포트 부인, 칩, 그리고 눈물을 보이는 모리스에 멈춘다.

칩 : 두 분은 행복하게 살겠죠, 엄마?
포트 부인 : 물론이지, 아가야. 물론이지.
칩 : (행복한 얼굴을 보이다가 당황한다) 저는 아직도 찬장에서 자야 하나요?

모리스는 허허 웃고 포트 부인은 아들을 안아주면서 웃는다. 카메라는 무도회장 전체를 비춘다. 왕자와 벨이 춤추는 장면이 서서히 멀어지면서, 마지막 유리를 비춘다. 유리에는 왕자와 벨이 가운데에 있고, 주변에 다른 사람들이 서 있다.

코러스 : (노래하며) *해가 동쪽에서 뜨는 것처럼*
오래된 사랑 이야기
미녀와 야수!
오래된 사랑 이야기
미녀와 야수!

점점 희미해지면서 크레딧이 뜬다.

끝.

- **pocket watch**
  회중시계
  A pocket watch is a watch that is made to be carried in a pocket, as opposed to a wristwatch which is strapped to the wrist

- **hug**
  껴안다
  When you hug someone, you put your arms around them and hold them tightly, for example because you like them or are pleased to see them

- **entire**
  전체의
  You use entire when you want to emphasize that you are referring to the whole of something, for example, the whole of a place, time, or population

- **certain**
  확실한
  If you are certain about something, you firmly believe it is true and have no doubt about it

Key Expressions

258 It is being bashed in by the Mob. 사람들은 문을 강타한다.

be being p.p.의 형태는 현재진행 수동태로써, 주어가 행위자로부터 당하고 있는 상황을 나타낼 때 쓰인다. 하지만 우리말로 해석할 때는 능동으로 하는 것이 자연스럽다.

· The cart is being pushed onto the truck. 카트를 트럭 위쪽으로 밀고 있다.

260 The mob succeeds in breaking in, and finds a grand entrance filled with assorted pieces of furniture, teacups, candlesticks, featherdusters and clocks.

가구, 찻잔, 촛대, 빗자루, 시계가 넓은 출입구에 조화롭게 배치되어 있다.

filled with는 '~로 가득 찬'이라는 숙어이다. full of와 같은 뜻이다. assorted는 '여러 가지'라는 뜻도 있지만 '조화로운, 어울리는'이라는 뜻도 있으니 함께 알아두도록 한다.

· The room was filled with the fragrance of roses.
방에는 장미 향기가 가득했다.

262 Belle, Maurice, Phillipe and Chip are making their way to the castle. 벨, 모리스, 필립과 칩은 야수의 성으로 출발한다.

make one's way to는 '~로 나아가다, 출발하다'라는 숙어로 자주 쓰이는 표현이다. 여기에 the best of를 더해 make the best of one's way라고 쓰면 '길을 서둘러 나서다'라는 뜻이 된다.

· Please make your way to the exit nearest you.
가까운 쪽 출구로 나와 주세요.

264 Beast has been provoked enough.

야수는 화가 머리끝까지 난다.

이 문장은 현재완료 수동태(have/has been p.p.) 문장이므로 형태에 주의한다. 이 역시 우리말로 해석할 때는 능동으로 해 주는 것이 우리말답고 자연스럽다.

· **Every seat in the cabin has been rebuilt.** 객실 내의 모든 좌석들을 개조하였다.

268 She stops crying for a second, then starts to back away. 그녀는 잠시 울음을 멈추고 뒷걸음질 친다.

stop ~ing는 '~하는 것을 멈추다'라는 표현이다. stop대신에 quit를 쓸 수도 있다. 한편 'stop to 동사원형'은 '~하기 위해 멈추다'라는 뜻으로 의미가 전혀 다르니 혼동하지 않도록 주의한다.

· **He stopped smoking. He's a man of strong will.**
그는 담배를 끊었어. 의지가 강한 사람이야.

270 I beg your pardon, old friend. 미안하지만, 친구.

I beg your pardon에는 두 가지 의미가 있다. 이 상황에서처럼 미안하다는 사과의 의미를 나타낼 수도 있고, 끝을 올려서 읽으면 상대방의 말을 못 알아들었을 때 되묻는 표현으로도 쓰인다. 그러므로 끝소리의 억양에 주의하도록 하자.

· **I beg your pardon? I couldn't hear you because I was putting on earphones.** 뭐라구요? 이어폰을 끼고 있어서 못 들었어요.

Certain as the sun Rising in the east
Tale as old as time Song as old as rhyme
Beauty and the Beast